PRODUCTIVITY

IS POWER

PRODUCTIVITY IS POWER

Five Liberating Practices for Undergraduates

HILLARY RETTIG

Infinite Art Press

ISBN 978-0-9899440-5-2 paperback
ISBN 978-0-9899440-6-9 ebook

Formatting and Interior Design by Woven Red Author Services, www.WovenRed.ca

To Jan Tobochnik,
a dedicated educator and
the best partner any writer could have

Contents

Vocabulary/Text Notes

Except where specifically indicated, I use the words "professor" and "teacher" interchangeably to refer to all educators, including tenure-track professors, adjunct professors, graduate student instructors, teaching assistants, coaches, tutors, advisors, and others.

I also use the words "college" and "university" interchangeably.

I use the words "productivity" and "creativity" interchangeably. (As opposed to labeling some kinds of work "creative" and others not: it's all creative.)

I use gender neutral pronouns (singular they/them) except when a person's pronouns are gendered, or when gendered pronouns are useful for clarity.

Except for my own personal autobiographical narratives in the Introduction and elsewhere, all of the examples and case studies in this book are either fictitious (but reflect real-life situations) or composites.

On Using the Correct Toolset

The techniques in this book have helped many, but no technique helps everyone, so feel free to skip any that aren't working for you. I'm unable to guarantee a positive result in any instance of using any of the techniques in this book.

Underproductivity often occurs alongside physical health problems (e.g., fatigue), mental health problems (e.g., anxiety or depression), and/or neurodivergence (e.g., dyslexia, ADHD, or Asperger's syndrome). In these situations, my techniques can be useful adjuncts to medical or therapeutic treatment, but should not replace it. If you are dealing with one of these types of conditions, or even if you think you might be, please consult a specialist.

Foreword

This book could be a lifesaver. Addressed to students struggling with the demands of college work and prey to procrastination, it offers a detailed and practical set of strategies for realizing their potential. As such, it should appeal to a broad audience. How many students today feel stressed by college workloads? Far too many. How many blame themselves for performing poorly? Again, far too many. But their distress is not inevitable. *Productivity Is Power* offers them a lifeline.

The reasons for student stress vary. Coping mechanisms that served well enough in high school may fail when confronted by the greater demands of college-level work. The cohort of friends that gave emotional support may have dispersed. Many students are living away from home for the first time, with the attendant temptations of life without parental supervision. Added to this mix is the fact that asking for help can be hard, especially if you have never needed help before.

But the main enemy, the author argues here, is perfectionism. Students want to do well, know they are underperforming, and then blame themselves, procrastinate, or both. Procrastination postpones what may seem an inevitable failure, yet also triggers a cascade of self-blame and further diminished performance. Simply put, self-punishment is a terrible motivator. There has to be a better way to succeed.

As this book makes clear, college support services and concerned faculty do offer counsel and guidance toward this goal. But their efforts are constrained by a lack of resources and time. Sadly, student demands for services often exceed the capacities of those equipped to offer them. No one on campus, least of all faculty, can do everything expected of them in the time available. Teaching, research, family obligations, committee service, and (one hopes) self-care all claim a part of faculty's daily schedule. Students can at best secure a sliver of adult attention when they need a generous slice, and are most often left to cope on their own.

Enter *Productivity Is Power*. The book offers both a nuanced set of diagnostics, enabling readers to discover where the root of their performance problems lies, and a wealth of practical solutions to set matters right. And whereas it offers students the tools and help they need, it does so without feeding their guilt for needing help in the first place. Instead, *Productivity Is Power* models the attitude the author wishes her readers to cultivate—kindness and understanding toward oneself, a sober analysis of poor academic performance, and confidence that one can improve.

Of course, validating students for who they are while still motivating them to change requires a delicate balance between acceptance and incitement. Students' self-criticism, feelings of unworthiness, or suspicion that they are perhaps the "admissions committee's big mistake" can easily rob them of the confidence and energy needed to address flagging productivity. Theirs is a problem that can be solved only if they believe that it's open to solution. As Hillary Rettig herself insists, guilt is disempowering. Encountering *Productivity Is Power* feels like entering a guilt-free zone.

It should be added that overcoming the syndrome of self-disempowerment and procrastination is a skill whose usefulness extends well beyond the college years. If the transition from high school to college tests students' coping skills, then the transition from college to postgraduate employment tests them all the more. Jobs in the "real world" come with deadlines and expectations of on-time performance. So do living with a partner and pursuing personal projects. Becoming reliably productive is in fact a life skill, and mastering it early pays dividends. This wise and timely book shows the way.

James Wilkinson
Senior Associate and Director Emeritus
Derek Bok Center for Teaching and Learning
Harvard University

Introduction:
A New Kind of Productivity Book for
a New Generation of College
Student

If you've picked up this book, I assume it's because you're a college student who would like to do great work as easily and effectively as possible. (Or perhaps you're someone who cares about such a student.) Maybe you'd like to get better at sticking to a schedule—and, especially, at starting your work on time. Or, at working steadily and with good focus for hours at a time. Or, at handing in your work on time, or maybe even a bit early.

Perhaps you'd even like to have fun while doing it all. That's not too much to ask! Maybe you remember a time when you were younger and did art, math, science, history, or some other creative or intellectual endeavor just for the fun of it.

This book will help you to reclaim that glory.

More specifically, it will teach you how to recognize, understand, and remove your barriers to joyful productivity, including procrastination, perfectionism, ineffective work processes, unhealed traumatic rejections, and unmanaged time.

Of course, there are plenty of "generic" productivity books that address these kinds of topics, some of them excellent. But I wrote this book specifically for undergraduates, for these reasons:

First, the undergraduate years are pivotal. Stay mostly on course during them and you can accelerate your progress and growth, both in college and beyond. But spend a lot of time lost in the weeds, as some of us do (see below), and you can struggle for a long time, and perhaps miss out on some valuable opportunities.

Second, the undergraduate years are uniquely challenging, productivity-wise. There's a lot going on, starting at the neurological and developmental levels. For one thing, our frontal cortex, which is responsible for much of our intellect, judgment, and decision-making, doesn't even finish developing until we're 25! Add to that the sudden transition from constant parental and teacher supervision to a much more independent lifestyle with many more opportunities—academic, extracurricular, and social—*and* distractions. Also, the fact that you're in a new community, surrounded (hopefully) by very different people and situations than those you grew up with.

It's a lot to handle.

In fact, I think that today's college students actually have it rougher than previous generations. The combination of soaring tuition, exploitative student loan programs, and the worst post-college job market in decades[1] has put enormous pressure on you. Meanwhile, your professors and the other school professionals whom you would naturally turn to for help are themselves under pressure from budget cutbacks and other factors.

As if all this weren't enough, you also have to contend with some of the worst political and social crises we've seen in decades, including rampant inequality, rising authoritarianism, the unfolding climate catastrophe, and the COVID-19 pandemic and its fallout. If you're distracted or upset by all of that, by the way, that just means that you're a good, caring person who's been paying attention. Don't worry: I'll show you some techniques for staying focused even during difficult and distracting times.

Finally, let's not forget social media, a complex subject from productivity and other standpoints. On the one hand, it's a fun and liberating technology that's an essential part of many people's personal and work lives. (And it can be especially liberating for those with disabilities, or who are isolated, or who belong to marginalized groups.) On the other hand, it's been linked to some serious productivity, health, and other problems; and the fact that it is both ubiquitous and constantly "on" only adds to those concerns. Throughout this book, I'll be discussing ways to keep your social media use in balance, and urge you to keep an open mind on this topic.

You do have one excellent thing working in your favor, however, and that's *you*. I have a lot of respect for today's college students and other young people. Generally speaking, I think you're far more astute—politically,

---

[1] See, for instance: https://www.cnn.com/2020/05/20/us/bad-job-market-graduates-coronavirus/index.html and https://abcnews.go.com/US/career-start-college-grads-face-bleakest-job-markets/story?id=70436676.

socially, and emotionally—than previous generations. Many of you also have a very healthy (for you *and* the planet) global and systems outlook. And many of you are also far more attuned to issues of identity, equality, justice, and inclusiveness than previous generations. These are all great things that will strengthen and enrich not just you, but everyone else.

One Student's Story

A long time ago, and at a university far, far away, a young woman graduated without a plan.

Actually, that was me! I was the one without a plan!

I had been an "accelerated" student, starting elementary school a year early and also skipping a grade. And so, I entered college at sixteen, full of accomplishment and confidence, ready to conquer the world. Instead, college wound up conquering me. I was clueless as to how to succeed, and hit so many roadblocks, both academic and personal, that it's a miracle I managed to graduate at all. Many stemmed from ignorance—I was the first person in my family to go to college, although at the time being a "first gen" wasn't yet recognized as a barrier to success—but I also had a bunch of personal and interpersonal issues I hadn't even yet recognized, much less begun to work on.

My grades in college were all over the map, covering the spectrum from A to D (somehow managing to elude the dreaded F). I also switched majors a lot, including once in my senior year. It was pure chaos, and I felt, often, like pure chaos.

Sure, some of my professors tried to help me. But it was a large school, and I was one of thousands. So "help" mostly consisted of a once-a-semester meeting with my advisor, plus meetings with my professors (or, at least, teaching assistants) whenever I reached out with questions. But what do you do if you don't even know what questions to ask?

What I don't remember is anyone ever sitting down with me and saying, "You look confused. Here's how this all works." I sure could have used that talk.

After college, I lacked a plan (as you already know), and so I spent the next few years hanging around my pleasant college town, taking easy secretarial and administrative jobs on campus. I then spent a couple of years traveling around Europe, before returning to my native New York City to write fiction ("the dream"). This was all in the mid to late 1980s, and financially, at least, I was in the right place at the right time, since I could easily support myself by working just a few nights a week in the "word processing department" of a financial services firm in Rockefeller Center. Sitting in a large, brightly lit, windowless room alongside a couple dozen other typist-dreamers—including many would-be actors, writers, artists, opera singers, etc.—I spent 12 hours typing and correcting memos, contracts, reports, and other capitalistic ephemera. The work was easy, my coworkers fun, and the pay *outstanding*: around $16 an hour in 1985 dollars, which would be around $38 an hour today. And because it was an overnight shift, the firm also paid for a luxurious Town Car to take us home in the morning. (I *loved* that Town Car.)

It was an easy and fun existence—but still, I was avoiding all forms of professional accomplishment. My fiction writing was going nowhere, mostly because, for years, I wrote and rewrote the same opening of a novel over and over. (Despite my confusions and disappointments, I must acknowledge my significant generational and other privileges at that time in my life. Meandering somewhat pointlessly through life is a lot pleasanter when you can do it on those good 1985 wages, versus the starvation wages most employers pay today. Also, white privilege, able-bodied privilege, and perhaps some other privileges played a role in my ability to survive on relatively easy part-time work.)

Things finally started to gel for me in my 30s, when I started doing freelance articles for computer magazines. This led to a job as an editor at a computer trade magazine, where I wrote business profiles and case studies. It wasn't the most glamorous writing job out there, but I loved it—largely because, most weeks, I'd have the opportunity to interview, in depth, at least one really smart and successful person on how they'd grown their business. As a perennial underachiever, I especially wanted to know how my interviewees had overcome their barriers to success, and many were remarkably candid on that.

After a few dozen of these interviews, let's just say I got a clue.

In 2000, the technology sector crashed, and I also got an obnoxious new boss. So I quit my job and, in the absence of other publishing options, took one as a business teacher and coach at a nonprofit entrepreneurship program in Boston. That's when things got really interesting, because, even though I hadn't planned it that way, I was now seeing the flip side of the entrepreneurial story, the ones who hadn't yet succeeded—and who, in some cases, would probably never succeed, because they couldn't manage their time or get motivated to do their work (write business plans, call mentors, etc.). To be fair, most of our clients were busy adults with jobs, kids, and other responsibilities, so their path was never going to be easy. But the goal, in many cases, was achievable, and we did have our successes.

Our clients were cool people, and it saddened me to watch them get in their own way. (Just as I'm sure it saddened some of my professors to watch me get in my own way.) And so—based on my accumulated knowledge of productivity, creativity, time management, and a few other disciplines—I created two new modules to add to our business curriculum: one on time management and another on overcoming "internal" barriers to success (e.g., procrastination, perfectionism, and ambivalence). I worried about the "barriers" module, in particular. Would our students—who were a diverse lot, of all ages and backgrounds—find it too "touchy-feely?" In fact, they loved both modules, and the barriers one especially. (I think it helped that I shared my own story and struggles, so that I was engaging with them on terms of equality.) I knew, after the very first time I taught it, that I was onto something.

One of the memorable pieces of advice I had gotten, back in my interviewing days, was to "focus relentlessly on your unique value-add"—meaning, the thing you do that is most valuable to the customer. (The guy who told it to me had grown a $250 million business from scratch, which was probably one reason it was memorable.) That was clearly my productivity work—and so, that's how I wound up with a career focused on helping people get productive. For nearly 20 years, I've been writing, thinking, teaching, and coaching on that topic: it's been a hugely rewarding path, and I'm especially pleased that my work seems to speak, in particular, to creative and values-driven people seeking to make a positive contribution.

Which brings us back to this book....

Why Productivity Is Power

A few words, before we continue, about my approach. People come to productivity work from different backgrounds, including psychology, education, management, and creativity. There's also an academic field of "procrastination studies." However, as Andrew Santella notes in his book *Soon*, an historical overview of procrastination, there's a lot of debate, among the field's experts, even on the fundamentals: "If you want to start a heated argument among a group of procrastination researchers, ask whether chronic deferral has more to do with our inability to manage time or with a failure to regulate our emotions." (To which I would reply, echoing the little girl in the popular Internet meme, "Why not both?")

As for me, I've come to the field, as discussed above, from the perspectives of entrepreneurship, education, social work, and creativity (from all those years studying writing). Crucially, however, I also come from the perspective of social justice. From a young age, I've cared deeply about injustice, and have sought to do my share in creating a fairer world. My activism has centered, over the years, on feminism, economic justice, free software, and veganism/animal rights; my very first book, *The Lifelong Activist,* was a self-help guide for progressive and Left activists.[2] It was, in fact, my social justice perspective that helped me to zero in on **disempowerment as the primary cause of underproductivity**—something that I don't think any other general-audience book has done. (Some works in critical pedagogy and related fields do discuss this, but their treatment tends to be much more theoretical, and much less nuts-and-bolts, than what I'm offering here.) This perspective has also helped me to recognize that **perfectionism is a much broader and more systemic problem** than it's often presented as.

Ironically, some progressives are skeptical of self-help books such as this one, mostly because the field has tended to minimize, or ignore entirely, the role of societal forces in people's struggles. Progressives can be even more skeptical of productivity and time management books—again, like this one!—because those techniques have often been used exploitatively to try to extract the maximum amount of labor from employees. Happily, this antipathy appears to be softening, with more and more people recognizing that it is possible to both acknowledge the societal roots of many of our so-called "personal" problems *and* to focus on improving our individual condition and coping strategies where we can.[3]

In this book, I'm fully committed to acknowledging the societal contributions to the problems I discuss. This commitment starts with my definition of **productivity**, which is: the ability to work as easily, effectively, and joyfully as possible on your schoolwork and other priorities, within the limits of whatever constraints you happen to be facing. You'll notice that this definition focuses on the *process* of doing your work, versus quantified goals (e.g., to be able to write X pages or do Y math problems per hour) or desired outcomes (e.g., to get great grades or a great job). We can't use quantified goals because everyone's different, every project is different, and our work capacities vary depending on the situation. We can't specify outcomes for the same reasons, and also because overfocusing on outcomes triggers perfectionism and procrastination. (I'll explain why later.) This doesn't mean that you shouldn't go for the great goals and outcomes. Of course you should! But you should hold onto those goals lightly, as opposed to with an iron grip, the way many perfectionists do. Besides, it's by focusing on process that you'll (somewhat paradoxically) have your best shot at attaining those great goals and outcomes. (Again, I'll explain why later.)

---

[2] https://lanternpm.org/books/the-lifelong-activist/
[3] See, for instance, *You Are Your Best Thing: Vulnerability, Shame Resilience, and the Black Experience,* a book coedited by activist Tarana Burke and self-help author Brené Brown.

Also, note the inclusion, in the definition, of those "other priorities." I want you to be "productive"—again meaning easy, effective, and joyful—in your self-care, relationships, recreation, and whatever other non-school activities are important to you. That's primarily because you're a human being whose needs deserve to be met, but also because our success usually rests on the foundation of a balanced, healthy, and well-rounded life.

Now for the second big word in my book's title, **power,** which I define as the ability to use your strengths, skills, talents, energy, focus, and other capacities to achieve meaningful outcomes in your schoolwork and other priorities. In college, these "meaningful outcomes" often come in the form of grades, but learning and growth are even more important, if harder to quantify.

Power also consists of the ability to influence and lead others without robbing them of their own productivity and power. Power *with* others, in other words, not *over* them.

Implicit in both definitions is that, as much as possible, you're doing stuff you really want to be doing—i.e., working and living as authentically as possible.

We might as well tackle the third word in my title, that "is." Yes, I'm saying that productivity (as defined above) is the same as power (ditto). The more productive you are, the more empowered you'll be, and vice versa. I'll also be explaining this later on: for now, just know that, whenever you see someone who is underproductive, you can be sure that that person is also disempowered. As some immediate proof, I'll point out that many people procrastinate only on one or two key projects, like their schoolwork or exercise, and are productive the rest of the time. So it's clear that they're not generally "lazy" or "undisciplined." Rather, something is preventing them from using their "power" (energy, focus, discipline, etc.) in the service of the projects in question.

So how does an underproductive, disempowered person get their power and productivity back? That's the life- and world-changing question this book answers.

Let's get started.

What to Do If You've Got an Urgent Deadline

This discussion is specifically for those who, right now, are facing an urgent deadline. If that's you, keep reading. If not, feel free to skip to Chapter 1. (I'll be covering all the points in more detail throughout the rest of the book.)

Here's what you should do if you're facing an urgent deadline:

1. **Clear your schedule.** Your most urgent needs right now are for time and energy, so make a list of everything you're supposed to be doing, including schoolwork, extracurricular projects, your job (if you have one), personal chores, and errands. Then, take a serious look at each item and ask yourself: *"Is it essential that I do this now?"* If the answer is "no," postpone it. (Or, if you don't have to do it at all, cancel it.)

   What about your self-care? (Sleep, grooming, exercise, medical and therapy appointments, etc.) Don't cut that: your health and well-being are important, and not just because they aid your productivity. However, if you're doing an intensive daily athletic or other practice, you might want to skip a few sessions.

   Your social life and recreation? Postpone or cancel most of your engagements, keeping just a few of the most fun. (We don't want you to get all cranky and isolated.)

   After you've finished, repeat the entire process and see if you can cut some more. (You often can.)

   This process should liberate lots of time for your urgent

project. Use two-thirds of it for the project, and the remaining third for some additional self-care and recreation.

2. **Ask your professor for a deadline extension.** They might grant you one, especially if you're late for reasons beyond your control, like an illness. Ask your professor sooner rather than later, however, because waiting till the last minute makes you look bad, and also leaves you working under unnecessary pressure and stress.

3. **Reduce your project's scope.** Meaning: figure out which parts you *don't* have to do, and eliminate them. Be ruthless! Instead of writing your paper on all the causes of World War I, for instance, maybe just focus on one or two. Or, if you're writing up a science project, maybe just discuss your key experimental finding in detail, and summarize all the rest in a paragraph.

    After you've eliminated all the unnecessary chunks from your project, start trimming bits and pieces. (They add up.) Do all this cutting sooner rather than later, so you don't waste time working on stuff you cut later. (If you're afraid of "overcutting," check with your professor. Chances are you'll be fine, because novice scholars—that's you!—tend to overstuff their projects.) Finally:

4. **Read—or, at least, skim—Part III.** It's loaded with techniques that will help you accelerate your work.

Good luck! See you after you're done.

PART I

EFFECTIVENESS

1. The Problem Isn't Laziness

You've probably noticed how people don't like talking about it when things aren't going well. "How are you doing?" you ask. If the answer isn't "Great!" it's usually "Good." Or, at worst, "Okay."

Sometimes a friend will tell you about their relationship, job, health, or even, if you're really close, money problems. But there's one thing that people have trouble opening up about to even their closest friends, and that's their problems getting their work done. There seems to be something uniquely shameful about underproductivity. Yet, so many of us have been there:

- The endless days and nights when you know you should be working, but are doing anything and everything but.
- The more-or-less constant feelings of guilt, shame, and fear.
- The lies. Such as telling yourself, "I'll work on it tonight," when you know you won't. And telling your friends, "I work best under pressure," when you know you don't. And telling your professor, "It's almost done!" when you know it isn't.
- The frantic couple of days before—or after—your deadline, when your fear finally builds to the point where you start working. Being fear-driven, however, you feel no real attachment to the work, and are super distracted and inefficient.
- The death-march all-nighters, when every second feels like you're dragging a heavy weight.
- The feeling of defeat when you finally hand the work in, knowing it could have been so much better.

- And finally: the humiliation of getting a mediocre grade, and maybe a comment from your professor like, "Great idea, weak execution," or, "Were you rushed?"

The problem is procrastination. Everyone does it, at one time or another, so why all the secrecy and shame? Well, it's probably because we misidentify the causes. **Many people think they procrastinate because they're lazy or undisciplined, but that's wrong: we procrastinate because we haven't been taught the attitudes and habits of productive work.** Even worse, we've been taught some *anti*productive attitudes and habits, like perfectionism.

And college can sure catalyze the problem. Get a group of smart people living and working together, set higher expectations for them than they've ever had to meet before, and grade them competitively, and you've created one heck of a pressure cooker. The pressure often leads to procrastination, as Sarah's story illustrates:

For **Sarah**, college had always been more than just "the next step": it was the place where she would finally get to be herself and find her community. Raised by a conservative family in a conservative Midwestern suburb, she hadn't fit in at either home or school. She was too artsy, too introspective, too concerned with events in the larger world, and too willing to question why things were the way they were. She was grateful for her small circle of high school friends, but was hoping that, in college, she would fit in better with the broader campus culture.

She also differed from many of the other high school students in not having a clearly defined career goal. Many of her classmates intended to go into medicine or engineering or business, but none of those appealed to her. This was yet another source of friction between her and her parents, and it also made it hard for her to figure out which college she wanted to go to. Eventually, however, a wise guidance counselor suggested that she do a double major in biology and anthropology/sociology, subjects that she found interesting, and that would prepare her for a potential career in many fields. (Of course, she could always change her majors later, if she wanted.) The guidance counselor also suggested that she attend a small liberal arts college (often abbreviated as a "SLAC"), where the emphasis would be on teaching, as opposed to research or sports, and where she'd get more individual attention.

Sarah followed all this great advice, and was thrilled when she got accepted into one of her top-choice schools. And for the first few weeks, at least, college was everything that she had dreamed of. She loved her classes, loved the political and cultural scene, and even loved her dorm, which was a lively and exciting place where there was always an interesting conversation going on.

She had finally found her community.

There were only two problems. The first was that she had more work to do than she had ever had before—mountains of it, it seemed, every week. She was in constant danger of falling behind, and the pressure was relentless.

The second was her grades, which were mostly low Bs and Cs. She wasn't happy with those, and also knew that they wouldn't get her into a good job or graduate school. Back in high school, she had always been one of the top students, a status that she had achieved without much effort, and that she had assumed she would maintain in college. Now, she felt as if she were surrounded by, and in constant competition with, students who were just as smart and well-prepared as she was, if not more so. It was a shock.

Worst of all, she couldn't come up with any solution other than to, "Just work harder!" And she couldn't even figure out how to do *that*. Along with the sheer quantity of work she had to get through, an old procrastination problem that she had struggled with on-and-off during high school had returned.

Things finally came to a head when she got a D on her chemistry midterm, the first D she had ever gotten. As she stared at the grade in disbelief and horror, she finally accepted that things had to change. Her advisor, who had been getting updates on her grades, had been urging her for a while to get some help at the Study Skills Center, but Sarah, who had been both embarrassed at needing the help, and convinced that she would somehow eventually manage to figure out things for herself, hadn't done so. Now she knew she had no choice.

Sarah's meetings with her Study Skills Center coach were revelatory. She learned that, like many students from even supposedly good high schools, she hadn't actually ever been taught how to study. Even worse, she had developed some unhelpful habits, like relentlessly focusing on grades (instead of the work itself), relentlessly comparing herself to others, trying to study in fun but distracting settings (like her dorm's commons areas), and doing a lot of her work at the last minute, often by pulling an all-nighter. These were humbling revelations, but they also pointed the way to solutions that would actually work—and that did, in fact, work for Sarah, whose grades soon started to pick up.

When you're stuck the way Sarah was stuck, the situation can seem hopeless. But it isn't! The first step to solving the problem is understanding the true nature of that complicated phenomenon we call "procrastination."

Sticking (or Not) to the Plan

Many people start the day with a plan. Maybe you write yours out in a planner, or maybe you keep it all in your head. It could be something like this:

8:00 a.m.	Get up; shower, dress, and eat breakfast
9:00–11:30 a.m.	Attend class
Noon–12:30 p.m.	Lunch
1:00–4:30 p.m.	Attend class
5:00–6:00 p.m.	Gym
6:30–7:30 p.m.	Dinner
8:00–11:00 p.m.	Study
11:30 p.m.–12:30 a.m.	Hang out; get ready for bed
12:30 a.m.	Go to bed

Procrastination is when you get derailed from your plan.[4] So, instead of getting up at 8:00 a.m., you get up at 9:00 (or 10:00 or 11:00). Or, instead of studying, you play video games.

Or, instead of eating a planned healthy lunch or dinner, you eat a bunch of junk food.

The key question is: what's derailing you? Often, we have a quick answer to that: "Me! I'm derailing myself because I'm lazy, undisciplined, uncommitted, etc." Not so fast! If you're like many people, you would do anything *not* to procrastinate, and have been trying for years to break the habit. So it's pretty clear that you're not really in charge.

I'll tell you who the "derailer" is in Chapter 11. For now, though, let's take a closer look at the phenomenon of procrastination, starting with five crucial points:

---

[4] And a "block," as in "writer's block" or "creative block," is a serious and sustained bout of procrastination. In this book, I mostly use the words "procrastination" and "block" interchangeably.

1. **Procrastination always has a cause, and it's not us.** We know this because many people who procrastinate do so mostly in one or two crucial areas, like schoolwork or exercise. Meanwhile, they're dynamos everywhere else. It's clear, therefore, that they're not generally lazy, undisciplined, or uncommitted, but are facing some additional barriers in those particular areas.

2. **Our reasons for procrastinating are always valid.** There are many reasons you might not feel like doing your work, including fatigue, illness, boredom, confusion, overwhelm, and distraction. These are all 100% legitimate—meaning, understandable, forgivable, and human—motivations, and so are the more frivolous-seeming ones, like that it's nice out and you want to spend the day outdoors, or that you're lonely and want to hang out with a friend. The problem, in other words, isn't that you don't feel like working, but how you respond to that feeling. Which brings us to…

3. **Procrastination isn't a sin or character flaw, but a suboptimal response to our obstacles and barriers to doing our work.**[5] We all procrastinate sometimes, and a little procrastination isn't going to hurt you. But if our reflexive response to every obstacle we encounter is to procrastinate, then we've got a problem, because most of us encounter dozens or hundreds of obstacles every day. (More on obstacles in Chapter 9.)

4. **You can't punish yourself out of a procrastination problem.** Think about it: if punishments—like shame, guilt, and deprivation—actually worked, wouldn't we all be super achievers by now? Most procrastinators have been punishing themselves, or been punished by others, for years, with zero effect except that the problem got worse.

5. **You can solve it, though!** In fact, I'm going to give you a whole bunch of really effective solutions. Implement them, and you can achieve the central goal of productivity work, which is to be able to work as easily, effectively, and joyfully as possible on your schoolwork and other priorities, within the limits of whatever constraints you may be facing. This goal actually encompasses two others: (a) the ability to optimize your use of your time, skills, energy, cognitive capacity (Chapter 45), and other resources; and (b) the ability to show up on time and do whatever work you're supposed to be doing

---

[5] I mostly use the words "obstacle" and "barrier" interchangeably. However, when such a distinction is useful, I use "obstacle" to refer to "mostly-internal" constraints like perfectionism, and "barrier" to "mostly-external" ones like a lack of financial or other resources.

with a high degree of clarity, engagement, focus, and fun! (Because we all need fun, and fun is motivating.)

First, however, let's discuss the true cause of procrastination.

2. The Problem Is Disempowerment

Why would someone who works productively at almost everything else be unable to do their schoolwork?

Why would a student who has never had any trouble doing their schoolwork suddenly find themselves blocked on their senior project?

Why do you get excited over a project when you happen to think about it while doing something else, but then that excitement is nowhere to be found when you actually sit down to do your work?

And why, when you sit down to watch television or play a video game "for just a few minutes," do you often wind up doing it for hours?

The answer, in all cases, is **disempowerment**, the state of being unable to use your strengths, skills, talents, knowledge, energy, enthusiasm, and other capacities. Some people exist in a state of general disempowerment, which means that they aren't able to get much of anything important done, while others are mostly disempowered in one or two key areas, or around one or two key projects.

As you will see, there are many situations, circumstances, and conditions that can disempower us. But how, exactly, does disempowerment cause procrastination? And how can the situation be remedied? To answer these important questions, you first need to understand that **every creative and intellectual act, including those you do as part of your schoolwork, is really an act of self-expression, self-assertion, and self-advocacy.** Whenever you share your work with others, you're revealing yourself at a pretty deep level. (Your thoughts, ideas, values, vision, voice, etc.) Self-expression and sharing almost always carry some risk, because you're exposing your ideas—and, sometimes, yourself—to criticism, judgment, and rejection. Even when delivered sensitively, that criticism, etc., can hurt. But if it's delivered cruelly or unjustly, as it often is, it can hurt a lot more. (More on this in Chapter 34.)

We procrastinate, in large part, to avoid that hurt. If you don't hand your work in, after all, it—and, by extension, you—can't be criticized or rejected. And even if you do manage to hand it in, procrastination provides a built-in justification for any bad grades or other disappointing outcomes you receive: "I was rushed." The problem, of course, is that, at the same time procrastination is keeping you safe from potential critics, it's also **isolating** you from, and thus rendering you **invisible** to, your essential audiences, including not just your professors, scholarship committees, and potential employers, but helpers, mentors, collaborators, and appreciators of all sorts. At its core, procrastination is a form of **self-silencing,** and sometimes, **self-censorship** (if you're specifically silencing ideas you think will offend, or be rejected by, others). It can also be a form of **hiding**—and, sadly, because your rushed work doesn't reflect your best efforts, it's often the best part of you, and the best of your ideas, that you're hiding.

Finally, procrastination is also often **hoarding**. "I'll hand in my work when it's ready," the procrastinator thinks—only, it never is. Or, "I'll hand it in after this last set of changes"—only, the "last set" leads to another, and another, and another. Or, even worse, "I know I need help with this project, but I need to get it into a little better shape before I show it to someone." But the need to get it "into a little better shape" never ends. (More on hoarding in Chapter 14.)

Isolation, invisibility, self-silencing, self-censorship, hiding, and hoarding are all highly disempowered responses to the risks of self-expression, and the "safety" they offer comes at a very high price: self-sabotage. Fortunately, there are more empowering responses to the risks, which I'll be discussing throughout this book.

Where the Disempowerment Comes From

Generally speaking, there are three main sources of disempowerment-based procrastination: your family, society, and certain life events. I discuss each below.

Family Disempowerments

Research has linked procrastination in teenagers to "untreated traumatic experiences"[6] and authoritarian—i.e., harsh and controlling—parenting. In the latter case, psychologist Timothy Pychyl notes that procrastination, "may

---

[6] https://www.hazeldenbettyford.org/articles/fcd/teen-mental-health

become one of the few means available to rebel against this [parental] control, a form of passive aggression."[7] We'll be revisiting this idea of procrastination as rebellion in Chapter 11.

In her excellent book *Adult Children of Emotionally Immature Parents*, psychologist Lindsay Gibson notes how insecure and controlling parents tend to discourage their children's self-expression, including their abilities to speak their truth and ask for help. At the same time, these parents tend to encourage "uncertainty and self-doubt," "guilt and shame over imperfections," and "stereotyped gender roles." Make no mistake: these children are being taught to silence themselves and hide their true selves—and absent some corrective therapy or mentoring, the need to do so will likely persist into adulthood, often resulting in a procrastination problem.

Societal Disempowerments

You don't have to have had a difficult childhood to be disempowered, however. Perfectionism, which I discuss in the next chapter and extensively in Part II, is highly disempowering, and it's rampant throughout our culture and media. You can also be disempowered by an ineffective work process (Part III), unhealed traumatic rejections (Part IV), unmanaged time (Part V), and a lack of planning and support (Appendix). And yeah: it's usually several of those happening at once.

On top of all this, many groups—including women, people of color, queer people, people with disabilities, poor people, and immigrants—experience **systemic oppression** and **implicit bias.** Generally speaking, the former is when an organization's policies intentionally or unintentionally lead to unequal outcomes for members of marginalized groups, while the latter is when the organization's policies aren't explicitly biased, but its members' attitudes and behaviors are. Many universities have worked hard to eliminate the former problem, but the latter remains prevalent (perhaps because policies are easier to change than people's attitudes). If you're a member of a targeted group, you unfortunately have the added, unjust burden of learning how to recognize and cope with barriers such as discrimination, harassment, stereotype threat, tokenization, and microaggressions. Your college hopefully has an office of diversity and inclusion, multicultural center, LGBTQ+ center, and/or other resources that can help; you should also check out

---

[7] https://www.psychologytoday.com/us/blog/dont-delay/200903/parenting-style-and-procrastination. Psychologists commonly recognize four general parenting styles: authoritarian (lots of rules and control, little affection and support), indulgent (few rules, lots of affection), neglectful (few rules, little affection), and authoritative (lots of rules, lots of affection). Authoritative is considered best.

online resources such as www.apiascholars.org, www.campuspride.org, www.hsf.net, www.nationalequityproject.org, www.nccsdonline.org, www.niea.org, and www.firstgen.naspa.org.[8] It's a shame that you might have to do such extra work, especially at an educational institution. But coping always beats non-coping, a.k.a., procrastination.

Our final source of disempowerment is...

"Life Events" Disempowerments

Some life events can also be disempowering. Obviously, the "bad" ones, such as an illness, job loss, or relationship breakup, can be, but even some "good" ones can be, at least temporarily. Transitions are inherently disempowering, and the transitions from high school to college, and between each year of college, are some of life's biggest. (See Table I.) True, these particular "transitional disempowerments" are made intentionally, with the goal of spurring your intellectual, creative, social, and emotional growth. But you still have to be able to cope with them.

Table I: Common Productivity Obstacles Caused by College Transitions

Transition	Common Productivity Obstacles
From High School to Freshman Year of College	• You've got a new home, role (college student), friends, community, etc. (Possibly all very different from what you grew up with.) • You've gone from having lots of supervision (from parents, teachers, guidance counselors, etc.) to very little. • The work is harder than in high school. • You're surrounded by high achievers: the competition is probably tougher than what you're used to. • You have more opportunities—academic, extracurricular, personal—but also more distractions.
From Freshman to Sophomore Year	• You're re-entering after summer break. Re-entries are tricky from a productivity standpoint: it can take more time than expected to regain your productivity after one.

---

[8] This article offers a great overview of the barriers faced by first-generation students and those from economically-disadvantaged or otherwise marginalized backgrounds, plus some solutions: https://harvardmagazine.com/2017/11/mastering-the-hidden-curriculum.

Transition	Common Productivity Obstacles
	• You're under more pressure now than you were in your freshman year. (E.g., the feeling that, "I should have school all figured out by now.") • If you're living off campus, you've got a more complicated housing and dining situation. • "Sophomore Slump," a kind of malaise often caused by being past the excitement of freshman year, but still miles away from graduation. • The work is harder. • You're now taking upper-level classes with juniors and seniors, which can be intimidating. • You're under pressure to choose a major (and career). • You may also be under pressure to get a summer internship, even though sophomore-year internships can be especially hard to get. • You've got yet more opportunities and distractions.
From Sophomore to Junior Year	• You're re-entering after a summer break or internship. • The work is harder. • Possibility of disillusionment if an internship was disappointing, or if your major isn't working out the way you had hoped. (Please talk to your advisor about this.) • Possible pressure to get a summer internship. • The need to start thinking about, and planning for, your life after graduation. (This can take a lot of time, and it can be scary.) • You've got yet more opportunities and distractions.
From Junior to Senior Year	• You're re-entering after a summer break, internship, or maybe a semester or year abroad. (Re-entry after time abroad can be an especially big challenge.) • Continued possibility of disillusionment. • The work is harder. In particular, your senior project or capstone is probably the biggest and most complicated project you've ever done. • The need to start detailed planning for your post-college career and life. (Time-consuming and stressful.)

Transition	Common Productivity Obstacles
	• You're anticipating post-graduation challenges (e.g., finding a job, housing, etc.) and losses (of friends, community, support systems, etc.). • "Senioritis," a decrease in motivation as graduation approaches. It's very common, and usually not a problem in small doses.

To make matters worse, many of your friends will probably be facing the exact same challenges that you are, and so you all probably won't be as helpful to each other as you'd like. Hopefully, however, you'll all be able to work together on the exercises in this book, starting with Exercise 1, below.

Exercise 1

Make a list of any transitional obstacles you're currently facing, and journal* about how each is affecting you and your ability to do your work. While writing, also take some time to appreciate how you've persevered—including by reading this book—in the face of all those obstacles.

*Whenever, in this book, I talk about journaling, I mean "free writing," also known as "stream of consciousness writing." Start with a question like, "How has the transition from freshman to sophomore year affected me and my work?" Then take your time writing out as complete an answer as you can. Let the words flow, and don't worry about spelling, punctuation, or grammar: you're not showing this to anyone. The goal isn't fabulous prose, but introspection: a better, clearer, more comprehensive introspection than you can achieve just by "thinking about the problem." Just remember to always write in a problem-solving way (e.g., "I can see at least three ways that the transition is affecting me...") and *never* in a shaming or blaming way ("I'm lazy, that's all!"). Always be your own best coach.

If you're worried that this journaling, or any of the exercises in this book, can themselves become a form of procrastination—or, more specifically, what I call Quasiproductive Procrastination (Chapter 5)—don't be: these exercises are specifically designed to help you feel more empowered around your work, and the more empowered you feel, the more you'll be able to, and the sooner you'll want to, get back to it.

Please do this and every exercise in this book with as much energy, focus, and dedication as you can. In the realm of personal growth, halfway measures usually don't get us far. (In fact, they're likely to be counterproductive, yielding all the pains of the effort with few or none of the rewards.) But putting your heart and soul into the quest can be transformational.

3. Procrastination and Perfectionism

In the last chapter, I discussed how a disempowering desire to self-silence or hide is often at the root of procrastination; also, how our disempowerment can arise from our childhood, society, or life events. But how is it that some who have experienced significant disempowerment can still manage to be productive? And why do so many who haven't experienced it still wind up procrastinating? Great questions! Let's answer them one at a time.

On the question of why some people are productive despite having had a disempowering childhood, or having endured other disempowering circumstances, please keep in mind that, just as procrastination always has a cause (or causes), so does productivity. Maybe the person was privileged and had the resources—like money and family connections—to overcome their barriers. Or, maybe they weren't that privileged, but had one or two key people who supported and mentored them. Or, maybe they had excellent skills in one or two key areas—technical, interpersonal, strategic, or otherwise—that helped them to break through. Or maybe they were lucky in some other way. (Most likely they were lucky in several ways.)

As to the question of why so many who haven't experienced serious personal disempowerment still procrastinate, there are three answers. First, procrastination is strongly habit-forming. Every time you do it, even if only for superficial reasons like boredom or distraction, you become a little more disempowered and fearful around your work, thus making it harder to do that work in the future. In some cases, procrastination probably crosses the line into an actual addiction—generally defined as a self-reinforcing or compulsive behavior with negative consequences. Hard as it is to overcome a habit, it's even harder to overcome an addiction.[9]

Second—and recalling that procrastination is often used as a way of hiding from possible negative reactions to our ideas—even many seemingly neutral or benign tasks actually do have a scary, self-revealing component. Having to memorize a long list of Italian irregular verbs may seem like a routine task, for instance, but if your studying Italian is expressive of a deeper desire to, say, travel or live in Italy, or to have an art history career, then any fears you have around that goal could manifest themselves in procrastination.

Please note that even a small amount of disempowerment can trigger procrastination, especially if it happens around an activity that's also challenging us in other ways. Worse still, if we happen to confide in someone about our challenges, we're often told to, "Stop whining!" "Stop complaining!" "Toughen up!" or, "Get over it!" This mentality is deeply perfectionist, which brings us to the third reason why even people who haven't faced serious personal disempowerment can have trouble working: **perfectionism**. It's probably the most disempowering force in many people's lives, not just because it's ubiquitous in our culture and media (more on that in Chapter 15), but because, along with being a barrier in its own right, it also blocks your ability to solve your other problems. It does that not just by making you think that you're lazy or otherwise "the problem" (as discussed earlier), but by swamping you with guilt and shame, emotions that aren't exactly conducive to problem-solving.

To sum up: perfectionism can cause you to procrastinate even in the absence of an authoritarian childhood or other barriers. Conversely, if someone is lucky enough to not be too perfectionist, they'll have an easier time coping with any barriers they might be facing.

Perfectionism is a complex phenomenon, and I discuss it in detail in Part II. For now, all you need to know is that it creates not just a fear of failure, but a terror of it. Many perfectionist characteristics, including the tendencies to: (a) define success narrowly and unrealistically, and (b) try to use punishment (e.g., harsh self-talk and deprivation) as a corrective or motivator, contribute to that terror. But the biggest contributor is probably that **perfectionists overidentify with their work**. To a perfectionist, every "success" is a source of personal validation, and every "failure" a devastating indictment. (I frequently put quotation marks around words like "success"

---

[9] Some experts do indeed believe that procrastination has much in common with "classic" addictions like alcoholism. See, for instance, https://www.cambridge.org/core/journals/behavioral-and-brain-sciences/article/abs/addiction-procrastination-and-failure-points-in-decisionmaking-systems/2255C0E5BE4D6A86ED9BE92646EE5819#.

and "failure" to indicate that these concepts are relative, and also that perfectionists often misuse them. See below, and also Chapters 22 and 23.) This overidentification not only wreaks havoc on your self-esteem—because, as I'll be discussing, perfectionists constantly see themselves as failing, even when they're not—it can also lead you to be constantly judging, evaluating, and critiquing both your work and yourself, all in a desperate, and exhausting, effort to stave off the inevitable "failures."

But wait! It can get even worse, because **perfectionists also constantly see themselves as failing**. Even at times when they've succeeded! (E.g., "An A- is okay, I guess, but I'm really bummed I didn't get an A.") That means that, because of their constant overidentification, they are also constantly in despair.

Overidentification can also manifest itself as:

Pathologizing, meaning that you interpret ordinary work obstacles and setbacks as a sign you're incapable of doing the work. Example: "It took me forever to find the bugs in my program, so I guess I'm just terrible at programming."

An overemphasis on external recognition and rewards—so that, for instance, a good grade or a compliment from your professor (or a friend or even a stranger) can put you over the moon. (And the obverse: an even slightly disappointing one can ruin your day.)

Using your work as a source of self-worth or legitimacy. "If I could *only* achieve X, then I would *finally* be Y," is a common perfectionist formulation. Example: "If I could *only* get on the Dean's List, then I would *finally* justify my parents' sacrifices in sending me to college." Let's be clear: the goal (in this case, Dean's List) is often fine and admirable! The problem is when your sense of self-worth or legitimacy hinges on it.

When you encounter someone who is generally productive but is procrastinating a lot on one or two key projects, it's a sure bet they're overidentified with those projects.

The Disempowerment Cascade

Perfectionism triggers procrastination in a five-step process I call **the Disempowerment Cascade**. Here are the steps:

1. While working, or attempting to work, you encounter one or (usually) more obstacles (confusion, boredom, distraction, overwhelm, fatigue, etc.).
2. You have a presentiment of failure. "Oh no!" you think. "My work's not going well! I'm going to fail!" Note that, for reasons I'll

28

be discussing in Chapters 13 and 14 (catastrophizing, negativity, shortsightedness, etc.), you're often afraid of failing not just at the current work session, but at the entire project—and even at the entire class, your entire college career, your post-college career, etc. That's a lot of fear! So, naturally...

3. You panic. Which then leads you to...

4. Urgently attempt to get yourself back on track. Unfortunately, most procrastinators know only one way to do this, a harsh and shaming inner monologue that goes something like this:

   "What's wrong with you? Why are you so lazy? This stuff isn't hard! Anyone could do it! Amy's already finished! Why can't you be disciplined like her? C'mon! If you don't get to work, you're gonna fail, and everyone's gonna know you're a loser...and did I mention that the stuff you've already done sucks?"

   I'll have a lot more to say about this monologue later, but for now let's just agree that all it does is add fear on top of fear. And so, eventually, your panic rises to the point where you must...

5. Escape ("derail") via procrastination. You start scrolling on your phone, or bust out a video game, or even do some tedious chores. (Because anything's better than facing your work, and that terrifying prospect of failure.)

Those are the steps—and it's important to note that they can happen at any point while you're working, or even before you start working. (In which case, you probably won't even start.) All five steps can, and usually do, happen in a flash, so that you might not even be aware of them. All you know is that you have a sudden, irresistible urge to do something—anything—other than your work.

The Disempowerment Cascade model shows that it's not the obstacles (confusion, boredom, etc.) that are the barrier to productivity, but our terrorized reaction to them. When we're terrified, we lose capacity—which happens to be the definition of disempowerment, remember? That's why the only "solution" we can come up with to our predicament is the unsatisfactory one of procrastination.

The Disempowerment Cascade model suggests two key differences between productive and underproductive people:

1. *Productive people learn to interrupt the Disempowerment Cascade.* Specifically, they replace the "panicking" step with problem-solving, with the goal of eliminating, or at least minimizing, the obstacle that is causing the derailment. This enables them to return to

work as soon as possible, as discussed in the next chapter and also Chapters 9 and 10.

2. *Productive people learn to minimize occurrences of the Disempowerment Cascade.* They do this by dealing definitively—or as definitively as possible—with their obstacles, so that they are either minimized or eliminated. If a productive person's workspace is noisy or uncomfortable, for instance, they'll quickly find a better one, and be more selective in the future. Or, if they get derailed after receiving an upsetting text message, they'll decide that, from that moment on, they won't check their phone until after they've done their work. **To outsiders, it looks like these productive people have phenomenal willpower, but what they're really doing is constantly removing obstacles to their productivity.**

Meanwhile, the underproductive people—who, let's not forget, are convinced that they themselves are the problem—tend not to recognize their true obstacles. This means, of course, that they are unlikely to be able to solve them.

And so those obstacles just keep reoccurring, and often get worse over time.

Exercise 2

Think back on a time when you were procrastinating and describe the roles that disempowerment and perfectionism played in that procrastination. Then, describe how disempowerment, procrastination, and perfectionism can all cause each other and be caused by each other.

4. A Quick Solution to Procrastination: Reclaiming Your "Lost" Options and Outcomes

Disempowerment often misleads us into thinking that we have fewer, and worse, **options** than we really have. Maybe you think, for instance, that your only options for a class are to "get an A" or "be a failure." Even if you do have a decent shot at getting that A, you're still putting huge pressure on yourself.

Here are some other examples of perceived poor options:

Marci feels stuck having to choose between a college major (and career) she loves but that doesn't pay well (music) and one that she is less enthusiastic about but that does pay well (engineering).

Chris feels that, because their laboratory partner is slacking off, they're stuck either having to do more than their fair share of the work or getting a bad grade.

A non-school example: Oliver feels like he must either stay in a bad romantic relationship or be doomed to loneliness.

Disempowered people also often perceive themselves as having only poor potential **outcomes**: meaning that, no matter how hard they work on a project, or how carefully they navigate a situation, they are doomed to failure. This often leads to feelings of hopelessness and futility, arguably the most disempowering emotions of all. (As the Star Trek "Borg"—who are constantly pointing out to their would-be victims that "Resistance is futile"—surely know.) Psychologists call the act of anticipating terrible outcomes *catastrophizing*, and many underproductive people do it a lot. They may think they're being "realistic" or "prepared for the worst," but what they're

31

really doing is being negative (see Chapter 13) and disempowering themselves.

Please note that, even though I've been talking a lot about feelings and perceptions, I'm *not* saying that the actual obstacles—poor musician pay, a slacking lab partner, and a bad relationship—aren't real and serious. Of course they are. The perceptual problem lies in believing that you have worse options and outcomes than you actually have. Catastrophizing can lead you to do this, and so can **dichotomizing**, another common perfectionist behavior in which you see the world in either/or terms. Notice how all of the above examples are dichotomized, with Marci feeling like she must choose between a career she loves and one that pays well, Chris feeling like they must choose between either doing more than their fair share of the work or getting a bad grade, and Oliver feeling like he's stuck between staying in a bad relationship or being lonely.

Like all perfectionism, negativity and dichotomization can shut your motivation right down. And so, **whenever you're feeling unmotivated, a good technique is to take a break from whatever it is you're trying to do, and either journal about the problem or talk it over with someone, with the goal of creating better options and outcomes for yourself.** Once you do that, you should find your motivation returning.

Back to our examples:

Instead of feeling stuck having to choose between a major she loves (music) and one that pays well (engineering), Marci could: (1) do a double major or a major/minor, (2) choose projects spanning both fields, such as audio engineering or computer-generated music, (3) pursue a musical career ultra-professionally so as to have the best chance of success, and/or, (4) pursue an engineering career in a way that supports her music. (For instance, getting a job in a "music town" like New Orleans, Seattle, or Chicago.)

Instead of feeling stuck between either having to do more than their fair share of the work or getting a low grade, Chris could, (1) talk with their lab partner. (The partner might be unaware of the problem, or doing more than Chris realizes, or have a valid or easily correctable reason for underproducing.) Or Chris could, (2) ask their professor to assign them another partner. Or, they could even cut their losses and: (3) settle for the lower grade (if the project isn't that important), or (4) just go ahead and do the extra work (if it is).

Instead of feeling stuck between either a bad relationship or a life of loneliness, Oliver could: (1) schedule more time with friends, (2) join a club or other organization where he'll meet new people, and/or (3) do some online dating. Or, if he feels the relationship is fixable, he could try to (4) get some relationship counseling.

In each case, we've gone from two bad options (and the associated bad outcomes) to four better ones—and whenever you use this technique, you should achieve a similar result. What you're really doing when you use this technique is re-empowering yourself. **If disempowerment is the state of being unable to access your strengths, skills, talents, knowledge, and other capacities, empowerment is the ability to access and use all of those.** Happily, as the above examples illustrate, shifting from one to the other state often comes down to a simple willingness to try to come up with some new options and outcomes.

Please note: I am *not* saying that the above solutions are easy, perfect, or even fair—only that they are all way better than procrastinating, which solves nothing and usually makes things worse. Besides, life can, and often does, surprise you. Especially once you've used this book's techniques to free yourself from the yoke of perfectionism, ineffective work processes, traumatic rejections, and unmanaged time, your options may, in fact, turn out to be much better than anticipated. As writer adrienne maree brown says in her wonderful book *Emergent Strategy*, "Creating more possibilities is...where we shape tomorrow towards abundance."

5. "Unproductive" Versus "Quasiproductive" Procrastination, and Other Distractions

People procrastinate in two main ways: "unproductively" and "quasiproductively."

Unproductive Procrastination (UP) is when, instead of your scheduled work, you do a low-value activity like gaming, social media, or television. (Yeah, they can sometimes be high value, but often they're not, especially if you're using them to procrastinate.)

Quasiproductive Procrastination (QP) is when, instead of your scheduled work, you do an activity that has some value. It could be other, less urgent schoolwork. Or you could go for a run, do some chores, or do a favor for a friend.

QP is sneakier than UP because it gives you the illusion of being productive. "Well, I didn't get any studying done today, but at least I got in a run," you tell yourself. Or "at least I cleaned up the place." Or "at least I helped a friend." Also, others will encourage your QP. The other runners will give you props for your dedication, your suitemates will be glad that you cleaned up, and your friend will be grateful for the help.

A common, and extra-sneaky, form of QP is when you procrastinate on one part of your project by overworking another. Examples include researching your paper to death but never writing it, and endlessly revising it but never handing it in. (See Chapters 31 and 32 for solutions to those problems.) And there are lots of other forms of QP, include overoptimizing (a.k.a., "letting the perfect be the enemy of the good enough"), ambivalence (which I discuss in Chapter 24), indecision, and "overthinking the problem" a.k.a. "analysis paralysis."[10]

As the 20th century humorist Robert Benchley put it, "Anyone can do any amount of work, provided it isn't the work he is supposed to be doing at that moment."

So how do you know when you're doing QP? First, remember that, as discussed in Chapter 1, the goal of productivity work is to be able to stick to your plan. So, if you had planned to do X, but are now doing Y, and Y is at least somewhat useful, there's a good chance you're doing QP.

Also, we usually *do* know, deep down, when we're procrastinating. So learn to listen for, and to, that small voice in your head that's saying, "I really ought to be doing something else."

Finally, overdo a QP activity enough and it will eventually become UP—and then you'll *really* know you're wasting time.

Debunking the Productivity Myths: "Good Procrastination," Multitasking, etc.[11]

Every once in a while, some expert claims that procrastination is "thinking time," and therefore useful. Or, that you can "productively procrastinate" on a big, scary task by doing lots of little, unscary ones instead. (Yup, they're actually *recommending* QP.) Or they offer some other rationale or justification for procrastination.

Repeat after me: **there's no such thing as "good procrastination."** (Or "positive" or "productive" procrastination.) Procrastination is *always* grounded in disempowerment, and disempowerment is *never* good.

I'm sure the people promoting these kinds of ideas are doing so in good faith. While I'm happy they've found a solution that works for them, that doesn't mean that you should assume it will work for you.

Similarly, every few years, multitasking (working on more than one thing at a time) gets hyped as a productivity technique. But it's really a sham, for at least three reasons: (1) most of us can't concentrate on more than one complicated task at a time—and when we try, our efficiency goes way down;

---

[10] Like this cat: https://youtu.be/p_17nvsuFFA.

[11] Citations for this discussion: Can't concentrate on more than one complicated task: https://sloanreview.mit.edu/article/the-impossibility-of-focusing-on-two-things-at-once/. Interruptions are expensive: https://www.npr.org/2015/09/22/442582422/the-cost-of-interruptions-they-waste-more-time-than-you-think. Social media degrades cognitive capacity of those around you: https://en.wikipedia.org/wiki/Cognitive_load#college_students; Cellphones degrade cognitive capacity even when not used: https://hbr.org/2018//03/having-your-smartphone-nearby-takes-a-toll-on-your-thinking.

(2) it takes way more time to get back up to speed after an interruption than most people realize; and (3) multitasking can lead to QP by encouraging you to focus on your easier tasks at the expense of your harder ones.

So don't multitask.

And, while I'm at it: don't mix work and social media. Research has shown that you can't work effectively while keeping one eye on your feed—which shouldn't be surprising, since social media platforms are literally designed to hijack your attention. In fact, the social media designers are so very good at their jobs that using social media degrades not just your own cognitive capacity (more on this in Chapter 45), but that of the people sitting around you! Research has also shown that just having your cellphone near you—even if you're not actively using it—can distract you! So either shut off your phone while studying, or leave it in a locker or other inaccessible location.

Be careful when studying with music. While some people can study with music in the background, or foreground, many can't.

Another way to put all of the above is: don't be what Cal Newport, in his book *How to Become a Straight-A Student,* calls a "pseudo-worker." "The pseudo-worker looks and feels like someone who is working hard—he or she spends a long time in the library and is not afraid to push on late into the night—but, because of a lack of focus and concentration, doesn't actually accomplish that much."

You may be the cosmic exception to all this: the rare person who can really multitask, or work effectively while also using social media. But you're probably not—and if you get this wrong, you're at risk for some serious self-sabotage.

Disconnecting Shouldn't Be Radical

One of productivity work's big divides is between those who try to work while connected to the Internet and its many distractions, and those who have figured out that that's a really bad idea. The second group understands the benefits of disconnecting at least part of the time, including not just increased productivity, but less stress, better health, and more enjoyment of life in general.[12]

Yes, of course I know that you need to be on the Internet sometimes. But you probably don't need to be on it as much as you think. You can, for instance, organize your work so that you do all your online tasks together in

---

[12] See, for instance: https://www.insidehighered.com/blogs/gradhacker/how-killing-your-home-internet-can-boost-your-productivity, http://www.theminimalists.com/internet/, and https://blogs.publishersweekly.com/blogs/shelftalker/?p=5127.

a batch, thus freeing you to disconnect for a while. And you can also train yourself to save minor online tasks—like looking up a date or writing a quick email—for your next online session, instead of constantly letting them interrupt your flow. (I keep some scratch paper near my computer so that I can write down such tasks as they occur to me.)

Another great technique is to download lectures and other videos so that you can listen to them offline. Doing this also gives you more flexibility, such as the ability to listen to lectures while driving or on the bus.

Ditto for reference materials: if you think you'll need certain formulas or constants to do your work, then download that information and organize it into a document before starting. (This, itself, could be a good learning exercise, so long as you don't overdo it and slip into Quasiproductive Procrastination.)

Even many people who think they must be online constantly for their work can cut back some—and, often, a lot. After writer and consultant Gregory Ferenstein started using timers to limit his social media use, for instance, he realized that:

> [T]here was hardly ever a time when I needed to constantly monitor social media. Even when I posted something that was popular, I rarely needed to spend more time than a few minutes on the app to meaningfully engage. The marginal utility [meaning, the additional value] from minutes 5 to 60 on Facebook and Twitter wasn't much more than the first 5 minutes.[13]

You don't hear much about it, but many people do disconnect regularly. (Again, see the links in Footnote 12.) Some only go online in the afternoons or evenings, after finishing their creative work; while others limit email and other online work to just once or twice a day; while still others shun certain applications—e.g., some social media platforms—entirely. Still others abstain on weekends, or go on multiday "digital detox" retreats. Novelists Zadie Smith, Isabel Allende, and Jonathan Franzen are famous "disconnecters," and so is Cal Newport, who's written two books on the topic: *Digital Minimalism* and *A World Without Email.* Programming legend Donald Knuth is a disconnecting pioneer, and in 1990 famously explained his decision to almost entirely dispense with email this way: "Email is a wonderful thing for people whose role in life is to be on top of things. But not

---

[13] https://www.forbes.com/sites/gregoryferenstein/2019/01/31/how-i-cut-my-social-media-use-with-app-limits/

for me; my role is to be on the bottom of things. What I do takes long hours of studying and uninterruptible concentration."[14]

Let's be clear, however, that even many who need to "be on top of things"—like, say, many activists or entrepreneurs—benefit from limiting their online time, both because their work does indeed have an intellectual or creative component, and because a lot of our online time is spent on low-value activities like social media and watching videos. Yes, of course, it's okay to do some of that! (And I allocate some time for it in Chapter 49's sample time budget and schedule.) But too much is problematic, not just from a productivity and effectiveness standpoint, but a mental and physical health standpoint.[15]

If all this sounds extreme, please remember that the choice isn't a dichotomized "always online" versus "always offline" one: it's about seeing the Internet and social media as the tools that they are, and figuring out how best to use them. It's especially about recognizing that the apps are designed by experts to suck you in, and that being sucked in is actually a form of disempowerment that, like all forms of disempowerment, you want to avoid. By the way, that "sucked in" experience has a name: a **ludic loop**. The classic ludic-loop-generating technology is the slot machine, which uses fun and flashy displays—plus the lure of the occasional small win, and the possibility of a (very rare) big win—to "hook" people and suck their time and (more importantly) money out of them. But many social media apps, television shows, games, and other escapist diversions are also designed to generate ludic loops. (In social media, the feeling that you're "winning" often come from people "liking" or "following" you, or responding to your posts.)

Once you do decide to limit your online time, you've got three main choices:

First, you can try a **WiFi /social media blocking app**, like Forest, Freedom, or Cold Turkey. If one of these works for you, that's great. But it's easy to get sucked into procrastination before and while using them, and also easy to "cheat" and restore your access. (No, I'm not going to say how.)

---

[14] https://www.calnewport.com/blog/2008/07/17/bonus-post-how-the-worlds-most-famous-computer-scientist-checks-e-mail-only-once-every-three-months/

[15] Mental health: See, for instance, research conducted by psychologist Melissa G. Hunt and colleagues on undergraduates that found a causal link between time spent on Facebook, Instagram, and Snapchat, and feelings of depression and loneliness. https://penn-today.upenn.edu/news/social-media-use-increases-depression-and-loneliness. And also see Chapter 17 and the citations listed in Footnote #35. Physical health: See, for example: www.mayoclinic.org/healthy-lifestyle/adult-health/expert-answers/sitting/faq-20058005, www.ncbi.nlm.nih.gov/pmc/articles/PMC5574844/, https://academic.oup.com/ije/article/41/5/1338/709862, and the citations listed in Footnote 23.

A better solution, in my view, is to **work in a space without WiFi**. Some of the top artist residency programs, including Yaddo and MacDowell, use this approach to support their visiting artists' productivity. They limit Internet access to just a library or other common area, leaving the rest of the campus, including the artists' studios, disconnected. Similarly, you can probably find a WiFi-free library, café, or other study space on or near your campus, where, like those pampered artists, you can work in luxurious disconnected peace and freedom. As a bonus, you'll probably find yourself working alongside some highly productive others who have also discovered the benefits of disconnecting. (Which should further boost your own productivity.)

The best solution to online distraction is to **do the bulk of your work on a computer from which you've deleted not just Internet connectivity, but (obviously) all games and other distractions**. In practice, this usually means using two computers: the disconnected one, on which you do your writing, programming, problem sets, and other work that requires sustained focus and concentration, and the connected one, on which you do your research, social media, gaming, etc. (In many cases, the disconnected computer can be an old one that you repurpose.) This two-computer system can not only boost your ability to concentrate, it can also help you create some empowering new options for yourself. One of my most effective productivity tricks, for instance, is this: every night, before going to bed, I shut down my "connected" computer while leaving my "disconnected" one on. That way, when I return to my office the next morning, it's the disconnected one that's "alive" and beckoning to me, and not the connected one. This simple-but-powerful ritual almost always ensures that I start right in on my work in the mornings, instead of getting waylaid by social media.[16]

If you do most of your work at home—or at an office, assigned library carrel, or other fixed location—working with two computers is pretty straightforward: you leave your disconnected computer at that location, and carry around your connected one (swapping files between them using thumb drives). True, the juggling gets more complicated if you're moving around a lot and/or working at multiple locations. Still, try to use a disconnected computer whenever you can. You could, for instance, bring your disconnected computer to the coffee shop, and use your phone for periodic email checks and other "urgent" online activities. (But keep your phone shut off most of the time, or you risk losing the whole benefit.) Then, when you

---

[16] Productivity expert Nick Wolny came up with a similar system involving the use of two smart phones—one optimized for work and the other for personal use: see https://debugger.medium.com/how-to-use-your-old-iphone-to-set-better-work-boundaries-741f3b00fcf8.

return home, you can boot up your connected computer and do the bulk of your online work or play.

Ultimately, you want to leave your connected computer off at all times except for those when you intentionally go online. Although it is probably harder to practice this kind of "digital minimalism," as Cal Newport calls it, in some fields than others, keep an open mind, and also keep trying out new ways to work—and play—disconnected. (See Chapter 44 for more tips on limiting your online time, and social media use in particular.)

Again, we're talking about a big divide here. Some people, when I suggest that they disconnect, understand why. But others are aghast, as if I had suggested that they disconnect an arm or leg while working. A college-aged reader of the manuscript for this book called the advice "peak Boomer," not realizing that many Boomers hate it, too! People of all ages have come to find the idea of disconnecting, even briefly, unthinkable. But ask yourself why that's so—and, also, who is benefiting from your spending long periods online in either low-value activities or corporate-engineered ludic loops.

Especially if disconnecting seems unthinkable, that's reason enough to give it a try. Few habits have as much potential to improve your productivity and life.

6. Building Your *Sitzfleisch*

Humans are social creatures, but studying is often a solitary activity—and so feelings of loneliness or isolation are a common obstacle to productivity. Happily, however, all it often takes to neutralize those feelings is a "study buddy" working quietly alongside you. They don't even need to be working on the same thing you're working on: just having the company is enough to keep you going.[17]

Not all study buddies are alike, however. I learned early on that the most helpful ones tend to be those who show up right on time (or a bit early) and work steadily throughout the interval. The less helpful ones show up late, and get up from their desks a time or two during the interval—each time interrupting my concentration and, I'm sure, their own. And the least helpful ones are in frequent motion, often leaving their desks.

The Germans have a handy word for the ability to sit still and stay focused on a task, *sitzfleisch.* (It translates roughly to "having a good sitting butt.") Probably the world champion of it was the 4th century philosopher Didymus of Alexandria, who wrote 3,500 books (actually, papyrus scrolls), and whose nickname, according to historian Stephen Greenblatt in his book *The Swerve,* was "Bronze Ass." Didymus probably wasn't a fan of what we now call "life balance," so you don't want to emulate him. Like all qualities, *sitzfleisch* is a double-edged sword: useful for some things (e.g., schoolwork and competitive chess), and not so much for others (e.g., staying healthy and fit).

---

[17] Good, local study buddies can be hard to find, so here's an article on apps that can pair you with remote ones: https://www.bbc.com/worklife/article/20200812-the-online-work-gyms-that-help-spur-productivity. Many people I know find https://www.focus-mate.com useful.

Of course, people have different ways of learning, and neurodivergence, disability, and other factors can play a role in determining how much *sitzfleisch* a person has. Still, for many people, the ability to sit still and stay focused for 30, 40, or 60 minutes at a stretch is both achievable and a good thing, productivity-wise.

Whatever your current amount of *sitzfleisch* is, you can increase it by using the below **Timed Work Intervals** technique.

First, some preliminaries:

Do all your preparation before starting your work session. This includes gathering your materials, refreshing your drink, arranging the temperature (or your clothing), and using the bathroom.

Next, **study in a space without clocks**. Yeah, that includes removing the clock from your computer desktop. You'll stop counting the minutes, and your sense of time will, somewhat magically, simultaneously seem to both expand (so you get more done) and go more quickly (so you get less bored and impatient). You know that daydream where time stands still, and so you finally have enough time to do everything you want to do? Working without a clock is probably the closest most of us can get to that in real life. (And yes, the technique also works for exercise and other activities where we're tempted to count the minutes.)[18]

Next, **grab a kitchen timer**—*not* your phone, which is distracting. (And has a clock!) Kitchen timers are cheap and come in many fun colors and styles: I highly recommend using them and other "props" whenever you can, because doing so adds interest and variety to your work.

1. Now you're ready to start your Timed Work Interval:
2. Pick a part of your project to work on. Pick one you truly want to work on, not one you think you should be working on. That feeling of wanting to work on something is called "inspiration," and you shouldn't waste it. (Find more techniques for recognizing and following your inspiration in Chapter 29.)
3. Set the timer to count down from three minutes. Or two minutes, or one minute, or 30 seconds: it's important to choose an interval you can easily complete.
4. Start the timer and start working. Work steadily, but without stress or pressure. Focus on the bit of work right in front of you, ignoring, for the moment, the rest of the project, and especially any concerns

---

[18] This "no clock" technique is also used by many stores, casinos, amusement parks, and other commercial spaces that want you to lose your sense of time so that you'll hang around longer and spend more money.

or expectations you have about the outcome. (And, obviously, any outside concerns, like your relationship or what you're having for lunch.)

If, during your interval, you feel yourself getting scared, stressed, distracted, judgmental, impatient, anticipatory, etc., *gently* talk yourself back to the work that's right in front of you. That fear and stress, by the way, is perfectionism—and so what you're also doing here is practicing nonperfectionism while working. Good stuff!

If you finish the bit you're working on, or find yourself getting bored or stuck, no problem. Immediately—and without fuss or drama—switch to another part of the project and keep working. (Repeat as necessary.)

5. When the timer goes off, take a break.
6. When you're ready, repeat Steps 1–4 either with the same or a different bit of work.
7. Repeat until you're done with your work session.

After you can reliably complete three minutes of stress-free (nonperfectionist) work, you can increase the timer to five or 10 minutes. Then, 15, 20, 30, 40 minutes, etc., until you reach your desired interval length. If, during an interval, you "accidentally" glance at the clock and are disappointed at how much time there is remaining in your interval, try reframing your situation more positively. Not, in other words, "30 more minutes!" *Groan.* "The time is crawling. I hate this!" But, "Wow, I still have 30 minutes left. What a gift of abundance! Okay, back to work...no rush...let's just have fun and see what I can do with these math problems."

If you ever find yourself having trouble completing your intervals, either because you're distracted or because the current project is especially difficult, don't hesitate to return to shorter ones. Remember, the important things are to: (a) finish your interval while (b) working nonperfectionistically throughout. (Eventually, you'll almost certain regain your "lost" *sitzfleisch*.)

Probably the biggest barrier to this exercise will be your Inner Perfectionist stepping in and saying something like, "Three minutes is nothing! We should go for three hours!" Feel free to ignore this misguided advice. (And we'll discuss how to deal with your Inner Perfectionist in Chapter 19.)

7. The Secret to Quantity *and* Quality

The goal of timed work intervals is not to get a lot of work done, or to do great work: it's to complete your interval while remaining nonperfectionist throughout. As Steven Pressfield says of his own work sessions in his book, *The War of Art*: "How many pages have I produced? I don't care. Are they any good? I don't even think about it. All that matters is I've put in my time and hit it with all I've got."

But wait! I hear you object. *I actually do want to get a lot of work done! And I also want to do great work!*

Fair enough—and the secret to achieving both goals is nonperfectionism.

Let's start with **quantity**. While it may seem sensible to set an ambitious page count or other "quantity" goal, doing so creates a perfectionist over-focus on product over process. (More on this in Chapter 13.) Think about it: if quantity goals worked, wouldn't we all be super productive by now? Most of us have been setting, and missing, such goals for years. But by setting a "process" goal of simply putting in your time while maintaining a focused but unstressed nonperfectionist mindset, you free yourself to do as much work as possible.

But don't many professionals use quantity goals? And what about my deadlines? If I don't set a quantity goal, I'll miss them all!

You're right, many professionals do set quantity goals. You can, too—*after you've overcome your perfectionism.* To set such a goal while perfectionism is still holding you back, however, is likely only to backfire. (As the Pressfield quote illustrates, many professionals—including me, by the way—continue to stick with process goals.)

As for deadlines, yeah, we do have a bit of a problem. We're aiming not for a quick fix, but growth; and growth takes time and can be unpredictable. For a while, your output might be lower than you'd like, or even lower than it is now. (Because you're no longer using fear and punishment as motivators.) That will be scary, but stay the course and things should soon start to improve.

Now onto **quality**. In their terrific book *Art & Fear*, David Bayles and Ted Orland tell a story of two groups of ceramics students, one of which was told that they would be graded based on the quality of their pots, and the other that they would be graded based on the quantity. (The more pots, the higher the grade.) I'll let them tell you what happened:

> Well, came grading time and a curious fact emerged: the works of highest quality were all produced by the group being graded for quantity. It seems that while the "quantity" group was busily churning out piles of work—and learning from their mistakes—the "quality" group had sat theorizing about *perfection*, and in the end had little more to show for their efforts than *grandiose* theories and a pile of dead clay. [Italics mine—and I'll have more to say about grandiose theories in Chapter 13.]

Quantity *creates* quality, in other words. Not only does aiming for quantity give you more practice, it defuses perfectionism by puncturing the illusion that you can do a perfect job. Even the most committed perfectionist is going to have to relax their standards when given just 15 minutes to throw a pot, or five minutes to write a paragraph.

The above story also illustrates another productivity truism: that most of the time—and almost certainly within the context of a well-run college course—you have everything you need to succeed. Enough ideas, skills, help, etc. This is crucial to understand because many perfectionists suffer from a "scarcity mentality" that convinces them that they don't, in fact, have enough. (More on this in Chapter 13.)

Just to be clear—and so I don't get hate mail from professors—when I say that you should aim for quantity over quality, I am *not* suggesting that you hand in sloppy work. What I mean is that you shouldn't overwork your projects in a perfectionist quest to eliminate every single possible error. "Excellence doesn't require perfection," as the English novelist Henry James noted. Even in the relatively few situations where the goal truly is "zero errors," like your resume and cover letter, you achieve that not by going over your work a zillion times (which doesn't even work, since we all tend to miss our own mistakes), but by working with others (e.g., a career coach and proofreader).

The above story also illustrates how even reasonable-sounding goals, such as "to do great work" or "get a great grade," are often perfectionist, reflecting an overfocus on outcomes and external recognition, shortsightedness, grandiosity, etc. These goals also can, and often do, trigger a deeply controlling (a.k.a., perfectionist) mindset where, consciously or unconsciously, you're trying to force the work in a certain direction. Creativity, however, is fundamentally an organic, nonlinear, and liberated process: try to control it, even a little bit, and you'll shut it right down. (More on this in Chapters 25 and 29.)

The *only* ways to maximize your quality creative input are to:

1. Become radically nonperfectionist, and use nonperfectionist work methods (see Part III), so that your ideas and inspiration (and work) can flow freely.
2. Do your time management (Part IV) to ensure that you have plenty of time not just to do your work, but to think, read, watch, listen, experience, experiment, play, etc.

One final tip for your intervals: **don't judge your experience of them.** Many perfectionists have such a strong habit of judging that, once they stop judging their work, they start judging their feelings while doing their work. "I did my work today but I didn't enjoy it," they'll grumble at me—to which I'll reply: "Fantastic! You did your work! That's the important thing. Now go out and celebrate." True: the goal is *joyful* productivity. But no one is joyful 100% of the time, and not all projects are equally fun. (And, as I'll discuss in Chapter 31, even fun projects typically have a "yuck" stage in the middle.) Your job is to continue working, while noting, but not giving too much attention to, any negative feelings that may arise. Do that, and the negative feelings will most likely dissipate, leaving you free to more fully experience the positive ones.

8. Working on the Right Stuff

"Effectiveness" means both doing the right stuff, and doing lots—or, at least, enough—of it. In this book, I mostly focus on the "doing lots" part, since it's really your professors' job to teach you what the right stuff is for their particular subjects. But here are a few general guidelines for making sure that you are, indeed, getting the most out of the time you're putting into your schoolwork.

First, always remember that the goal isn't to study, it's to learn. Memorization and knowing how to look stuff up are important parts of learning, but not the whole thing. True learning only occurs when you engage deeply with the material. As Paulo Freire noted in his classic *Pedagogy of the Oppressed*, "Reading is not walking on the words; it's grasping the soul of them."

Think, for instance, of your favorite book, film, album, etc. Probably you've read or seen or listened to it many times and know parts of it by heart. Perhaps you've thought about its various meanings and how they relate to your life experiences and situation. Maybe you've even read the artist's biography, researched their techniques and influences, and thought about why they made the choices they did.

And maybe you've even created your own work in response to theirs.

That's engagement, and you should seek to engage similarly with the people, places, times, ideas, principles, practices, and methods you're encountering in your classes. Here are some techniques for doing that:

Seek out the best teachers. Especially for difficult classes. A great teacher can not only help you learn, they can open your mind and transform your life. Now, some teachers are natural performers: their classes are always lively and fun and snapping with all kinds of intellectual razzle-dazzle. Go

47

ahead and take their classes. But don't overlook the less flashy teachers who show their caring and commitment via well-prepared lectures and course materials, homework that's returned on time and with substantive comments, and a willingness to go the extra mile for a student.

Word of mouth—and especially recommendations from good students—is probably the best way to find out who the best teachers are.

Read (and reread) the syllabus. It's an important document that should not only provide you with a helpful overview of the class, but other information that will help you to study more effectively.[19]

Resource yourself as abundantly as possible. Excellent supplies make the job easier and more fun. Obviously, many students don't have a lot of cash, but to the extent that you do, you should invest it in tools (like ergonomic furniture, see Chapter 9), supplies (like timers, or those fancy colored markers you've been coveting), and services (like tutoring, see Chapter 47) that help you to learn. Speaking of which…

Get the textbooks. I know that some students try to do without, in part because of the high prices, but they are invaluable. If possible, get the paper versions, and buy instead of rent, because marking up your books is part of an active and engaged learning process.[20] (Some rental services do let you mark up books, but the risk is that you'll receive a book that someone else marked up, which lessens the utility of the book and makes it less fun. So if you can afford to buy new, then do that.)

Learn the subject's "best practices." Meaning, the best ways to do the work, including how to avoid or overcome common obstacles. Ask your professor, and also do a Web search on "how to study [subject name]."

Read critically. In their book, *How to Study in College*, Walter Pauk and Ross Owens suggest that, when reading for an assignment, you first skim the assigned section, and then go back and read it closely—and maybe more than once. While reading, stop frequently to restate things in your own words, and to ask and answer questions. (E.g., "Why did it happen this way, and not that way?" and, "How does this reflect what we've been discussing in class?" and "How does [specific example] fit into this analysis?")

Pay attention in class. Shut your phone and laptop off[21] and really focus on the professor. If you want to take extensive notes, record the lecture and take them later from the recording. (But always ask your professor's permission before recording.) Listen actively and critically, really thinking

---

[19] Snoop Dogg agrees! See https://youtu.be/aL_fP5axQV4.

[20] https://www.affordablecollegesonline.org/college-resource-center/reduce-the-cost-of-college-textbooks / offers some good options for purchasing lower-cost textbooks.

[21] See, for example: https://www.nytimes.com/2017/11/22/business/laptops-not-during-lecture-or-meeting.html.

about (and questioning) what the professor is saying, while also working to connect the information with what you already know.

Have a learning goal for each study session. Not, for instance, "to do my reading," but, "to understand the causes of the Cold War." And not, "to do my problem set," but, "to learn how to solve complex differential equations."

Team up. Work with motivated study buddies, and they will not only help you to learn, but inspire you with their ideas and enthusiasm. (And you will, of course, do the same thing for them.)

When asking for help, get specific. Don't hide behind generalities: tell your professor exactly what you're having trouble with.

Get visual. Create flow charts, diagrams, timelines, bubble maps, and other visual aids that convey the material in fresh and useful ways. (Just be careful not to overdo this, so that it becomes a form of Quasiproductive Procrastination.)

Teach someone else. Even your dog, cat, fish, or ferret! Or, if no one's around, pretend that you're explaining the topic to a five-year-old. It's when we try teaching others that we truly understand what we know and don't know.

Write it out. Another sure-fire way of finding out what you know and don't know.

During tests, first calculate how much time you have for each problem, and then do the easiest problems first. (If they're easy enough, you might wind up with some extra time for the harder ones.) Stay mindful of the time, and watch out for Beginning Bias (Chapter 32).

And a few other tips specifically for **solving math, science, engineering, and other technical problems**:

Read the entire problem, and think for a moment about the entire problem, before trying to solve it. Some students "jump the gun" and start trying to solve problems without having fully read or thought about all the information presented. (And, needless to say, some homework and test questions are worded in such a way as to trick you into doing just that.) A good preventive against doing that is to underline everything in the problem's text that you think you'll need to use in the solution. (See, also, Chapter 26's discussion of "slow work.")

Write out the solution's basic steps or logic without doing any of the research or calculations. Be sure to include the units (e.g., kg, mol, m/sec^2), however, since making sure that your answer includes the correct one(s) is an important way of checking your work. This kind of "problem sketching" is useful for helping you figure out which approaches make the most sense, and especially for avoiding false starts or other time waste during tests.

After you've solved a problem, **try explaining your solution in non-technical language.** Again, try teaching that hypothetical five-year-old. (Bonus points if you also explain what *doesn't* work.)

This has been a tiny overview of a vast topic. For follow-up reading, I recommend Walter Pauk and Ross Owens's *How to Study in College*.

9. The Re-Empowerment Process I: Overcoming Your Obstacles

Creating options, as we did in Chapter 4, is a quick and easy way to re-empower yourself, and it's particularly useful when you're in a rush. To get maximally productive, however, you should take the time to systematically identify and resolve all your obstacles to doing your work. I discuss the first part of this process, obstacle identification, in this chapter and the second part, obstacle resolution, in the next.

Obstacles fall into six general categories:

1. **Project-Related.** Your project is difficult, confusing, boring, overwhelming, etc. Or your teammates aren't doing their job.
2. **Course-Related.** There's a mismatch between you and the course. Maybe you lack the right skills or preparation for it. Or maybe it's badly organized or taught.
3. **Resource-Related.** Your workspace is uncomfortable, inconvenient, noisy, or ill-equipped. Or you lack a well-functioning computer or other necessary piece of equipment.
4. **Time-Related.** You don't have enough time.
5. **Personal Issues.** You have physical or mental health challenges, or a learning difference.[22] Or you're dealing with perfectionism or one of the other barriers to productivity I discuss in this book. Or,

---

[22] As per the "On Using the Correct Toolset" note at the beginning of this book, if you're dealing with a physical or mental health issue, or a learning difference, please consult a specialist.

you're dealing with serious relationship, financial, and/or other problems. (Or are worried about someone else who is.)

6. **Societal Issues.** You're distracted by events in your community or the larger world. (And perhaps, also, anxious, depressed, or grief-stricken about them.)

A word about that "Resource-Related" category: it's more important than it might seem because **a lot of procrastination begins in the body**. (You feel a bit uncomfortable, and that feeling builds until you have to get up from your chair.) There's also a safety issue, because a bad setup can cause an injury. (Once, after working on a too-high desk for just a few weeks, I got an elbow injury that took *two years* to heal.) So, always use a comfortable and adjustable ergonomic setup.[23] Many dorms and study spaces now provide good desks and chairs, but if you need to get your own, there are lots of cheap sources.

In ergonomics, seemingly "little" things can make a big difference. I'm a big fan of adjustable book stands, which are cheap and make reading (especially big textbooks or reference books) far easier on your neck and shoulders. If you're doing a lot of typing I really recommend using a "wavy" keyboard that lets you hold your wrists at a natural angle. (Try one in a store for just a moment, and I think you'll be sold.) Footrests are also cheap—or free, if you create yours from a cardboard box. (Top it off with a spare pillow or bit of foam for extra comfort.)

Don't forget lighting! Adjustable, variable-setting desk lamps are also cheap.

I know many students don't have a lot of money, but to the extent you have it, investing in furniture and supplies that make studying easier, safer, and pleasanter is an excellent choice. It also sends the crucial message to both yourself and others that, "This work is important, and I'm committed to it. And my health and safety are also important."

Returning to the entire list, that's a lot of potential obstacles! Picture each as a string, and all of those strings snarled up in a giant ball; then, picture that giant snarly ball blocking—as in "writer's block" or "creative block," get it?—the "path" you're trying to walk along. (Meaning, the plan or schedule you're trying to follow for the day.) Some people visualize their block as a boulder or wall, but I think a snarl is a much more useful representation because it reflects the fact that your block is actually made up of multiple

---

[23] Here are two good, quick ergonomics primers: https://youtu.be/i1wIcVRP9xQ and https://youtu.be/9mJDs2CGZRI. And for a deep dive: https://ergo.human.cornell.edu/ergoguide.html.

smaller "strands" (obstacles) that you can "untangle" (resolve) one at a time. Even better, the more untangling you do, the easier the rest of the snarl becomes to deal with!

The next time you feel tempted to procrastinate, therefore, don't waste time with negative self-talk. Instead, just grab your computer or notebook and make a list of all the obstacles that are blocking your ability to do your work. Be sure to include any "small" ones, such as that your chair is uncomfortable and your lighting poor. The small ones do add up—and, like icebergs, are often bigger than they seem.

Table II shows a sample Obstacle List for a student stuck on an art project.

Table II: Sample Obstacle List

Category	Obstacles
Project-Related	1. I've got a whole bunch of pieces and don't know how to put them together (a.k.a., confusion or overwhelm). 2. No matter how hard I work, this project is destined to fail (a.k.a., futility). 3. I'm so bored with this thing!
Course-Related	4. The instructions were confusing. I don't actually know what I'm supposed to be doing. 5. My professor can be hard to reach, so I can't ask questions. 6. They can also be harsh, so I'm afraid to ask. 7. Also, I don't want to let them know how little I've gotten done!
Resource-Related	8. The art studio is way on the other side of campus. It's hard to get to, especially during winter. 9. It's also cold and uncomfortable. 10. There aren't enough paints and other supplies.
Time-Related	11. Not enough time! I've got a ton of other stuff to do.
Personal Issues	12. I'm exhausted. I never get enough sleep. 13. My brother is going through a hard time, and I'm worried about him. 14. I'm also worried about whether my scholarship will be renewed for next year.
Societal Issues	15. The current political situation really upsets me.

Fifteen obstacles may sound like a lot, but it really isn't: most people come in at anywhere between 10 and 40. (Yes, 40.) In fact, many people are shocked at the number of obstacles they come up with, because much of the time we're often only half-aware of many of our obstacles...which is why you should do Exercise 3!

Exercise 3

Make an Obstacle List for a project you've been procrastinating on. After you've finished, take a moment to reflect on it, and especially to feel some compassion and respect for yourself. Maybe at times you've bashed yourself for your supposed laziness or lack of discipline. (Or others have.) Now it turns out you've actually been struggling honorably to do your work in the face of many obstacles.

Note: What's even better than doing an Obstacle List to help you identify your barriers while doing your work? Doing one before you get started, so that you can identify potential barriers and nip them in the bud! Get in the habit of doing such a "preemptive" list, especially before your big, complicated, important, or otherwise difficult projects.

Obstacle Resolution

After you've created your Obstacle List, start listing possible solutions to each obstacle, and then implement the best solutions. Table III shows the beginning of our art student's solutions list.

Table III: Sample Solutions List

Category	Obstacle	Possible Solutions
Project-Related	1. I've got a whole bunch of pieces and don't know how to put them together (a.k.a., confusion or overwhelm).	1. Use journaling to clarify exactly what the problem(s) are. 2. Ask the professor for help. (Or another professor or a teaching assistant, if that's easier.) 3. Ask a classmate or an artistic friend for help. 4. Make a to-do list; tackle one item at a time. 5. Use the solutions in Parts II and III of this book to help defuse perfectionism.
	2. No matter how hard I work, this project is destined to fail (a.k.a., futility).	1. Journal for clarity: is there a specific reason you feel this way and can it be addressed? 2. Are you being perfectionist? (See Part II.) 3. Discuss with your professor or another helper.
	3. I'm so bored with this thing!	(See solutions in Chapter 32.)
Etc.		

Two very cool things happen when you start coming up with solutions:

1. **You empower yourself.** Every problem-solving step you take—from identifying the problem, to journaling about it, discussing it with others, listing possible solutions, trying out a solution, improving that solution, and implementing the improved solution—empowers you some, thus making it easier for you to take the next step. It's a virtuous cycle! (The opposite of a vicious cycle.) And the more empowered problem-solving you do, the more empowered, in general, you become.
2. **You become less afraid, and more optimistic.** That's partly because of the empowerment, and partly because the solutions often turn out to be easier than we expect. You write, "ask a

classmate for help," for instance, and immediately think of a nice person you can ask. Or, "get more sleep," and immediately think of some evening events you can cancel so that you can do that. However, even with the solutions that take more work, or even years of work (e.g., learning to cope with a chronic physical or mental health condition), and even for the problems that will never be fully solvable (e.g., a difficult family situation), or are largely out of your control (e.g., the societal problems), you're still way better off problem-solving than procrastinating.

Some of your solutions, especially for problems in the Personal category, may involve seeing a counselor or therapist. Most colleges do offer such services but limit you to just a few appointments, which usually isn't enough. See if your insurance will cover additional appointments with a therapist in the local community. Or, if not, whether there's a therapist who offers a "sliding scale" fee structure. If you have to pay out of pocket, and are in a position to do so, then do it—good therapy is one of the best investments around. (I speak from experience, by the way.)

Your therapist should not only offer services congruent with your needs—trauma work, eating disorder work, relationship counseling, addiction recovery, etc.—but feel like a good fit in terms of personality and communication style. And after the first couple of getting-to-know-each-other sessions, your work together should start yielding meaningful change in your life. If your first therapist isn't doing all this for you, then keep looking until you find one who does.

Exercise 4

Come up with solutions for the obstacles you listed in Exercise 3 and start implementing the best ones.

10. The Re-Empowerment Process II: Getting Help and Resolving Conflicts

Got a problem?

Well, someone you know probably has a solution.

Oh, I know, I know: you don't want to ask for help. You're afraid you'll look "dumb"—although asking for help is the opposite of that. Or you don't want to "impose" on anyone—even though, in college, you are literally surrounded by people who are being paid to help you. Or you think it's somehow more admirable to go it alone. Sure: try that, for a little while, anyway. But if you really need help—and why wouldn't you? We all do!—it's best not to be in denial about that, because: (1) as discussed in Chapter 2, the desire to go it alone, no matter how well-rationalized, is often rooted in deeper issues; and (2) a failure to ask can lead to some spectacularly time-wasting forms of Quasiproductive Procrastination (QP), such as:

1. Trying to figure out which direction to take your project, when your professor can tell you in a flash.
2. Struggling endlessly with a computer problem, when the friendly gurus at your college computer center know exactly how to fix it.
3. Wasting time, and risking failure, doing a difficult project from scratch when a more-experienced person can tell you what works and doesn't work. (Otherwise known as "reinventing the wheel.")
4. Having both halves of a conversation in your head when you really should be talking to the other person. (An incredibly common form of QP.)

The bottom line is that isolation, no matter how tempting, is not your friend—and asking for help is really one of the most empowering things you can do. The latter is probably why, often, after someone emails me for help, I'll get a second email from them a few minutes later saying, "Never mind! I figured it out for myself!"

You'll also be further empowered, of course, by the actual help you wind up receiving, as well as by your strengthened relationship with your helper. (Who will themselves be further empowered by having helped.) So many great outcomes just from the simple act of asking for help! And so, **you should ask for help early and often**. Ask when potential problems are still small, so that you can nip them in the bud. Or, ask even before they arise, so you can avoid them entirely. (Example: "Hi! I'm planning to do X. Can you tell me the best way to do it? Also, what problems do people typically encounter, and how can I avoid those?") Do this not just for your school-work, but all your important endeavors.

Unfortunately, there can be barriers to asking for help, especially for students from disadvantaged and nontraditional backgrounds. In his book *The Privileged Poor*, Anthony Abraham Jack notes that college students from poor backgrounds who had attended elite public or (via scholarship) private high schools were, like their more affluent classmates, "at ease and proactive in connecting with faculty, building support networks, and asking for help." But those from poor backgrounds who had attended (often) overcrowded and under-funded non-elite public high schools often weren't. "Faculty and administrators, for them, remain authority figures who should be treated with deference and left unburdened by their questions and needs."

Of course, there can be other reasons why a student from *any* background would be reluctant to reach out. They might be shy or overwhelmed, or stuck in a hoarding situation (as described in Chapter 2). But Jack is clear that a reluctance to interact with faculty and administrators comes at a great cost:

> Face time with faculty and administrators matters. … I saw again and again that forging these relationships was not just the way students got help with assignments and homework. Help on these kinds of specific tasks was just the tip of the iceberg. Relationships were a gateway for securing support for and achieving success in future endeavors. Developing rapport with key faculty and administrators was the road not just to assignment extensions, but also letters of recommendation, on-campus jobs, and off-campus internships. And these connections also meant so much more: having a faculty member or dean in your corner often meant getting the benefit of the doubt when in a

bind; or the single in the dorm with the nice windows; or introductions to corporate recruiters and help with negotiating job offers.

You should also be connecting with your peers. Obviously, it's good on a personal level to have friends, but it also turns out that it's good for you academically. A recent study shows that having a "peer social network" can increase your chances of succeeding in even a tough STEM (science, technology, engineering, and math) field.[24]

Let me say it again: isolation, no matter how tempting or well-rationalized, isn't your friend.

Resolving Conflicts

Sooner or later, one of your solutions will conflict with someone else's needs. When that happens, I recommend a conflict resolution technique I call **Cooperative Problem-Solving**. It's based partly on one in Adele Faber and Elaine Mazlish's famous parenting book, *How to Talk so Kids Will Listen & Listen So Kids Will Talk*, which I recommend to everyone, whether or not they have kids, because it's an excellent and fun communications guide.

Cooperative Problem-Solving consists of eight steps:

1. **State the problem** and how it makes you feel.
2. **Listen with patience, care, and respect** to the other person's response. That's not only kind, it motivates them to work with you, and also provides you with the information you need to craft a mutually acceptable solution.
3. **Restate** the other person's points. That shows that you've been listening, and also helps ensure that you're on the right track in terms of coming up with a solution. Please note that you want to "restate" and not "repeat." Verbatim repetition can not only be annoying—kids often do it to tease each other—it can (somewhat paradoxically) convey the impression that you actually haven't been listening. (Think of a classroom full of kids being forced to repeat what their teacher says, and just droning away mechanically at it.)
4. **Get the "yes"**—meaning, their agreement that you've restated their views accurately. You do this by asking, after restating, "Did I get that right?" or something similar. If they reply, "Yes," then good work! But don't worry if they say, "no." Just ask them to repeat what they said, and try restating again. (And again, if necessary, until you get your "yes.") By the way, a "no" doesn't necessarily mean that you

---

[24] https://advances.sciencemag.org/content/6/45/eaba9221

weren't listening well: it could be that the other person didn't express themselves clearly, or were clarifying their thoughts as they spoke with you. (That actually happens a lot.)

5. After you get your "yes," you can move onto...

6. **Brainstorm solutions.** You and the other person each list possible solutions *without judging or evaluating them.*

7. **Negotiate.** It's interesting how late in the process this step occurs. Conflict resolution really is mostly listening! You typically negotiate by first vetoing the solutions each of you finds wholly unacceptable, and then figuring out a good compromise among the rest.

8. **Restate the agreed-upon solution** and **get the other person's "yes."** And if you don't get a "yes" the first time around, repeat Steps 6 and 7 (and 5, if necessary) until you do.

9. **Express *sincere* gratitude.**

Here's how the steps work in action:

Hector has become increasingly concerned and frustrated that his suite has become "Gaming Central." Practically every night, one of his suitemates, Lou, has some friends over; and they spend all night gaming in the common living room. The noise makes it impossible for Hector to study, and some-times to sleep. Also, Hector would sometimes like to sit in his own living room and watch TV!

He's tried dropping hints, but that hasn't worked, so he knows he has to discuss the problem with Lou. And so, one afternoon he knocks on Lou's door and asks if he has time to talk. Lou invites him in, and here's how the conversation goes:

> **Hector (Stating the Problem):** Hey, I'm wondering if we could do something about the constant gaming in our suite. It's keeping me from studying and sleeping, and it's really stressing me out, especially with finals coming.

> ***Note:*** It would be great, at this point, if Lou responds with something like: "Sorry! I didn't know it was a problem. Tell me what I can do to make the situation better." And you know what? People often do re-spond with that kind of ready helpfulness and consideration. For the sake of this example, however, let's assume that Lou doesn't.

> **Lou:** Really? It's bothering you? No one else has complained.

Hector: Maybe that's because my room is closest to the living room, or because Bert and Jackie spend more of their studying somewhere else. I can't really speak for them. But the situation isn't working for me. And, you know, another problem is that sometimes I want to sit and watch TV, but you guys are monopolizing it.

Lou (defensively): Well, what do you want me to do?

Hector: Look, I appreciate your willingness to talk it over, and I know it's not the easiest conversation to have. But why don't you tell me your take on the situation? (Now he **Listens with Patience, Care, and Respect.**)

Lou: Well, it's supposed to be a commons area, isn't it? I've got as much right to use it as anyone. Also, we've got the best gaming system in the dorm.

Hector: (Restating and **Getting the Yes)** You're right: it is everyone's area to use. And since we've got the best gaming setup in the dorm, of course everyone wants to use it. Is that right?

Lou: Yup.

Hector: (Brainstorming) Well, can we come up with any solutions?

Lou: Well, you could always study in the library. That's what it's there for.

Hector: Okay, that's one. Any others?

Lou: You could wear noise-canceling headphones.

Hector: Okay. Any others?

Lou (thinks for a moment, then shrugs): Not really.

Hector (Negotiation): Okay. The headphones idea isn't bad. Still, I feel like I should be able to study in my own room, if I want. And I need to be able to sleep without you guys waking me up all night. Isn't that reasonable?

Lou: Yeah, I guess so.

Hector: So how about this: your friends can hang out in our living room until 9:00 p.m. After that, you'll all go somewhere else to game.

Lou: How about 10:00?

Hector: How about 9:00 on weeknights, and midnight on Fridays and Saturdays?
Lou: And Sundays?

Hector: It's gotta be 9:00. Sundays are study nights.
Lou (sighs): Okay. But how about 1:00 on Fridays and Saturdays?

Hector: Sure. Also, I'll go ahead and buy some earplugs, but could you guys also lower the volume?
Lou: Okay.

Hector: And no gaming at all during midterms and finals weeks, okay?
Lou: How about just in the afternoons?

Hector (thinks about it, then reluctantly nods): I guess afternoons are okay...I can always go to the library. But nothing after dinner, okay?
Lou: Okay.

Hector: (moves onto **Restating** and **Getting the Yes**) Okay, so we agree that you guys will shut off all the games at nine, except on Fridays and Saturdays, when you'll go till 1:00. I'll get some earplugs, you'll lower the volume, and no gaming after dinner on test weeks. Is that all okay?
Lou: Yup.

Hector: (Gratitude): Thanks a lot for talking with me about this. I really appreciate it.

If the other person won't engage in this process, or won't compromise at all, that's too bad. Do your best to create some acceptable options for yourself. Or, you could ask a mutual friend, or someone in authority—in the case of housing disputes, maybe a residence advisor—to mediate. But even if you get a poor outcome from all of this, you'll still be glad you advocated for yourself, and be more empowered and skillful (for example, at negotiation) for having done so.

11. The Best Solution to Procrastination

The best solution to procrastination is, obviously, to not need to do it in the first place—and you can achieve this, at least mostly! To see how, let's take a closer look at our friend the Disempowerment Cascade. Turns out, it's an interaction among three internal personae (or "voices"). They are:

The **Fragile Creator.** The persona who's trying to work. They're fragile not because you're weak, but because the work is challenging and you're facing many obstacles.

The **Terrified and Terrorizing Perfectionist.** (Also sometimes known as the Inner Critic or Inner Bully.) This persona is both hypercritical and terrified of failure, which isn't a great combination. They're also almost certainly suffering from some other problems that I'll be discussing in Part II, including shortsightedness, negativity, and a fixation on supposed personal "flaws." They are, in fact, the persona responsible for Chapter 3's disempowering monologue: "What's wrong with you?," "Why are you so lazy?," etc. And when the pain they cause becomes intolerable, the third persona is invoked...

The **Rebellious Procrastinator.** Contrary to what you might guess, they are *not* your enemy. Their job is to rescue the fragile Creator from the bullying Perfectionist, and in some ways they represent the best part of you: the part that is willing to fight for freedom, authenticity, and self-expression, and against bullying, coercion, and injustice. The problem is that they are invoked in circumstances of panic and stress, and are therefore disempowered and not great at problem solving. In fact, the only "solutions" they can come up with to address the problem of the perfectionist bullying are:

1. *Rebellion.* As in, "Why am I stuck inside doing this stupid work when everyone else is outside having a great time? It's not fair! Screw it, I'm going out!" (Recall Timothy Pychyl's point, from Chapter 2, about how procrastination often originates as a rebellion against authoritarian parenting.)
2. *Helplessness.* As in, "I can't even try to get started on my work."

Here's the tricky part: although your Inner Procrastinator can only come up with those two bad solutions, they can come up with infinite ways to "sell" them to you. So if it's not, "It's nice out and dammit I deserve a break!" it's "I should do all these less-important tasks first so that tomorrow I can focus better on my big project." Or "A little TV won't hurt." Or "[Insert your favorite rationalization for procrastination here.]"

Always remember that **the fundamental goal of productivity work is to be able to show up on time and do what you had planned to do.** Maybe not every single time—we all have emergencies and "off" days. But most of the time. When you accept that foundational truth and stay mindful of it while you work, you will become much less susceptible to your Inner Procrastinator's manipulations.

Of course, the best solution would be to retire your Inner Perfectionist persona, because it's in response to them, and as a protection from them, that you invoke your Inner Procrastinator in the first place. I'll discuss ways to do that in Part II.

PART II
COMPASSION

12. Perfectionist Myths and Realities

Note: The first quarter (roughly) of this section (Chapters 12–15) provides an overview of perfectionist attitudes and behaviors. After that, I'll discuss solutions (Chapters 16–23). And I'll end (Chapter 24) with a discussion of ambivalence, which is closely linked to perfectionism. Also, just to remind you: in this section and elsewhere in the book, I do some labeling, dichotomizing, and generalizing to keep the prose concise. So you'll see a lot of "Perfectionists do this…" and "Nonperfectionists do that…" In real life, however, I would avoid doing that. (It's okay to label a behavior, but not a person—and anyhow, no one is entirely perfectionist or nonperfectionist.)

Perfectionism is a set of attitudes and behaviors that make it hard, or even impossible, to do your work. Unfortunately, there's a lot of confusion out there, with many people confusing perfectionism with "having high standards" or "caring about my work," and some even thinking, "It's good to be a little perfectionist." That can make it hard to even identify the problem, much less solve it.

Let's, then, be crystal clear: **perfectionism is *never* a good thing.** It *never* helps, and *always* hinders, your creativity and productivity. It can also hinder you in other areas of your life, including your relationships and health. After you've finished this section, I hope you will commit to rejecting perfectionism in all its forms, and in all areas of your life. I especially hope you'll reject it at times you feel you've failed or had a setback. At such times, the temptation to revert to guilt, shame, deprivation, and other perfectionist punishments will be strong. But you need to be stronger. (More on that in Chapter 22.)

Beth's story, below, shows us how perfectionism can create serious problems for a student—but also how, with the right support, that student can overcome her perfectionism and resolve those problems.

Procrastination had never been a big problem for **Beth**, a creative writing major. Her fiction had always come easily, and had always been well received by professors, classmates, editors, award committees, and others. And so, she hadn't really expected to run into any problems with her senior project, an interconnected series of five short stories based on her family history and centering on the small farming community where she had grown up.

But she was running into problems. She was determined to create as true and nuanced a portrait of her family as she could, including both the positives (the close family ties, hard work, and perseverance in the face of obstacles) and negatives (poverty, addiction, and loss), but she was finding it hard to balance all those elements. At the same time, she was constantly worried about how her family would react to the stories when they read them. Would they see her as "airing dirty laundry" or, even worse, holding them all up for public judgment and ridicule? There had already been grumblings from home about some of her other autobiographical works.

Beth felt trapped, in other words, between telling the stories she wanted to tell and the knowledge that doing so was likely to upset those she loved. That wasn't the only thing blocking her, either: last year, a semi-famous writer who had been a visiting instructor in the creative writing program had harshly critiqued one of her stories, calling it "clichéd" and "derivative." Fortunately, it had happened during a private critique meeting, and so the rest of her class hadn't heard it—but Beth still cringed to recall it. She was now constantly on the alert lest any other bit of her writing be clichéd.

Beth also faced another source of pressure, which was that this was the project she was hoping would launch her literary career. If her stories turned out well, her plan was to, first, get them published in literary magazines, and then later expand them into a novel. It was important to her that she have some early success with her writing, both because a writing career had always been her dream, and because an early success would vindicate her insistence on majoring in creative writing, versus what her parents had considered a more practical field like teaching or nursing. Besides, nearly every time she read a literary blog or listened to a literary podcast, she heard about yet another 20-something writer who had gotten a book contract: why, she thought, shouldn't she be one of the "young successes?"

Beth knew she should be setting all of these concerns aside while writing, but she was having trouble doing that. Her worries kept crowding into her thoughts and crowding out the stories she was trying to tell. Her writing "pace" had consequently become slowed to a crawl, and it didn't help that she was also very unhappy with the quality of what little she was managing to produce. Whenever she compared her prose to that of one of her idols, like the short story master (and Nobel laureate) Alice Munro, she felt like crying.

Eventually, things got to the point where she couldn't even bring herself to go near her computer.

Finally, in desperation, she consulted her school's writing center. (She had previously ignored it, thinking that a "serious writer" like herself shouldn't need it.) Fortunately, the writing coach they assigned her—let's call him "Muse"—was himself a creative writer who also happened to have a lot of experience helping people overcome their procrastination, perfectionism, and other barriers. Along with helping Beth to recognize how, exactly, those barriers were blocking her ability to write, Muse also showed her how to do Timed Work Intervals (Chapter 6), Quickdrafts (Chapter 30), and other techniques that supported and encouraged her creativity. Beth embraced these methods and, sure enough, was able to start writing again.

In a follow-up meeting, Beth summoned the courage to tell Muse what the visiting instructor had said about her work. When she finished, Muse shook his head angrily. "We heard a lot of complaints about him," he said. "Apparently, he critiqued all the students' work very harshly. We told the Creative Writing Program that he shouldn't be invited back." Beth was incredibly relieved to hear that her work wasn't as bad as she had feared, and readily agreed to Muse's suggestions that she: (a) do her best to ignore the harsh instructor's comments, and (b) show her story to the professor supervising her senior project for some more balanced and useful feedback.

As for Beth's concerns about offending her family, Muse told her that that was a very common concern among writers of autobiographical fiction and nonfiction. His advice was that Beth, "write the stories you want to write, and that want to be written. Then, later on, you can decide whether you want to show them to your family or anyone else outside the Creative Writing Program." Beth found that advice incredibly liberating.

Finally, Muse raised a concern of his own: Beth's unrealistic career strategy. "The fiction world is *really* competitive," he said. "Contrary to all the media hype, almost no one gets a book published soon after college. You need a more realistic plan." This was hard for Beth to hear, but it also came as a relief because, underneath it all, she had known that her career plan was unrealistic. Muse aided her in coming up with a more realistic one whereby she would build up a meaningful body of work over time, while at the same time supporting herself by working at media or other jobs that would get her the connections she needed to accelerate her publishing success.

With all this great help, Beth was able to regroup, have more realistic expectations, and get more relaxed about her writing—all of which meant that she could be more productive, and...

...finish her senior project on time.

13. How Perfectionists Think

In this chapter, I discuss the most common perfectionist attitudes; and in the next, I discuss some common perfectionist behaviors. Obviously, there's a lot of overlap between attitudes and behaviors, with the attitudes often causing the behaviors. But the attitudes discussed in this chapter can cause many different types of antiproductive behaviors, and so it's useful to discuss them separately.

(1) Perfectionists devalue process and overvalue product/outcome. For them, it's all about the grade. (Or getting the scholarship, landing the job, etc.) Nothing else matters, including how hard they worked, what they actually accomplished (in terms of learning, performance, etc.), what internal or external barriers they overcame, and any intelligence, courage, kindness, integrity, or other admirable qualities they may have displayed along the way. This viewpoint isn't just fundamentally unfair and inhumane, it creates vast pressure *and* sucks all the joy out of your work.

Also, reducing the actual work you're doing to a mere "means to an end" makes it hard to stay motivated on big projects in particular.

Overfocusing on outcomes is actually dangerous, because you're never guaranteed a good one. You could be really well-prepared for a test, for instance, and still do disappointingly because it was poorly designed or happened to focus on your weakest area. Or you could prepare like mad for a job interview and still not do well because you got nervous or the interviewer was inept. Or, you could ace the interview and still not get the job because of nepotism, discrimination, or (more benignly) a budget cut. True: most of the time your grades and other outcomes should be commensurate with your efforts. If they're not, something's wrong, and you should consult your advisor and other mentors. It's also okay to hope for a good outcome,

71

so long as you don't get too attached to that hope. But, for the most part, you want to avoid having any strongly held expectations.

(2) Perfectionists define success narrowly and often unrealistically. To them, only an A—or, better yet, A+—is acceptable.

A professor comments that your paper was "very good"? Big deal! If it wasn't "excellent" or "outstanding" you've failed.

You're a runner-up in a tough academic, athletic, arts, performing, or other competition? Who cares? You didn't win.

Obviously, this attitude also creates vast pressure. It also redefines your successes as failures, which is one of the most demotivating, demoralizing, self-sabotaging, and pointless things you can do. (As already noted, the perfectionist tendency to confuse "success" and "failure" is why I frequently put those words in quotation marks.) See Chapter 21 for more on the difference between realistic and unrealistic definitions of "success," and Chapters 22 and 23 for more on "failure" and "success."

(3) Perfectionists are grandiose. Grandiosity is when you think the normal rules of productivity don't apply to you, or—put somewhat differently—that things that are difficult or even impossible for others should be easy for you. This can lead to:

- Unrealistic goal setting. ("Sure, I can handle five classes, a research project, and a job!")
- Underestimating the difficulty of challenges. ("This will be a piece of cake!")
- Unwillingness to research and plan ("Boring!") or ask for help. ("I'll figure it out myself.")
- Expecting yourself to succeed despite being under-resourced. ("Last year, it took five people and $500 to do this community project, but we should be able to do it this year with only three people and $300.")
- Tendency to take shortcuts. ("I'll just do the bare minimum for this class, and then make it all up on the final.")
- Tendency to think you or your project is special or even unique. ("My project is so intellectual/cutting-edge/original/etc. that there are no role models, and no one I can turn to for help.")
- Lack of respect for experience and expertise. ("I know my professor wants us to do the problems this way, but I'm going to do them that other way because it's faster.")
- Silly pointless rebellions. ("I won't bother getting a haircut for my job interview because my resume says it all.")

- Stinting on self-care. ("I only need four hours of sleep a night." Or "I don't need to see a counselor for my depression.")
- Trivialization of your pain or suffering. ("Who cares if I'm unhappy? It's my work that matters.")

Grandiosity can also cause you to take on overly ambitious projects. The underlying problems here are often insecurity and a desire to impress others. I can usually tell if someone's fallen into this trap because: (a) the project in question is too huge a leap from their previous work, (b) they lack the training and/or preparation to do it, (c) they're overfocused on externals (e.g., creating a fancy explanatory slideshow) versus the nuts and bolts of the work, (d) they're overfocused on others' anticipated glorious reactions to their work, (e) they're isolated (no mentors, collaborators, etc.), and/or (f) their plan has an overintellectualized or overcomplicated quality. (Out of all of those, I would say that (e), the lack of mentors, is the biggest red flag.) Don't get me wrong: ambition is great! But taking on an overly ambitious project is, like all perfectionism, a dead end. Overly ambitious projects tend to bog down in Quasiproductive Procrastination (QP) because the person won't let the project go, but also has no real idea of how to proceed—and so, they wind up burying themselves in pointless, and often repetitive, busy work. Then, when they can no longer maintain even the illusion that they're making progress, the QP usually devolves into full-blown Unproductive Procrastination (UP), at which point it's only a matter of time before they abandon the project.

To be clear, this particular problem should never happen in college, since your professors should be assigning projects at the appropriate level of difficulty. But sometimes they screw up or (gasp!) students don't follow instructions. (And then isolate themselves when they run into problems.) And sometimes projects just mushroom out of control. That last is actually a good problem to have, because what it's really indicating is an "excess of inspiration." But it's still a problem you need to solve. (Again, talk with your professor.)

Perfectionists usually have a compelling-sounding (to them, at least) rationalization for their grandiose ideas. Point out, for instance, that a perfectionist is overscheduling themselves, and they'll reply that they are "efficient" or "well-organized." Or, point out that they need to plan their big project, and they'll reply that they're "good at winging it." But the rationales fall apart at even the slightest scrutiny. No one, no matter how well-organized, can cram 10 hours of work into five hours, for instance. And while you may be able to "wing" a small or unimportant project, winging a big or important one is a recipe for disaster.

(4) Perfectionists overidentify with their work. As discussed in Chapter 3.

(5) Perfectionists are shortsighted. They live in one big, hyperjudgmental "now," in which every project (or task) is of the utmost importance. Even worse, every *moment* of every project is of the utmost importance. **The perfectionist, in other words, is constantly comparing their work and progress to an idealized version of what they think should be happening.** Even worse, they're constantly thinking that they're falling short, and constantly bashing themselves for that. (More on comparisons in the next chapter.)

Shortsightedness doesn't just result in a highly pressured and miserable work experience, it's also **one of the main reasons perfectionists quit projects.** (And classes, schools, careers, etc.) Whenever a perfectionist hits a "bump" in their project—even a small and/or ordinary one—they can't see their way past it, and get so discouraged they quit. Obviously, pathologizing, if present, will contribute to this predicament, and so will the disempowered belief that you have fewer options than you really do.

How does a perfectionist quit a project? Often by glomming onto a shiny new one that they hope will be, "the one that finally keeps me interested enough to finish." But it never is, for the simple reason that the problem isn't the projects, it's the perfectionism. (And if you're thinking that some people do the same thing with their romantic relationships—perpetually ending them when they get challenging and moving onto others they hope will magically go better—yeah, you're right.)

(6) Perfectionists are impatient. Because of their overfocus on product, overidentification, and shortsightedness, they need—no, crave—their success *now*. This impatience doesn't just make for a miserable work process, it compromises the quality of your work and is a barrier to learning (Chapter 26) and, more generally, health and happiness (Chapter 42).

Perfectionists are also impatient in their careers, craving youthful success. Many see life as a kind of race, and are constantly comparing their progress to that of their friends, acquaintances, siblings, and others, including media celebrities. The ubiquitous "30 Successful People Under 30"-type articles only feed this impatience, and they also have another big problem, which is that they heavily favor the privileged. As podcaster Kristen Meinzer puts it: "What would happen if [those types of articles] excluded people whose parents paid for their college, paid the down payment on their first place, or paid the bills while they worked unpaid or low-wage internships?"[25] (More on competition in the next chapter.)

---

[25] https://twitter.com/kristenmeinzer/status/1281287686662377476

(7) Perfectionists are negative. As noted in Chapter 4, they habitually underestimate and devalue their available options and outcomes. Even worse, they devalue their accomplishments, others' accomplishments, and others' willingness and ability to help them. They also mentally filter out positive results and outcomes, seeing only their "mistakes" and "failures." Tell a perfectionist you think their work is excellent except for one tiny thing, and they'll only hear the tiny thing—and probably inflate it into a Great Big Thing.

This negativity can lead to an even more disempowering **scarcity mentality**, in which you think that you either "aren't enough" (not smart, disciplined, creative, or attractive enough, etc.) or "don't have enough" (money, time, help, ideas, etc.) to succeed. Negativity and scarcity can also contribute to hoarding (Chapter 14), since they can convince you that your work is lacking—research, polish, originality, etc.—and so you hold onto it hoping that you can improve it. (See, also, Chapter 14's discussion of fixations, and note how this scarcity mentality aligns with the idea of not having enough good options or potential outcomes.)

A scarcity mentality can also manifest itself in the belief that it is somehow nobler or more impressive to succeed in the absence of adequate resources. Examples range from the centuries-old "starving artist in the garret" stereotype to the more recent "I ate ramen for five years before my big break" media profiles of successful artists and entrepreneurs. Please note that what I'm objecting to here is not scarcity itself—scarcity is neither a virtue nor a vice, just an unfortunate circumstance that some people must deal with—but a romanticizing of scarcity. It's vital that you not buy into this romanticizing, because, perfectionist myths aside, it is very hard—and, often, impossible—to succeed when you're under-resourced.

(8) Perfectionists distrust success, and often reframe their successes as failures. If a perfectionist gets a good grade, they'll come up with five reasons the achievement should be dismissed. (E.g., "the project was easy" or "the teacher's an easy grader.") And if their work is going easily, they'll worry that they're not challenging themselves enough. They might even add some unnecessary work to their project, just to make it harder!

There can be a cultural component to this problem. You may have been taught, for instance, that humility is a virtue, and that talking about your successes, even to yourself, is boasting. There's a difference, however, between taking pride in your achievements and boasting about them. Pride is based on an objective and humane assessment of yourself and your work. It's an emotion that you primarily communicate to yourself, although others can certainly sense and respond to it. It is also incredibly motivating, so you don't want to cheat yourself of it.

Boasting, in contrast, is usually grounded in insecurity, and primarily aimed at others. (Who aren't fooled.) I'll be discussing it some more in the next chapter.

Remember that the word "humble" derives from the same Latin root as "humus," meaning earth or ground. The classical virtue of humility isn't about being self-effacing or overly modest: it's about being grounded.

Perfectionists can also suffer from **impostor syndrome**. It's can take several forms, including the belief that you haven't earned your success or are somehow fooling everyone with it, and the belief that you really don't belong in the professional or other communities you wish to be a part of. Those from marginalized or under-represented communities can be especially vulnerable, as can those who have personally experienced harsh criticism or rejection. (See Part IV.) Even in such cases, however, dealing with your perfectionism can help alleviate the problem.

(9) Perfectionists are rigid. This shows up, especially, in a tendency to stick with a solution long after it's clear it's not working. If a perfectionist keeps getting distracted by their phone while they're trying to work, for example, they'll "keep trying till I can concentrate, dammit!" Or, if they're in a contentious relationship, they'll keep using the same ineffective coping strategies over and over again.

Perfectionists can also be rigid about their career choices. For them, it's "medical school or bust!" or "Employer X or bust!" with no backup plan. It's fine to have a cherished dream, and to work hard to achieve it. (The Appendices tells you how.) But it's always dangerous to not have a backup.

I've saved the worst for last:

(10) Perfectionists try to use punishment as a motivator. It usually takes the form of either a shaming label (e.g., "I'm such a loser for not doing well."), a threat ("If I don't do well, then I'm really going to be in trouble."), or deprivation (e.g., "I'm going to sit here until I get it right. No breaks!"). What's confusing is that these tactics sometime seem to work in the short term. But **punishment always leaves you more disempowered around your work and, thus, less able to do it in the future.** (Which is why I say perfectionists "try to" use it as a motivator.) Also, we become habituated to punishment, so that it eventually stops working even in the short term. The first time we call ourselves, or someone else calls us, "lazy," for example, it feels terrible, and might actually shame us into doing our work. But the fifth or 10th time? Yawwwwn.

Because perfectionists are constantly feeling like they failed, they are also constantly punishing themselves—which, needless to say, is a terrible way to live. Punishment is also alienating, and it provokes opposition. That's easy to spot when the "punished person" and "punisher" are different people—

think of a teenager rebelling against their domineering parents. But it also happens within us, when we respond to our bullying Inner Perfectionist by calling up our rebellious Inner Procrastinator. (As discussed in Chapter 11.)

The biggest problem with punishment, however, has nothing to do with whether it works: it's that it's inhumane and immoral. You should never do it to yourself or anyone else.

Those are the main perfectionist attitudes. See how they can all work together to create a trap? Overfocus on outcomes and define success narrowly and grandiosely, and you're pretty much guaranteed to "fail," especially if you're both impatient for your success, and mistrustful of any successes you happen to achieve. Overidentify with that "failure," and you'll feel even worse, especially if you can't shortsightedly see past it. And respond to all this by punishing yourself, and you're guaranteed to feel not just miserable, but hopeless—especially if you rigidly refuse to consider any other way of approaching your work.

And procrastination will start to make sense as an escape from all that pain and hopelessness.

14. How Perfectionists Behave

Below are some common perfectionist behaviors, all of which derive from one or more of the attitudes discussed in Chapter 13.

Labeling. By now, I hope you understand why you shouldn't use punishing/shaming labels like "lazy" or "undisciplined." But even positive labels can be problematic. Being labeled as "gifted" or "talented" can put a lot of pressure on you, leading to perfectionism and procrastination. (Also see Chapter 16's discussion of "model minority.")

Some people get into trouble by overidentifying with a professional label such as "artist" or "engineer." It's okay to use those labels, only don't do so in a way that increases the pressure on yourself or limits your options. Beliefs such as, "an artist should be willing to sacrifice everything for their art" and "an engineer should only be concerned with data and never feelings" are both incorrect and unhelpful. (Also notice both statements' grandiosity.)

Be careful even with more objective labels. You might think of yourself as "pragmatic," or "idealistic," or "caring," for instance. That's wonderful—until you take things too far and your pragmatism becomes stodginess, your idealism becomes shallow fantasy, and your caring becomes overgiving (Chapter 48). As it turns out, many of our vices are simply our cherished virtues taken just a bit too far.

You also want to avoid labeling your work. A professor once told a friend of mine that her paper was "brilliant": she spent the rest of the semester terrified of not living up to that high standard. Perfectionists also often label their projects as "hard" or "easy," then dichotomize those labels so that "hard" becomes, in their mind, impossible, and "easy" trivial. This leads to a lot of fear (in anticipation of your supposedly hard stuff) and discouragement (when your supposedly easy stuff turns out to be harder than anticipated). Better to let those labels go, and let your work just be your work. And when praising someone else's work, it's a good idea to follow psychologist Carol Dweck's advice from her bestselling book *Mindset*, and praise not their outcome or what you consider to be their intrinsic talents (e.g., intelligence), but their "growth-oriented *process—what* they accomplished through practice, study, persistence, and good strategies." (Italics mine.)

The worst labels tend to be **hyperbolic**. Statements like, "my paper is garbage," "my workout is hell," and, "I'm the worst girlfriend ever" do nothing but increase your fear and disempowerment around the activity in question. And while we're on the topic of word choice, be aware that there are a few seemingly benign words that, all by themselves, are enough to make a statement or thought perfectionist. One is "just," as in the statement, "It's just 10 math problems." The implication—and dangerous expectation—is that your work should go quickly and easily. Ditto for "only," which is often used the same way. Another "stealth-perfectionist" word is "should," as in, "I should be able to handle five courses, a sports team, and a job." (An assumption or expectation that often turns out to be grandiose.)

In my writing productivity classes, we often do an exercise entitled "Perfectionism Test," where students identify the perfectionist elements in a group of sentences. After we're done, I say, "Hey! There's one more perfectionist thing on the page—can you find it?" Most students can't. "It's the title!" I point out. "Why call this a 'test?' Why not call it an 'exercise' or even a 'game?'" The simple act of swapping in "exercise" for "test" causes everyone in the room, including me, to relax.

These kinds of perfectionist word traps are everywhere. So please watch your words, and keep things as light and playful as possible.

Comparisons. Perfectionists constantly compare themselves to anyone and everyone, including family members, friends, strangers, and famous people both living and dead. They'll compare themselves on any criterion, including grades, looks, popularity, wealth, and possessions. They'll even compare themselves to *themselves* at a higher level of performance. A perfectionist who was once able to write an "A" paper overnight, run a four-and-a-half-minute mile, or perform a faultless Brahms piano sonata will constantly expect themselves to repeat that exceptional achievement, and constantly bash themselves for failing.

Speaking of Brahms, he was, relentlessly and from a young age, compared with Beethoven, to the point where people would joke that his First Symphony would actually be "Beethoven's 10th." And you know what? It took him *21 years* to produce that symphony. The miracle was that he was able to produce it at all, given the enormous pressure and public scrutiny he labored under. "You can't have any idea what it's like always to hear such a giant marching behind you," he bemoaned in a letter to a friend.

Many perfectionists also constantly compare themselves to—and constantly bash themselves for falling short of—an idealized version of an identity or role that's important to them, such as the "good student," "dedicated activist [or artist]," or "dutiful child of immigrant parents." Philosophers call this the "Nirvana Fallacy," and it is an especially demoralizing and exhausting habit. Many perfectionists also constantly compare their work sessions to an ideal, and constantly bash themselves for supposedly (not really!) falling short in terms of quantity or quality. They'll even compare themselves, in the midst of all that constant pressure, to some mythical creator for whom the work is always easy and joyful—and then bash themselves for falling short of that ideal as well.

Comparisons can obviously be a useful analytical tool. A perfectionist comparison rarely is, however, because the goal of a perfectionist comparison isn't objective analysis, but to shame yourself into doing better. One sign that your comparison is perfectionist is that it leaves you feeling bad; another is that it omits crucial information. A perfectionist poetry student, for instance, might bash themselves because their poems aren't as good as the ones in their textbook, ignoring the crucial points that: (a) the latter are considered to be, by the editor at least, "the best of the best," and (b) many of those elite poems were probably written when the poets were much more experienced than our student. Post-college, our poet might obsess over the fact that they are making less money in their editorial job than a friend is making in finance, omitting the crucial points that they love their work and would hate finance.

Whenever you feel bad about yourself or your work, there's usually a perfectionist comparison involved.

Competitiveness. Often goes hand in hand with competition. Sure, competition can be fun and help you excel. But perfectionists often focus just on winning, and they'll also try to compete in situations that aren't, or shouldn't be, competitive. That gratuitous competition is a drag in real life—no one enjoys being around the person who always has to win. But it's even worse, in some ways, on social media. Many platforms explicitly or implicitly encourage constant comparisons, either with your friends or, worse, with the carefully curated and photo-edited feeds of celebrities and "influencers." Psychologist Melissa G. Hunt, whose research on the mental health harms of social media I cited in Chapter 5, says that these constant "social comparisons" are among social media's worst aspects.

Perfectionists also often forget that, in an unfair world, even many fair-seeming comparisons and competitions really aren't. As politician

Alexandria Ocasio-Cortez put it, "A lot of people...haven't realized yet that what they're actually competing with is intergenerational wealth."[26] (She then added this wise and empathetic advice: "Be patient and kind to yourself.") Also see Kristen Meinzer's quote about the "30 Under 30" articles, cited in the last chapter.

Boasting and Misplaced Pride. Perfectionists often feel the need to boast about how hard they're working, or the massive sacrifices they're making. "Yeah, I probably shouldn't have pulled three all-nighters last week," they'll say, sounding rueful and abashed. But you can hear the pride underneath.

Boasting is tedious and rude, and it doesn't fool anyone.

Another common type of perfectionist boast is about how tough their class or major is. Examples: "[Insert name of major]: only the strong survive," "This class is designed to weed out the weak," "In [insert name of major], they don't baby you," and, "You can't learn this stuff—you've either got the talent or you haven't." Along with also being tedious and rude, this kind of boasting can discourage students from under-represented groups and those who haven't had the privilege of an elite high school education,[27] *and* it also lets bad teachers off the hook. (So perhaps it's not surprising that some academic professionals, who ought to know better, also repeat these boasts.)

Hoarding. As noted earlier, perfectionists hoard their work. Unfortunately, the more you do that, the more scared and disempowered around your work you become, and the more you need to do it. (It's a vicious cycle, in other words.) Another way to visualize this is that the hoarding creates a wall between you (and your work) and those with whom you should be interacting, including not just your professors, but potential collaborators, mentors, employers, and audiences. To be clear, you're not just keeping your work behind the wall, but advice, support, and opportunities outside of it. And the more you hoard, the bigger, taller, and more impenetrable that wall gets. (Solutions to hoarding in Chapter 32.)

Fixating. Perfectionists are generally self-critical, but they also often have one or two areas where they are especially self-critical. I call these "fixations," and they often start when someone harshly or publicly criticizes you or your work, and that criticism then becomes a part of your self-image that you struggle with. Especially if the critic is someone you respect (Chapter 34), the criticism—be it, "Math isn't your strong point, is it?" or "You've got some weird ideas, don't you?"—soaks right in and becomes something

---

[26] https://twitter.com/AOC/status/1208258894323015680

[27] https://www.nytimes.com/2020/11/16/science/weed-out-classes-stem.html

you dwell on. (Beth, from Chapter 12, is another example, perpetually worrying about her work being clichéd.) As with many of the problems I discuss, it's often the most caring and dedicated students who fall prey to fixations, because their caring makes them vulnerable.

Of course, our society and media are themselves hugely fixated on certain things, including wealth, looks, and popularity (including social media popularity), so it's easy to get fixated on those even if no one directs a criticism specifically at you. Society also fixates on glamorous intangibles like "talent" and "originality," so it's easy to get personally fixated on those as well.

Again, notice how all the perfectionist behaviors can reinforce each other, so that, for instance, labeling and comparisons can cause a fixation, which, in turn, can cause hoarding—which you might then try to cover up, or compensate for, via boasting. Notice, also, how all the perfectionist characteristics I've been discussing both in Chapter 13 and this chapter are prevalent in academic settings. And notice, finally, how *exhausting* it all is. Constantly struggling against perfectionism will wear you out until you have no energy or enthusiasm left for your work or anything else.

Exercise 5

Go ahead and expand Exercise 3's (Chapter 9) Obstacle List using the perfectionist characteristics we've been discussing in Chapters 13 and 14. If you're overfocusing on outcomes, narrowly defining success, overidentifying with the work, etc., describe the effect that that behavior is having on your productivity, and on your overall health and happiness.

Exercise 6

List all the perfectionist attitudes and behaviors you see in Beth's story (Chapter 12) and discuss how each might be blocking her ability to do her work.[28]

---

[28] Some answers (you may find more): narrow definition of success (wants to create, "as true and nuanced...a portrait...as she could"); an overfocus on others' response (fear that she would be accused of betraying her family); grandiosity (expectation of easy success and an initial reluctance to ask for help); impatience (both with the writing process and in her desire for a quick career success); yet more grandiosity (anticipating a "home run" career, especially without a viable plan for achieving it); comparisons (and with a Nobel laureate!), labeling ("serious writer"), fixations (worries about her writing being clichéd or derivative), rigidity (rewriting the same story over and over); and overidentification (wanting the project to confer legitimacy and validate her choices). Whew!

15. Where We Learn Perfectionism

The perfectionist attitudes and behaviors discussed in the previous chapters all have one thing in common: they go against accepted best practices for productivity, learning, and growth. So where do we get the idea that they're useful? From the media, to start with. Perfectionist narratives tend to be simple and compelling, and so the media loves them. That's why you constantly see:

- Stories of "spectacular," "easy," "overnight," "solo," and "against-all-odds" success in education, business, sports, romance, etc.
- Stories that gloss over the process a person used to succeed, focusing instead on the glorious outcome.
- Stories that glamorize or exalt poverty, deprivation, and suffering. (For instance, depictions of "starving artists" who don't seem to mind their poverty.)
- Stories that exalt punishment, suffering, or "tough love."
- Stories where the characters live in what I call "magical affluence"— e.g., the barista or freelance writer who somehow manages to afford a fabulous New York City apartment. These households also always seem to magically clean and stock themselves, which is also perfectionist.
- Stories where the person supposedly has the high-paying job needed to support the fancy lifestyle, but you never actually see them doing that job. (In the real world, high-paying jobs tend to dominate your life.)

- Stories that trivialize the realities of human existence and relationships. If you've read *Atlas Shrugged*, for instance, you may recall how, at the end of the book, Ayn Rand's capitalist heroes all manage to live together in effortless peace and harmony despite their many economic and romantic conflicts. Come on! Have you ever seen that happen in real life? (For the record, Rand's own personal relationships were, to put it mildly, a mess.[29])

A lot of **advertising** is also perfectionist. Many ads overfocus on product at the expense of process ("Just do it!"), grandiosely trivialize human suffering ("No pain, no gain!"), depict narrow and unrealistic outcomes ("Use this mascara and you'll look like a supermodel!"), use flawed comparisons ("before and after"), promise quick solutions to difficult problems ("Lose 10 pounds in two weeks!"), and trivialize human relationships ("Drink this booze and you'll be sexy and popular.").

The Parents' Trap

Perfectionism is so pervasive that even many **parents, teachers, coaches, and other mentors** have internalized it. See if you can identify the perfectionist characteristics in these common parental statements:

1. "How come you only got a B?"
2. "It's easy!" (When you're struggling with something.)
3. "Why can't you do as well as your brother?"
4. "Get over it!" (When you're hurting from a painful rejection.)
5. "Sam is great at science, and Amanda is great at art."[30]

Make no mistake: just as it's often the most dedicated and caring students who fall prey to perfectionism, it's also often the most dedicated and caring parents who do. But it can still hurt, as this real-life episode illustrates:

A while back, a friend got a call that her 12-year-old daughter had broken her wrist during soccer practice and was on her way to the emergency room with her father, who had been coaching. My friend hurried to meet them there, but when she arrived, she unexpectedly found a daughter who wasn't just injured, but irate. Apparently, at

---

[29] See Barbara Brandon's biography, *The Passion of Ayn Rand*.
[30] Some answers (you may find more): (1) narrow definition of success; (2) overfocus on product /trivializing of process; (3) comparison; (4) grandiosity (you shouldn't feel pain); (5) comparison.

some point during the drive, Dad had told Daughter, in response to her crying, to "stop being a wimp." Talk about *literally* adding insult to injury! Small wonder, then, that Daughter's first words to her mom weren't, "Ow, my wrist really hurts!" but an outraged and accusatory, "He called me a wimp!" The emotional and moral pain of being perfectionistically labeled had completely trumped her actual physical pain.

Dad, meanwhile, just stood there looking guilty and confused. What had he done wrong? He hadn't meant to cause his daughter additional pain, of course. But he, too, had grown up surrounded by perfectionism, and had internalized many of its messages.

Sometimes, during discussions of perfectionist parenting, someone pushes back on the whole don't-pressure-or-punish-your-kids idea, saying something like, "My parents pushed [or punished] me, and *I* turned out okay." Of course, we have no idea, in such cases, what kinds of pushing and punishments actually took place, or how the person's life might have differed had they not been subject to them. Perhaps the pushing and punishments were relatively mild and occurred in a context of authoritative parenting (with lots of rules but also lots of affection), rather than authoritarian parenting (with lots of rules but little affection). (I discussed this in Chapter 2.) Or, perhaps the person had an exceptionally kind person in their life, and that kindness helped to neutralize the perfectionism and other harshness.

Or perhaps they were resilient for another reason.

No matter. As discussed in Chapter 13, it doesn't matter whether punishment "works," or seems to. It's an inhumane practice that you should take an ethical stand against, both for yourself and others.

Situational Perfectionism

People often ask me whether someone can be "born perfectionist." It's a good question. Every parent knows that kids are born with different temperaments, and that some kids definitely do have a tendency to be critical and/or judgmental. Such kids, if they're lucky enough to receive compassionate parenting, can usually avoid the trap of perfectionism. Unfortunately, what most of us get, in a perfectionist society, is perfectionist parenting, and so, even if we weren't born with an especially critical temperament, we still wind up falling into the trap. (And, obviously, those who were born with a critical temperament are at risk for having that tendency reinforced.)

Many events can also trigger what I call **situational perfectionism,** which is when an event or circumstance causes your perfectionism to spike. These include:

- A transition, like those discussed in Chapter 2.
- A perceived failure or rejection (Chapter 22 and Part IV) that makes you more afraid of possible future failures.
- A perceived success (Chapter 23), if it causes you to feel more visible and scrutinized. An extreme example of this would be the writers, like Ralph Ellison and Harper Lee, who, after having had a notable success with their first book, either failed to produce a second or took decades to do so. (A phenomenon so prevalent it's got a name: "the second book problem.")
- An opportunity you're afraid of squandering. For instance: "Now that I've got this scholarship [or new computer, or paid tutoring, or some other advantage], I'd better get all As!" Or, during winter break: "I've got a whole month off, so I'd better make the most of it!" (Either in the sense of having fun or studying for the next semester.)
- A need to justify others' efforts on your behalf. Even students from affluent backgrounds can feel pressure to justify their parents' tuition payments, but those from working-class or poor backgrounds can obviously feel that pressure even more. As a student once told me, "My mom spent the last 20 years cleaning rich people's houses so I could be here [at college], so I'd better do well."
- Being a first-generation student, or one from an under-represented group, especially if your situation causes you to feel extra-scrutinized, or that your "success" or "failure" reflects on your group. Speaking of which...

Members of so-called **model minorities** face a particular challenge. That stereotype—of an ethnic or immigrant group whose members excel academically and professionally—is problematic on several levels. It's a trigger for situational perfectionism, with everyone, including maybe you yourself, putting more pressure on you because of your heritage. (The cliché that "a B is an Asian F" is as perfectionist as it gets.) Also, like all stereotypes, it erases your individuality, reducing you to a type. It also creates competition, resentment, and other barriers between you and others, both within and outside your group.[31] And it can lead some to trivialize your achievements by either crediting them to your culture or making the assumption that you didn't face any barriers.

If you're a member of a supposed model minority, or subject to any form of situational perfectionism, that's just one more hurdle you'll need to overcome in your quest for joyful productivity. Remember: **there's nothing wrong with wanting to do great work. The problem is when you cross the line into perfectionism and your work becomes painful, stressful, or deprivational.**

Exercise 7

Reread Beth's case study (Chapter 12) and list all the factors that might be creating some situational perfectionism for her.[32]

Exercise 8

Take another look at the situation you examined for Exercise 3 and see if you can find some situational causes that caused your perfectionism to spike.

Note: We've finished our discussion of the nature and origins of perfectionism. Time to move on to the solutions!

---

[31] See, for instance: https://www.npr.org/sections/codeswitch/2017/04/19/524571669/model-minority-myth-again-used-as-a-racial-wedge-between-asians-and-blacks.

[32] Some answers (you may find more): senior project (a special project, and also a longer and more difficult one than she had ever done), "lifelong dream," and challenging (highly personal and complex and emotionally fraught) subject matter. Also, earlier successes setting up an expectation of success, while at the same time—and, yes, paradoxically—last year's harsh critique set her up for a simultaneous terror of failure. Also, framing the project as the vindication of her major, culmination of her college experience, and foundation for her post-college career. Finally, the fears of being criticized by family and community, and of betraying them by doing a bad job.

16. Nonperfectionist Attitudes and Behaviors

Nonperfectionists hold the opposite of the attitudes, and do the opposite of the behaviors, described in previous chapters. Specifically, they:

(1) Focus on the process of doing their work. Meaning their actual math, English, political science, etc.—as opposed to the grade or other desired outcome. A process focus not only takes a lot of the pressure off, it helps connect you with the work's intrinsic pleasures: and that, in turn, helps you stay motivated. As Steven Pressfield puts it in *The War of Art*, "The professional has learned that success, like happiness, comes as a by-product of work. The professional concentrates on the work and allows rewards to come or not come, whatever they like."

(2) Define success broadly and holistically. Yes, nonperfectionists want that great grade. But mostly they measure success based on whether or not they've done their best—meaning, whether they've worked steadily and with good focus. After that, it's whether they've accomplished some good learning, with "learning" interpreted broadly. (Sometimes, as per Chapter 28's discussion of trial and error, the valuable lesson is a greater understanding of what *doesn't* work.) Other important accomplishments might be staying cool under pressure, treating others well under difficult circumstances, overcoming (even partially) a personal or institutional barrier, connecting with a new mentor or collaborator, and having enjoyed the work.

It's worth repeating that excellent Steven Pressfield quote from Chapter 7: "How many pages have I produced? I don't care. Are they any good? I don't even think about it. All that matters is I've put in my time and hit it with all I've got."

Another example of a broadly defined success is when someone joins a sports team not just, or primarily, to compete, but for the health, recreational, teamwork, camaraderie, coaching, and other benefits of participation. (Ditto for someone who joins a musical, artistic, or other group for similar benefits.)

(3) Stay grounded. Nonperfectionists know that grandiosity is delusional. (It's actually a gambler's mentality and linked to low self-esteem.[33]) So, they try to err on the side of humility and do *extra* planning, get *extra* help, etc. They also choose their projects for the right reasons—e.g., out of a sincere interest, rather than a need to impress. And they take their time management (Part V) seriously: never, for instance, trying to pack 10 hours of work into an eight-hour workday.

(4) Maintain a healthy emotional distance from their work. Nonperfectionists know that even their "important" work is merely something they do, and not a justification for their existence or a window into their innermost soul. They also know that obstacles are a normal part of any project and not a reflection on them personally, and so when they encounter one, they don't pathologize. They also know that everyone is better at some things than others, so they don't expect themselves to be exceptional in every area. (Or, necessarily, in *any* area: as discussed in Chapter 13, you should avoid having a lot of expectations.)

(5) Take the long/broad/high view. Nonperfectionists understand that there's a point in pretty much every big project—and, sometimes, more than one—where you feel stuck and hopeless. (See the discussions of the Anti-Honeymoon and Vast Middle in Chapter 31.) Also, that a lot of problems that seem serious at the time turn out not to be (Chapter 22). And that *all* projects, including the biggest and most important-seeming, are mere "station stops" along the journey of their life and career.

These and other long-range perspectives help them to stay grounded and motivated, even in the face of setbacks.

(6) Are patient. Nonperfectionists understand that it takes time to do quality work—and, often, way more time than we anticipate. (More on this in Chapter 26.) They also understand that, perfectionist fixations on youthful success aside, most successful careers are built gradually over time. And they understand that, when they rush their work or other activities, they not only compromise their chances of success, but cheat themselves out of potential joy and fulfillment. (More on the evils of rushing in Chapter 42.) So, they strive to remain patient and to work systematically and with deliberation, even when the pressure's on.

---

[33] https://pubmed.ncbi.nlm.nih.gov/29455443/

(7) Are positive. Nonperfectionists work to stay objective—or, even better, a bit positive. Positivity (a.k.a., optimism) is often disparaged as naive or childish, but it is a fantastic basis not just for joyful productivity, but a happy life.[34] Sure, it's a form of expectation, so you don't want to overdo it. But a little too much positivity is way better than negativity, and way, way better than cynicism (which is when you expect the worst from everyone and everything around you). Not only are negativity and cynicism profoundly disempowering, they repel others, and so can damage your professional and personal relationships.

Nonperfectionists also have an **(8)** "abundance mentality" that encourages them to not only fully utilize all available resources, but to persevere in finding new ones. They explicitly or implicitly grasp, in other words, a key foundation of productivity work: that you are enough, and have enough, to succeed. Enough talent, originality, and other personal qualities, for one thing; and also enough time, help, and other resources. Just to be clear: this doesn't mean that you have every single quality or resource you want, or could use. Probably no one has that! But enough, at least, to get you mostly where you want to go. (Important note: I'm *not* denying that many people don't actually have enough money, time, connections, or other resources, due to either their personal circumstances, systemic inequalities, or both. The specific problem I'm addressing here is the many people who do actually have enough, but don't think they do.)

(9) "Own" their successes. Nonperfectionists are comfortable "owning" and celebrating (Chapter 23) their successes. If anything, they take some extra pride and satisfaction from them—always taking care, however, to avoid the trap of overidentification—since it never hurts to err a bit on the side of nonperfectionism. This is an area where hanging out with the right crowd can really make a difference. Be among people who are comfortable owning their successes, and it will become easier for you to own yours.

Nonperfectionists also don't waste time questioning whether they are challenging themselves enough. If they're in any doubt, they ask their professor—who, let's not forget, happens to be an expert in evaluating student potential.

Nonperfectionists also know that it's perfectly okay—and a wise strategy, actually—to take on the occasional easy project and to benefit from the occasional lucky break.

---

[34] Also, a healthier and longer one: https://www.ny-times.com/2020/01/27/well/mind/optimism-health-longevity.html.

(10) Reject impostor syndrome. Nonperfectionists recognize that impostor syndrome is a story we tell ourselves that has the power to harm us. They therefore do their best to reject that narrative and eliminate any perfectionism that might be contributing to it. If actual incidents of exclusion have contributed to the problem, they work to heal from those, perhaps with the help of counseling. (Again, this is an area where hanging out with the right people can really help.)

(11) Are flexible. If a solution isn't working, nonperfectionists don't sit there and try to make it work: they quickly seek out another one. They also always have a "Plan B," just in case their primary plan doesn't work out.

(12) *Never* punish themselves. Unfortunately, even after you intellectually and ethically reject punishment, it can still be a hard habit to break. (Chapter 20 offers some suggestions for dealing with that.)

Relatedly, nonperfectionists also understand that **there is no cheating in antiperfectionism work**. I don't mean that you shouldn't cheat: I mean that you literally can't cheat. The minute you overfocus even a little on product, or put even a little pressure on yourself, or try even a little to control your outcome (Chapter 28), you're back in the realm of perfectionism.

(13) Resist labeling and hyperbole. Whenever possible, nonperfectionists use precise and nuanced descriptions, such as: "I've got 10 pages to read tonight," "I've got a 60-minute workout," or, "I need to learn to follow through on my commitments better." This precision may sound boring in comparison to perfectionist labeling and hyperbole, but at least you aren't disempowering yourself via your language.

(14) Avoid comparisons. Nonperfectionists are comfortable evaluating their achievements on their own merits, without constant comparisons. While they may look to more successful people as role models and inspirations, they avoid strong or over-direct comparisons, especially if they don't know the whole story behind the other person's success. Especially, they are careful not to get sucked into comparisons on social media.

(15) Nonperfectionists also avoid **envy**, which accomplishes nothing except for making the envious person miserable. (It's the only one of the so-called Seven Deadly Sins that is no fun!) Nor do they dwell on their former successes, except to: (a) appreciate them and (b) figure out, and try to replicate, the conditions that made them possible.

(16) Avoid excessive competitiveness. When nonperfectionists compete, their goal is not to triumph over others, but to do the best they can while, as much as possible, enjoying and otherwise benefiting from the experience. (If they win, that's just the icing on the cake.)

Ultimately, nonperfectionists understand that creative and intellectual endeavors are fundamentally individual journeys of discovery—as is life itself. (More on this in Chapter 25.) While it is possible, and essential, to learn from others, in the end, we each need to chart our own course. As the novelist Bernard Malamud put it, "Eventually everyone learns his or her own best way. The real mystery to crack is you."

The creative journey is fascinating and important. But a habit of relentlessly comparing yourself to, and competing against, others can undermine it.

(17) Don't boast or indulge in misplaced pride. If they feel the need to do so, they take that as a sign that something's wrong. (Boasting is often a sign of insecurity.)

(18) Share their work early and often. Nonperfectionists know that, in contrast to the "walls" that hoarding builds between you and others (Chapter 14), sharing creates "bridges." They also understand that the more, and earlier, you share, the more bridges you create, and the easier it becomes to keep sharing, both with your current project and future ones. So, they share early and often. Early on in a project, for instance, a nonperfectionist might share their idea and project plan with their professor and get feedback on those. Then, as they proceed with their work, they'll share bits and pieces of it with their professor, teaching assistants, tutors, advisors, classmates, and friends. Sometimes they'll do this in the context of asking a question. ("Here's what I've done so far; what do you think?" Or "I'm not so sure about my conclusion, is it okay?") And sometimes they'll share just for the heck of it, because they know that sharing is empowering. ("Hey, I love this thing I just wrote, just wanted to show it to you, no reply needed.") (Obviously, the more casual forms of sharing are best done among friends.)

(18) Hand their work in on time. Nonperfectionists don't give themselves permission to routinely miss deadlines. A great technique for achieving this, by the way, is to **give yourself an "early deadline" that occurs somewhat sooner than your real one**. Tell yourself often enough that your problem set is due on Wednesday, for instance, and you'll eventually start to believe it—and then it will come as a pleasant surprise when you realize that the deadline is actually Friday, and so you have a couple of extra days to finish. (Of course, sometimes we miss a deadline due to an extenuating factor, like an illness or family crisis. That's a different situation from what I'm discussing here, which is a habit of missing deadlines even when there is no extenuating circumstance.)

(19) Don't sit around waiting for the grade After they've handed in their work, nonperfectionists **don't sit around waiting for the grade** or other outcome, but move right on to the next project. This not only helps them get more done; it also helps them to not overreact when the grade or other outcome, be it "positive" or "negative," finally does arrive. Yes, you want to pay serious attention to the feedback you get on your work: that's a crucial part of learning. But it's possible, and advisable, to do that without getting too emotionally caught up.

(20) Work to overcome their fixations, and to avoid developing new ones. Nonperfectionists use journaling and, if necessary, counseling to help overcome their fixations. They might even take a media literacy class to help them better understand media manipulations and machinans. And they are also careful to filter their media and other inputs to limit their exposure to unhelpful and sabotaging messages.

Nonperfectionists also understand that, while some fields—like, say, theoretical physics and professional athletics—do have extreme requirements of one kind of another, most of the time we actually do have sufficient intelligence, creativity, talent, originality, and other personal qualities to succeed at our goals. (Even in the "extreme" fields, hard work and a willingness to ask for help will often take you further than you might think.) Nonperfectionists also understand we mostly use labels like "talent" and "originality" retroactively after a creative work or career turns out well, and so it's best not to get too worked up about them. As novelist Stephen King puts it: "Talent is cheaper than table salt. What separates the talented individual from the successful one is a lot of hard work."

Ditto for money, time, help, and other resources. As discussed above, many people who think that they don't have enough of these actually do, especially if they're willing to ask for help.

So that's our list of nonperfectionist attitudes and behaviors. Do nonperfectionists do all of these things 100% of the time? Of course not: they have their slip-ups like everyone else. (And that "100%?" Perfectionist!) The important thing is that, when they do make a mistake, they skip the self-reproach and focus on learning from the experience and making a plan to do better in the future.

I'll share the techniques nonperfectionists use to overcome their perfectionism starting in Chapter 18. But first (after the exercise), we need to discuss the three most critical things every nonperfectionist knows.

Exercise 9

Is there an activity you love but aren't perfectionist about? (Sometimes called a hobby.) Maybe you love to cook, even if your meals aren't gourmet quality. Or knit, just for fun. Or swim, even if you're not on a team. Maybe you've even had a "disaster"—like a meal where everything went wrong, or a scarf where you dropped a whole bunch of stitches—and been able to laugh it off. That's some excellent nonperfectionism right there! See if you can bring that same playful and process-focused approach to your school-work and other "serious" endeavors.

If you don't have such a hobby, I urge you to develop one, as the benefits will be many. Perhaps there's an activity you've always wanted to try, but haven't yet. If so, go for it!

17. The Three Most Important Things Nonperfectionists Know

The three most important things nonperfectionist people know are:

(1) All perfectionist narratives are lies. Poke any perfectionist statement and all kinds of inconvenient truths come flying out: the "overnight success" turns out to have worked for years prior to their breakthrough; the "young" or "solo" success was helped by family money and connections; the "natural beauty" required days of preparation before the photo shoot, plus photo-editing afterwards; and the "glamorously" broke artist or activist didn't actually enjoy being broke (and their work suffered).

Nonperfectionists also know that social media is a horror-show of comparisons, competitiveness, and pretty much every other perfectionist characteristic we've been discussing. They may also be aware that, largely because of its perfectionism, psychologists have linked social media use to depression, anxiety, and, sometimes, suicide in teenagers and young adults.[35] And so, nonperfectionists use social media judiciously. In particular, they: (1) limit their use (it helps to develop some offline interests), (2) are media-savvy, especially about how advertising and celebrity culture use social media

---

[35] See, for example: https://www.nytimes.com/2017/10/11/magazine/why-are-more-american-teenagers-than-ever-suffering-from-severe-anxiety.html, htttps://www.ny-times.com/2019/02/20/health/teenage-depression-statistics.html, https://www.cbsnews.com/news/a-lost-girls-diary-alexandra-valoras/, and https://www.theatlantic.com/magazine/archive/2015/12/the-silicon-valley-sui-cides/413140. If you're having suicidal thoughts please call the National Suicide Prevention hotline at 1-800-273-8255 (TALK). And here's a list of global anti-suicide resources: https://www.speakingofsuicide.com/resources.

to sell images of bogus perfection, and (3) are selective about whom they hang out with. (More tips on how to safely use social media in Chapter 40.)

All this brings us to the second important thing nonperfectionists know, that...

(2) Perfectionism *never* helps and *always* makes things worse. And not just with your work, but your life in general, as illustrated by a high-school student's poignant response to the Quora.com question, "What's it like to be a straight-A student?":

> Naturally I am already a perfectionist...I spend hours and hours doing my work to make sure that I can get a 100 to keep my grades, and I am worn out and exhausted. I never feel the joy of receiving a good grade anymore because I expect myself to do that well. On the flip side, I am completely devastated every time I make anything less than a 95. I am constantly comparing myself to my best friend (she is also my academic competitor). I find myself hating others when they score higher than me and smiling when they do not do as well as me. This is completely awful of me, and I am trying to slowly change, but my academic pressures prevent me from going back to my old, relaxed self.[36]

As mentioned earlier, we should ethically reject perfectionism's punishments regardless of whether or not they "work." But really, they don't work. The truth is that we succeed *despite* our perfectionism, not because of it. **One of the very worst perfectionist lies is that you need to suffer to succeed.** (More on this in Chapter 20.)

So, yes: work hard. Work a lot. Make your commitments, investments, and sacrifices. But don't work past the point of health, happiness, and a balanced life. And don't work just to beat someone else. (Especially a friend!)

Try, in other words, not to act out of fear, but love: love of the subject, and of learning itself.

All of which brings us to the most important thing nonperfectionists know:

(3) *"Never go there"*. Never succumb to the urge to do the things I discussed in Chapters 13 and 14. Now, that's easy enough to do when your work is going well. But we all have times when we're underproductive or otherwise think we've "failed," and when that happens, the temptation to revert to pressure and punishments can be strong. But you need to be

---

[36] https://www.quora.com/What-is-it-like-to-be-a-straight-A-student/answer/Cathy-Tran-5

stronger. The key is understanding, not just intellectually, but deep in your bones, that perfectionism *never* helps and *always* make things worse.

This may all sound philosophical, but it is deeply practical. By refusing to give in to the temptation to be perfectionist, nonperfectionists not only keep themselves healthy and safe, but ensure that they are able to get back on track with their work as soon as possible.

"Never go there" is a very strong instruction, but strength is exactly what's needed. **Procrastination and perfectionism are strong and sneaky habits that are fed, often, by denial and self-deceit: you won't get far trying to counter them with weak, wishy-washy measures.** You need to confront them with strength, certitude, fortitude, and the conviction that, "I never pressure or punish myself or anyone else."

18. The Nonperfectionist Mindset: Introducing Your Inner Compassionate Adult

Nonperfectionism is a collection of attitudes and behaviors that support your ability to do your work. Unfortunately, just as there are myths around perfectionism, there are also myths around nonperfectionism. Many people confuse it with "having low standards," "being self-indulgent," or "not being accountable for my mistakes." Not so! It's about doing your best and holding yourself accountable, but not crossing the line into immoral and counterproductive punishments.

Remember the three personae from Chapter 11's Disempowerment Cascade: the Fragile Creator, Terrified/Terrorizing Perfectionist, and Rebellious Procrastinator? Someone's missing, and that's the Compassionate Adult. That's the persona who doesn't just understand and respect your ambitions, but actually knows how to do the work, and is an expert at recognizing and overcoming obstacles.

They are the persona, in other words, who should be leading the others.

The core work of overcoming perfectionism, therefore, is developing your Inner Compassionate Adult persona/voice. Below are two techniques for doing that. They're relatively simple, but don't let that fool you: they are powerfully transformational.

Reframing to Compassion

The first is a **reframing** technique: you catch yourself thinking perfectionistically—often after some kind of mistake or "failure"—and GENTLY interrupt that train of thought and reroute to nonperfectionism.

Instead of thinking: "I did badly on that test. I'm stupid."

You think: "Well, I'm disappointed in my grade. But it was a hard test, in a hard subject. Even so, I know I should have studied more, and I also should have gone to the Test Prep Center a couple of times. Well, I won't waste time feeling bad or calling myself names. Instead, I'll just make a plan to do better next time."

Instead of thinking: "I can't believe I didn't get that internship. I'm such a failure."

You think: "I knew I should have practiced more for that interview! Well, I'm pretty disappointed, but will try to get past that. I'll apply for some other internships this week. Also, I hear that the career center can record you doing a practice interview and give you suggestions for improvement. So maybe I'll try that."

Instead of thinking: "I can't believe I dropped my phone and broke the screen. What a klutz!"

You think: "Well, that sucks, especially since I don't have the money to fix it right now. But getting upset won't 'unbreak' it and, besides, everyone drops stuff. But yeah: in the future, I'll definitely be more careful when taking my phone out of my bag."

Notice how the nonperfectionist statements are longer than the perfectionist ones. That's because, in contrast to reductive perfectionism, nonperfectionism aims for a more nuanced and accurate view. Notice also how, even though the nonperfectionist statements skip the guilt, shame, blame, and other punishments, they still maintain accountability. Nonperfectionism isn't about giving yourself a pass (a perfectionist's worst fear). Rather, nonperfectionists know that you don't have to punish yourself to learn, grow, and improve.

A good way to locate your nonperfectionist voice is to ask yourself, "What would I tell someone else in this situation?" That works because we're often more compassionate with others than with ourselves. Treating ourselves worse than we treat others is a common mistake, and a grandiose perfectionist might mistakenly feel some pride about doing that. But it's as misguided as every other perfectionist behavior. We need to be *at least* as compassionate with ourselves as with others.

Some have described the nonperfectionist voice as that of the "good grandparent" or "wise teacher." These adult designations are no accident:

nonperfectionism is an empowered mature viewpoint. Your Inner Creator, Inner Perfectionist, and Inner Procrastinator are all fearful, and thus at least somewhat psychologically regressed—because fear causes us to lose our capacities—which is why they keep coming up with the same ineffective solutions. But once you introduce an Inner Compassionate Adult into the mix and let them lead, your Inner Perfectionist will start to relax, as frightened children do when a competent adult steps up. Then your Inner Procrastinator will see that they are no longer needed and gracefully exit the scene.

Leaving your Inner Creator free to do their job!

If the idea of reframing your thinking (or your inner monologue, see below) sounds silly or shallow, remember that perfectionism itself is a learned behavior that harms you every day. So why not work to replace it with something better? When you do, you should see a boost not just in your productivity, but your mood. In fact, the more reluctant you are to do this reframing, the more you probably need to do it.

I sometimes tell people that they shouldn't "indulge" in perfectionist thinking. What I mean by that is that, despite all the pro-perfectionist societal conditioning out there, perfectionism is ultimately a choice that you make, and so is nonperfectionism. Yes, change can be weird, as I'll discuss in Chapter 20. But commit with all your heart to overcoming perfectionism, and a new and better world can open up to you.

Developing a Nonperfectionist Inner Monologue

It's great to interrupt a perfectionist self-criticism and replace it with something more self-affirming. But it's even better not to have that self-criticism to start with. Replacing your perfectionist inner monologue with a nonperfectionist one will strengthen your nonperfectionism and make it less likely that you'll succumb to perfectionism during times of trouble.

Perfectionists, as discussed earlier, live with a more-or-less constant sense of failure, which is fed by a more-or-less continuous self-critical inner monologue: "What's wrong with you? Why you so lazy?" etc. You need to replace that monologue with a nonperfectionist, self-affirming one like this:

"Okay, let's get started...Good work starting on time...Okay, that sentence has got a few problems, but I can fix those later...And hey! That's a really great point I just made! Let's have some fun expanding it..... Okay, that part doesn't really work, but let's just leave it there for now. Got plenty of time to fix it later...This is turning into a really interesting topic. I'm so glad I chose it..."

This kind of monologue helps to build your confidence and enthusiasm—and, again, please note that you are not abandoning your critical judgment and accountability. You still see the problems with your work and are committed to fixing them: you're just not panicking or shaming yourself over them.

Pay particular attention to your monologue at the beginnings of work sessions because that's when your fears tend to be at their highest. If your monologue, at that fragile moment, is all about how, "My homework is a chore...How tedious...I'd rather be partying...Why me?...This sucks...etc.," *of course* you're going to have trouble starting your work. (When I sit down to work, I actually greet my project like an old buddy: "Hello! How's it going today?" Weird as that may sound, it sets a casual, relaxed tone that helps defuse any initial fear, and also provides a graceful entry into "our"—meaning, my project's and my—creative conversation.) Instead, monologue in an affirming way that also helps you reconnect with the interesting ideas or problems that brought you to the project to start with. For instance: "Okay, time to do my philosophy reading. Spinoza's kind of difficult reading, so I'll have to go slow. But I love that he's so humane and nonjudgmental and secular. Also, he was *way* ahead of his time in terms of seeing humans as an integral part of nature. With the climate crisis and everything, he's really relevant right now." This kind of inner monologue, especially when combined with the nonperfectionist work habits I'll be describing in Part III, can mean the difference between wanting to avoid your work, and actually being impatient to get started. So, try it! Please note that, in many cases, it's worth taking the time to actually write out your monologue, both because the act of writing can yield clarity and strength, and because what you write can often transition seamlessly into your actual work. (For instance, if our student has to write a paper on Spinoza, or even just organize their thoughts for a class discussion.) Go ahead and set your timer for a Timed Work Interval (Chapter 6), and go to it.

The above techniques will help you develop a nonperfectionist mindset that will make it easier for you to do your work at just about any time. One word of caution, though: try not to rush or put pressure on yourself while learning to use them, because that's perfectionist. Yup, I'm telling you not to be perfectionist in your quest for nonperfectionism. (It happens!) **You'll know you're doing your nonperfectionism right when you're able to sit down and do your work when you had planned to do it, and for as long as you had planned to do it.** Also, because you're doing less self-censoring, you'll start getting more and more ideas for your work, even when you're away from your desk. There you'll be, minding your own business on the bus or at the grocery store, when wham! You get a good one!

Maybe it's a clever new idea for that paper you're writing, or a new angle for that math or chemistry problem you've been wrestling with. Please, please, please: record it. (Use your phone's voice recorder or notepad feature.) What productive students, and others, know is that there aren't just a few good ideas out there, but lots of them. You just gotta: (a) be nonperfectionist and (b) take notes.

But what about when perfectionism strikes hard during a work session and you're tempted to procrastinate? The next chapter tells you how to deal with that.

Exercise 10

Table IV, below, contains a list of all the perfectionist attitudes and behaviors discussed so far, as well as their nonperfectionist replacements. First, cross out any that you don't think you do very often. Then, of the remainder, choose one or two you'd like to start working on replacing with their nonperfectionist equivalents. Work gradually (as described above) on replacing them.

Every time you eliminate, or mostly eliminate, one behavior, start working on another.

Remember to be patient, and to give yourself lots of affirmation for your successes; also, to ignore any "failures," except to learn from them.

Table IV: Perfectionist Attitudes and Behaviors and Their Nonperfectionist Replacements

Perfectionist	Nonperfectionist	Perfectionist	Nonperfectionist
Overfocus on product and external recognition and rewards.	Focus mostly on process and the intrinsic rewards of doing the work.	Rigidity	Flexibility: tries new solutions; has a Plan B.
Narrow/unrealistic definition of success.	Expansive/holistic definition of success.	Attempts to use punishment as corrective or motivator.	*Never* uses punishment.
Grandiosity: e.g., inadequate planning, an over-reliance on luck,	Groundedness: accepts help, does a lot of planning, and chooses	Labeling/ Hyperbole	Uses precise and nuanced descriptions.

Perfectionist	Nonperfectionist	Perfectionist	Nonperfectionist
and/or choosing overly ambitious projects.	projects at the right level of difficulty.		
Overidentification and pathologizing.	Maintains a healthy emotional distance from the work; doesn't pathologize.	Comparisons/ Competitiveness/ Envy	Resists comparisons except for informational purposes. Competes healthily, with more focus on doing good work than on winning. Avoids envy.
Shortsightedness	Takes long/high/wide view. Doesn't overreact to problems or setbacks.	Boasting/False Pride	Feels truly proud of one's self and one's achievements, so no need to boast to impress others.
Impatience: craves success NOW.	Patience: understands that (in contrast to media hype) success is something that you build, and thus takes time.	Hoarding	Shows work early and often.
Negativity	Neutrality or (better) slight optimism.	Fixating	Works hard to defuse persistent self-criticisms.
Distrust of success/ impostor syndrome	Recognizes success when it happens, and "owns" it.		

Exercise 11

Here's a sweet little exercise that packs a nonperfectionist punch. All you have to do is send out some emails or texts with intentional errors in them. Those errors could be anything from aN typo, to a mispeling, to some wEiRd formatting, to any kind of random STR*&^qq(ANGENESS.

That's it! "What's the catch?" I hear you ask. The "catch" is this: perfectionists *hate* this exercise. They hate making errors, and the idea of making one intentionally is simply *inconceivable* (as Vizzini would say). Yet, what's the harm? (So long as you're sending them out to friends and not, say, the chair of the scholarship committee.) This exercise is useful in both helping you to see just how perfectionist you are, and in helping you to loosen up a bit and build your nonperfectionism.

I've seen people try to cheat at this exercise by sending "artful" errors, "clever" errors, "subtle" errors, and "faux," "ironic," and "meta" errors. Don't do any of that! I want full-on silly, stupid, and goofy errors. (Remember: there's no cheating in antiperfectionism work.) It's okay, however, to let your friends know what you're doing, and why—and if you encourage them to respond similarly, you'll be helping them to develop their own nonperfectionism!

19. Interrupting the Disempowerment Cascade

Perfectionism doesn't just show up and announce itself. ("Hello! My Name is Perfectionism.") Mostly what happens is you start feeling guilty, stressed, scared, stuck, or otherwise bad about your work—a feeling that's followed, pretty quickly, by an urge to do something else. Instead of letting yourself get derailed, however, try writing out a dialogue between your Inner Perfectionist and Inner Compassionate Adult. Here's an example:

Inner Perfectionist: (panicked) What's wrong with you? Why are you so lazy? This stuff isn't hard! Anyone could do it! Amy's already finished! Why can't you be disciplined like her? C'mon! If you don't get to work, you're gonna fail, and everyone's gonna know you're a loser…and did I mention that the stuff you've already done sucks?
Inner Compassionate Adult: (keeping cool) Okay, I hear you! And I really want to address the problem. But no name-calling, okay?

IP: But it's hopeless! We've got to stop being so lazy!
ICA: (kindly but firmly): I mean it. We can talk about everything you want to talk about, but you have to be respectful. And factual too, okay? No more hyperbole like, "It's hopeless!"

IP: (glumly): Okay, I guess.
ICA: Great! Can you rephrase your concerns?

IP: Our paper's in really bad shape, and it's due on Friday.
ICA: Okay, I hear you! Do you have any suggestions?

IP: We could stay up all night working on it.
ICA: That's one option. But is it really a good idea?

IP: I guess not. We probably wouldn't get that much done, and it would wreck tomorrow.
ICA: Anything else?

IP: Not really…so what are *your* ideas?
ICA: Maybe we should delete that third section. It's got a lot of problems, and I don't think we need it. What do you think?

IP: (resignedly) If we do that, the paper won't be as good, so that's kind of disappointing. But I guess this is an "emergency," and so we should delete it.
ICA: Great! The paper just got way easier, didn't it?

IP: I guess so.
ICA: How about if we go to the writing center for some help with the organization and grammar?

IP: (glumly) You *know* I hate asking people for help.
ICA: Oh, I know…but is that a good thing?

IP: I guess not.
ICA: We should probably also find someone to take Thursday night's shift at work.

IP: (a bit shocked at this "radical" suggestion) Really?
ICA: Sure! We need all the time we can get.

IP: (starting to panic again) But I don't know who to ask!
ICA: Well, we took Jasmine's shift last month when she had a test, so let's see if she can take ours. If she can't, maybe Michael can. We took a shift for him last month.

IP: Okay.
ICA: Hey, so now we've got a lot less work to do, and a lot more time to do it in. It all seems more doable now, doesn't it?

IP: (now a bit optimistic) Yeah, I think so!

The more you use this dialoguing technique, the more you'll internalize the Compassionate Adult's voice and problem-solving wisdom—until, eventually, you skip the perfectionism entirely, and go right to the wisdom.

It's especially useful to do this dialoguing at times you think you've "failed." At such times, the perfectionist voice tends to be ascendant, and so you need to do everything you can to neutralize it.

Incidentally, the above example is short compared with many real-life dialogues. As with all the exercises in this book, be sure not to rush it.

How to Stop Fighting Your Inner Perfectionist

Did you notice how, when the Inner Compassionate Adult refused to let the Inner Perfectionist bully and insult them, it set the stage for a productive conversation? That's no accident: "limits are love," as the parenting manuals say. When the Adult set some limits, it helped the Perfectionist manage their fears.

Also, did you notice how the Inner Compassionate Adult refused to accept the Inner Perfectionist's fake solution of pulling an all-nighter? Many Inner Perfectionists have:

1. good *general* goals (do excellent work, meet deadlines, etc.)
2. terrible *specific* goals ("Get an A or die trying"), and
3. ridiculous solutions ("stay up all night," "take no breaks," "never ask for help," etc.).

That's a confusing mix, but it's the Compassionate Adult's job to respect and act on (1) without indulging in (2) and (3). Use the above dialoguing technique, and your Inner Perfectionist will eventually realize that your Inner Compassionate Adult is not only serious about achieving your goals, but has some good strategies for doing that. Then they'll relax and retire from the scene, taking your now-unneeded Procrastinator with them.

20. Overcoming a Punishment Habit

Many people are afraid that, if they stop punishing themselves, they'll lose whatever shreds of willpower they have. As already noted, however, many of us have been punishing ourselves, or been punished by others, for years or even decades: if punishment really worked, we'd all be superachievers by now. The truth is that many of us are productive in spite of the punishments we've endured, not because of them. As the 20th-century psychologist B.F. Skinner said, "A person who has been punished is not less inclined to behave in a given way; at best, he learns how to avoid punishment."

You'll probably pass through three stages, as you work to overcome your perfectionism/punishment habit:

Mostly Perfectionist. You're still mostly perfectionist, but occasionally catch yourself at it and self-correct to nonperfectionism.

Mostly Nonperfectionist. You're now mostly nonperfectionist, although you occasionally lapse into perfectionism during stressful times, or when you've made a mistake, or are in the midst of an especially challenging project.

Nonperfectionist. You remain resolutely nonperfectionist even during times you're tempted to "cheat" with a little harsh self-talk or deprivation. (Again, there's no cheating in antiperfectionism work.)

It's the bone-deep knowledge that perfectionism *never* helps that will help you to move as quickly as possible through the stages.

Like any behavioral change, the shift to nonperfectionism can feel weird at first. And giving up punishments (e.g., harsh self-talk and deprivation) can feel especially weird, because:

- We're so used to our punishments that they feel normal.
- Society keeps telling us that our punishments are useful.

- We often use punishment performatively to reassure ourselves (and others) that we're taking our work seriously.
- We often use our punishments as a form of penance or atonement for perceived underachievement. (Another type of performance.)

If you're having trouble kicking your punishment habit, ask yourself which of the above purposes, or others, it might be serving. (Journal about it!) That knowledge, combined with your obstacle resolution process (Chapter 9) and other tools, plus your foundational ethic of non-punishment, should help you liberate yourself from the habit.

Once you stop punishing yourself, however, you'll probably encounter yet another barrier to progress and productivity. Both procrastination and perfectionism are dramatic and noisy habits. (All that monologuing, justifying, rationalizing, denial, distraction, shame, blame, guilt, regret, remorse, etc.) When you start to give them up—meaning, when you start to be able to sit down and do your work with a minimum of fuss—the simplicity, ease, and quiet can be unnerving. Plus, you now suddenly have lots more time on your hands (because you're no longer procrastinating) that you're not exactly sure how to use. Not coincidentally—because procrastination often is, or resembles, a kind of addiction, as discussed in Chapter 2—this is all pretty similar to what many addicts experience during the early stages of recovery.

You'll need to learn to tolerate all this weirdness, at least for a while. You'll especially need to make sure that it doesn't send you spiraling back into perfectionism and procrastination. Persevere gently—always gently— and the weird feelings, which are kind of like "perfectionism's last stand," should eventually go away. Meanwhile, time management (Part V) will help you to deal with the "problem" (not really!) of "too much time."

Hopefully, you'll eventually decide, at some not-so-distant point, that, "Dammit, I am *not* going to treat myself badly anymore, no matter how badly I think I've screwed up! It's not worth it, it feels terrible, and it doesn't help anything." *That's* when you'll know you've turned the corner away from perfectionism, and toward a brighter, happier, kinder, more abundant, and more productive future.

Exercise 12

Think back on times you've punished yourself, and answer the questions below about the incidents. (Journaling works well for this exercise, and you may also wish to discuss your answers with a sympathetic friend or counselor.)

1. Were there unspoken motives underlying the punishments? Did you, for instance, punish yourself because you thought you were "supposed" to do that? Or because you didn't know what else to do in the face of a "failure"? Or, were you using the punishments performatively to show yourself, or others, that you were serious about the work?
2. How did the punishments affect you and your work?
3. What might have been healthier and more productive ways to respond to the situations in question?

21. How to Distinguish Between High Standards and Perfectionism

High standards are great, and so are ambitious goals. But how do you know when you've crossed the line into unrealistic standards, otherwise known as perfectionism? This is yet another confusing area, but here are some guidelines:

Unrealistic standards are often realistic ones taken a bit too far. Right now, for instance, you might be capable of reading 10 pages of your textbook in an evening, but not 11. Or of doing math problems for two and a half hours, but not three. Or of getting a B+ or A- in a course, but not an A.

We all have limited time and energy. In addition, we all find some subjects, and projects, harder than others. Productivity work is all about getting real, especially about our all-too-human limitations. Sure: you can, and should, aim for improvement—and that's kind of the point of education. But bashing yourself for not being where you'd like to be, or not progressing fast enough, is perfectionist.

Unrealistic standards are often the wrong standards. Grades aren't the most important thing: doing your best is.

A high salary isn't the most important thing in a job: a healthy and humane work culture is.

Some people aim to never disappoint their parents, but a better goal is to have a healthy and loving relationship with them—which inevitably means disappointing them from time to time. (You need to be able to stick up for yourself.)

Obviously, I'm dichotomizing: you can get As *and* learn, get a job where you're paid well *and* treated well, and please your parents *and* have a healthy relationship with them. But one goal should be paramount, and perfectionists often choose the wrong one.

Expecting a certain outcome when you don't have all the information or control needed to achieve it is unrealistic, and therefore perfectionist. And, as noted in Chapter 13, we *never* have all the information or control. So keep your focus on process, and keep your expectations moderate.

Unachievable goals are grandiose, and therefore perfectionist. *Really?* I hear you say. *Why would anyone set an unachievable goal? That doesn't even make sense!* You're right, it doesn't. But people set unrealistic goals for themselves all the time, and you've done it too, if you've ever...

- Taken on an overly ambitious project, as discussed in Chapter 13.
- Taken on more work than you could possibly accomplish.
- Expected any outcome to be 100% positive. (See Chapter 23.)
- Expected yourself to stay healthy and productive while stinting on self-care.

There are many other examples. Many working parents, for instance, bash themselves when they are working and not with their kids, and also when they are with their kids and not working. Basically, they're bashing themselves for not being in two places at once, which is pretty grandiose. (And deeply unfair.)

Finally, and most confusingly:

The same goal can be perfectionist and nonperfectionist at different times. It can be more reasonable to expect a high grade in some classes than others. Or, for some projects than others. Or at certain times of your life more than others.

That's why your final and most important clue as to whether you've crossed the line into perfectionism is this: perfectionism hurts. If you're feeling stressed, pressured, or otherwise bad about your work, that means that you've probably crossed the line into it. Stop what you're doing and do some journaling and obstacle resolution work (Chapter 9), so that you can get back on track as soon as possible.

22. Learning the Art of Failure

The most important time to put your Inner Compassionate Adult in charge is when you've "failed," experienced a rejection, or had some other kind of setback. It's a natural temptation, during such times, to get self-critical, but nonperfectionists have better ways of coping. They know that:

Everyone fails. It's an ordinary part of life. In fact, successful people probably fail more than most because they take more risks. To be precise: they're successful both because they take the risks, and because they react productively—meaning, in the ways described in this chapter—to the inevitable failures.

Failure is essential. You learn things from it that you never would from success, including resiliency, humility, how to compromise, and how to play defense. (As well as, of course, how to avoid or correct the mistakes that caused you to fail in the first place.) As Malcolm X said, "Every defeat, every heartbreak, every loss, contains its own seed, its own lesson on how to improve your performance next time." And as adrienne maree brown says in *Emergent Strategy*: "I don't experience failure much these days; I experience growth." Which brings us to...

There's no such thing as a complete failure. Nearly all failures yield at least some positive outcomes, and even the worst are valuable learning opportunities. The more serious a failure seems, the more important—and healing—it is to actually sit down and list those positives.

Most failures turn out to be unimportant. This includes even some that seem awful at the time. A week later, you wonder what you were so upset about, and a month later, you've forgotten the entire incident.

A surprising number of "failures" turn out to be lucky breaks. Like when you get rejected for a job you later realize wouldn't have been a good fit. Or rejected romantically by someone you later realize wouldn't have been a good partner.

A failure can also clear the way for you to start on a new and better path. As the Chinese philosopher Lao Tzu put it, "New beginnings are often disguised as painful endings."

Only rarely is one person responsible for a failure. So, yeah, someone could fail a test because they didn't prepare well. But if the class happened to be badly taught or the test badly designed, those absolutely would be contributing factors. And if the student were distracted by personal or family problems, or had some bad luck with their schedule (e.g., two tests in one day), that might also contribute.

It's important to acknowledge all the causes of a failure, not to negate your own responsibility, but so that you don't take on an unjust burden of shame. (To be clear, you shouldn't feel ashamed even in situations where you did do something wrong: see below.) This is even more important in the work world than in school, by the way. In school, your professors and the other institutional employees are ethically—and, in some cases, legally—obligated to at least try to look after your interests. No such obligation exists in much of the work world, however, and so many employees do wind up getting mistreated. A common scenario is when an employee is given a project but not the support or resources needed to succeed. Then, when they inevitably fail, they're unfairly blamed and penalized (up to and including being fired). This is not only devastating when it happens, it can lead to years or even decades of shame.

Situations where you did your best but still got a suboptimal outcome aren't failures. They're just life! Again: none of us ever has 100% control over our outcomes.

You have to be really, truly willing to fail. These days, many people do, in fact, understand that, "you have to be willing to fail." But ask them what they mean by that and they'll say things like, "Well, I wouldn't want to get less than a C," or, "I'll be really disappointed if I'm not in the top 10." The problem is that, even though these kinds of goals sound reasonable, they're still overfocused on outcomes. If you find yourself getting stuck, therefore, ask yourself if you're really, truly willing to fail, or just think you are. If you really are, then you'll be focused mainly on process, and thinking only a little about outcomes.

What "being willing to fail" really means is that you are prepared to get an F, come in last, bomb, embarrass yourself, even. Obviously, we all hope that that doesn't happen *this time*, but it probably will happen eventually if you're taking some good risks. When it does, it probably won't feel so bad if you're focusing on process, maintaining a proper emotional distance from the work, not being shortsighted, etc.

Last, but definitely not least, the most important thing nonperfectionists know about failure is that regret, remorse, shame, blame, and other negative reactions are pointless. So skip them! **The *only* useful way to respond to a failure is to: (a) analyze what went wrong, (b) make amends to others if needed, (c) make a plan to do better in the future, and (d) move on.**

Or, as the spiritual teacher Ram Dass put it, "It is important to expect nothing, to take every experience, including the negative ones, as merely steps on the path, and to proceed."

Exercise 13

Examine some of your "failures" from the standpoint of the information in this chapter. Were they really complete failures, or did they actually have some positive aspects? Has time revealed them to be less important than they initially seemed? Were you really 100% responsible, or did others, or bad luck, play a role? Write out your answers and, if desired, discuss them with a friend or counselor. Hopefully, after you're done, you'll feel more at peace with these incidents.

23. Learning the Art of Success

Do we really have to learn how to succeed? Isn't success simply the party that comes after all the hard work? Not quite. Success is great, and I wish you lots of it. But it can complicate things, and even lead to situational perfectionism (Chapter 15). Lao Tzu, who obviously thought a lot about the whole success/failure thing, put it pretty plainly when he said, "Success is often as dangerous as failure."

Perfectionists often gloss over their successes—or, worse, reframe them as failures (Chapter 13). But nonperfectionists are careful to recognize and celebrate their successes. Doing so is not only fun, it helps to neutralize perfectionism and fixes your successes in your memory so that you can call on them when needed for motivation. ("Okay, I'm feeling stuck, but I remember that, just a few weeks ago, I felt equally stuck. But I persevered and everything turned out fine. So I guess I'll just persevere now, too.")

Recognition involves four steps:

1. Write down a list of the parts of your project, or the aspects of it, that succeeded. Be sure to define "success" as broadly as you can: remember, from Chapter 13, that it's not just about the grade.
2. For each of those successes, list the skills and personal qualities— e.g., intelligence, patience, kindness, nonperfectionism, persistence, resourcefulness, etc.—that helped you to accomplish it.
3. List any problems you solved, and the skills and personal qualities you used to do that.
4. List any barriers you overcame, and the skills and personal qualities you used to do that.

You'll also want to consider the parts of the project that didn't go so well. As noted in the last chapter, do that efficiently and nonjudgmentally, and then move on.

By **celebrate**, I mean, first of all, taking some time to feel truly proud of what you've accomplished. (As written up in the above "recognition" document.) If you want to go beyond that and treat yourself to a dinner out, a new outfit or piece of gear, or some other splurge, go for it! Obviously, the magnitude of your celebration should roughly correlate with the magnitude of your success—maybe save the big trip for after graduation—but it's okay to be a little generous with yourself, to the extent your budget allows.

Be sure to recognize and celebrate even your "small" and partial successes. For one thing, they're often bigger and more important than they seem. Even something as "small" as reviewing your notes for a project you've been avoiding can take real courage, so why not recognize and celebrate that? (Especially since doing so will empower you to take further steps.) Also, recognizing and celebrating your small and interim successes can help you to stay positive and motivated throughout the course of a long project. In fact, big successes, as such, don't really exist—they're just accumulations of small ones. George Eliot didn't cough up her fantastic epic novel *Middlemarch* all at once like a hairball, for instance: she created it one paragraph, page, and chapter at a time. And before she even started it, she had successfully written many smaller pieces, and had also succeeded at a lifetime of study and other preparation. (Your own college graduation will similarly be a "big" success that is really an accumulation of small ones.)

Of course, the minute you do try to celebrate your small successes, your Inner Perfectionist will likely show up to scorn you as unambitious, self-indulgent, etc. As always, treat them with compassion, but don't let them abuse you, and *don't* take their advice.

While understanding that recognition and celebration are important, nonperfectionists also know not to take things too far. In particular, they know that your successes shouldn't be a source of exaggerated pride (e.g., "I'm king of the world!"), self-justification ("That'll show 'em!"), or professional legitimacy ("After I'm published, then I'll be a *real* scholar."). Your successes should also not be a route to popularity, love, sex, status, or any other form of personal validation. All of these attitudes are *extremely* overidentified—and so, to some degree, this problem is theoretical, because people who view success in these kinds of ways tend to be much too terrified of failure to do their work.

The Costs of Success

Nonperfectionists also know that:

Success leaves you busier. Many successes create more work: for example, when you win a fellowship and then have to do the project. Success also can be a magnet that draws new people and projects to you. Don't get me wrong: these are excellent problems to have! But they're still problems. (See Chapters 46 and 47 for solutions.)

Success raises the stakes. It causes you to ask questions like: "What if my next paper [or performance, etc.] isn't as good as this one?" Or, "Now that I've gotten that great job, what if I can't handle the responsibilities?" Or, "Now that the newspaper is publishing my editorial, what if I get blowback on social media?" Or, "Now that I've gotten a date with this person I've been crushing on, what happens if it doesn't work out?" These kinds of questions are all natural—and I'd actually be worried if you *weren't* asking them. But dwelling on your fears or, even worse, letting them dictate your behavior, won't get you far. Instead, **always answer your rhetorical questions.** What *will* you do, for instance, if your next paper isn't as good? (And what does "good" mean, in this context, anyway?) Or if you can't handle your new job's responsibilities? (And which responsibilities are we talking about?) Answering these types of questions is not only empowering in and of itself, it gives you a chance to avoid, via planning and consultation with mentors, the potential problems.

Last, but definitely not least,

Success always involves at least some compromise, loss, or sacrifice. Some examples:

1. When you're a student, you may decide to forgo partying for a weekend so that you have a better chance of doing well on a test. (Or, to forgo a whole bunch of parties so that you have a better chance of getting into graduate school.)
2. Later on, you may decide to give up your dream of living in the mountains so that you can pursue the big-city career you want. (Or vice versa: maybe you settle for a less-ambitious career so that you can live in the mountains.)
3. Do well at your career and you might become a public figure, losing some of your precious privacy.
4. Find a wonderful romantic relationship, and you lose the ability to mostly do whatever you want, whenever you want, without having to consult anyone else.

You need to be aware of these kinds of losses because it's easy to get caught off guard by them; also because fear of them—a.k.a., **fear of success**—is a major cause of hoarding and procrastination. **Now we see that procrastination's "purpose" isn't just to protect us from potential criticism or rejection (Chapter 2), but potential loss.** That's a powerful double punch, so be sure to use your journaling, discussions with mentors, counseling, and other techniques to not just identify your potential losses, but figure out how to minimize or prevent them. Minimization Step 1 is to stop dichotomizing: in the above examples, you can still go to some parties, live near the mountains if not actually in them, retain some of your privacy, and retain some of your autonomy. You also want to do the work of **mourning and accepting those losses you can't avoid**, so that you can proceed wholeheartedly and unambivalently with your work. Journaling and discussions with friends (or a counselor) work well for this, or you can go deeper via a spiritual discipline like Buddhism or a secular one like Acceptance and Commitment Therapy. Russ Harris's book *The Happiness Trap* is a good starting point for the latter, and there are also counselors who specialize in it.

Despite the complex nature of success, including all the attendant losses, I hope you have a lot of practice coping with it!

Exercise 14

Journal about a school or other project you're procrastinating on to see if any success-related fears and potential losses are contributing to that procrastination. If so, keep journaling and, if necessary, consult a friend or counselor, with the goal of defusing the fears and eliminating, or at least minimizing (and mourning), the losses.

When you're done, hopefully you'll be able to approach your work with less ambivalence and procrastination.

24. Overcoming Ambivalence

Ambivalence is when you're caught between two or more contradictory goals or motives. Ambivalence about small things—"Should I have a doughnut or a muffin, I can't decide!"—is no big deal. (Unless it becomes chronic, in which case it's Quasiproductive Procrastination. See Chapter 5.) But ambivalence about bigger things, like your schoolwork, relationships, career, or identity can be awful. You're stuck in an exceptionally uncomfortable and confusing place, often doing the one-step-forward-two-steps-back kind of behavior that is so frustrating to you and those around you.

Here are some examples of ambivalence:

- Your parents want you to spend winter break with them, but you would rather do something else. But you are reluctant to have that conversation, and so wind up procrastinating on your travel plans until all the cheap flights are gone.
- You hate your job, but don't want to go through the hassle of finding another. So you stay put, only you keep getting less and less motivated and focused on your work until, eventually, your boss fires you.
- You've taken on an extracurricular project that you don't have time to do. So you procrastinate on it, hoping that some time will magically open up. Only that doesn't happen, and so you wind up, finally, handing in only a part of what you promised to do, thus disappointing everyone involved, including yourself.

As these examples show, ambivalence is a disempowered—and, often, passive-aggressive—response to pressure that is often characterized by indecision, dithering, and busy work. Yup: we're talking Quasiproductive Procrastination *big time*. Two important things to keep in mind, however, are that:

1. Although the ambivalence is, like all forms of procrastination, a disempowered reaction to pressure, it also, as discussed in Chapter 11, represents the best part of you: the part that is fighting for freedom and authenticity and self-expression, and against bullying and coercion.
2. We're often ambivalent not just because others are pressuring us, but because we at least partly agree with their viewpoint—so that, for instance, while you don't really want to go home for the holidays, a part of you thinks you should.

We see both of these dynamics in Jeremy's story:

From elementary school onward, **Jeremy's** passion had always been art. In high school, he had been "the guy with the sketchpad," known for his short, ironic comic strips highlighting aspects of school life that he drew for the school paper. His dream was to one day create graphic novels, and he spent as much time as he could in his school's art studios, working on his projects, helping the teachers prepare for class, and sometimes, even, helping to teach.

When it came time to think about college, however, art school wasn't an option. Jeremy's family had always struggled financially, and while his parents had always been proud of his artistic ability, they had also impressed upon him and his younger sister the importance of choosing "practical" careers that offered financial security. Jeremy decided to do pre-medical studies, hoping to also be able to minor in art.

Mostly for financial reasons—the tuition was cheap, and he could live at home—he attended a nearby state college. To his surprise and dismay, however, he found himself struggling from the very beginning of his freshman year. His biology and chemistry courses were much harder than he had anticipated, and he was also much busier than he had anticipated. Between the class time, laboratories, piles of homework, "optional" (but, he felt, necessary) test prep sessions, *and* his commute and part-time retail job, he was constantly rushing from one commitment to the next.

Something had to give, and it turned out to be his art class, "Introduction to Digital Methods." It was his favorite class, and he felt comfortable with both his teacher and the other students in a way that he didn't in his other classes. Given a choice, he would have gladly spent most of his time, as he had in high school, hanging out in the studio. Being perpetually rushed for time, however, he couldn't do that. In fact, he wasn't even able to spend enough time there to do his assignments properly. More and more, he was doing them at the last minute, which wasn't fun and yielded only mediocre grades. He did manage to pull himself together for his final project, however, and wound up getting an excellent grade on that. "Where have you been hiding all semester?" his professor joked.

Jeremy ended the semester with two good grades (art and a required freshman writing course) and two mediocre ones (his sciences). His advisor warned him that he would need to do better in the spring if he intended to go to medical school. She also suggested that he not take the second semester of the Digital Methods course, so that he'd have more time for what she called his "important" courses. Jeremy was disappointed but had to agree, and so he signed up instead for a less time-intensive Art History elective.

During winter break, he went through the motions of the holidays with his family, but emotionally he was elsewhere. He felt a constant turmoil of anger (mostly at himself, but also at his parents and the college), confusion (how, exactly, had everything gone so wrong?), shame (that he was letting his family down and setting a bad example for his younger sister), and fear (that the next semester would be the same, or even worse). Nearly every conversation with his parents seemed to escalate into conflict, so Jeremy started taking extra shifts at his job just to get out of the house. And when he was at home, he spent most of his time alone in his room.

Spring semester, his grades picked up some—at first. But then they dropped again. His science classes turned out to be even harder and more competitive than the first semester's, and he was also having a harder time concentrating. At the same time, his social life had also taken a downturn. His best friends had all been in his Digital Methods class, and now that he wasn't taking the follow-up, he wasn't seeing them.

Feeling more and more hopeless and discouraged, Jeremy started skipping classes.

One day when he was at a real low point—it was mid-afternoon and he still hadn't gotten out of bed—he felt a powerful inspirational surge. Leaping out of bed and to his desk, he started sketching, for the first time in ages. He soon found himself creating a series of comic strips entitled "College: The Dream Versus the Reality," that told a fictionalized version of his freshman year experience. He worked on it for a week, devoting every spare moment he could to it. When he was done, he was prouder of it than anything else he had accomplished that year.

He posted a couple of the strips on his social media—and was caught entirely by surprise when, just a couple of minutes later, his sister Callie showed up at his bedroom door. "The strips are great!" she said. "But what's up with school? Something's obviously wrong."

Jeremy tried to evade the question, but she wouldn't let him. She invited herself into his room and made herself comfortable in his reading chair, and asked again: "Seriously, what's up?"

It was hard for Jeremy to open up, but once he started, he couldn't stop. He told her everything that had happened since he had started school, including all his fears, discouragements, and confusions. When he was done, she said, with true sisterly candor, "I didn't think the pre-med thing was going to work out. You need to switch majors."

"I know!" Jeremy said, amazed and relieved to have finally heard the obvious spoken aloud. "But to what?"

"Duh...art!"

"Mom and Dad will freak out if I do that. They want us to earn money, remember?"

"They're freaking out now, in case you didn't notice," said Callie. "Anyway, whose decision is it?"

Jeremy paused. The truth was, he didn't really know. "Well, Mom and Dad should have a say, they're paying for a lot of it..." he began. "And they're right: there aren't a lot of jobs out there..."

"C'mon Jer, it's got to be *your* decision," she said. "It's your life, not theirs. Anyhow, I do think there are jobs out there. You know Frankie, from down the street? Her best friend's sister's girlfriend majored in something like 'Applied Art,' and she got a great job at some kind of high-tech firm."

"But how do you get those jobs?"

"*I* don't know," she said, rolling her eyes. "Why don't you ask your professor? And after you do, then come back and have the conversation with Mom and Dad. You know I'll have your back."

Jeremy made an appointment to talk with his Digital Methods professor. The professor listened sympathetically as he told him about his situation, then reassured him that there were, indeed, jobs for art graduates with lots of enthusiasm and a great portfolio. "Film-making and video game design are the 'glamour jobs,' right now, and there's a lot of competition for those," he said. "But there are also good jobs available in advertising, product design, Web design, marketing, and some other fields."

The professor suggested that Jeremy do a double major, saying, "That will strengthen you on the job market, and it will also be good for your art. Psychology, sociology, marketing: those are all good choices." Then he handed Jeremy a couple of brochures on arts careers. "Read these, and then give them to your parents. Don't forget to tell them that, when you start looking for work, you can contact people in the school's Alumni Network for advice, or to get an 'in' at companies you want to work for. That's helped a lot of students."

The professor then said, "You know, if it would help, and with your permission, I'd be happy to talk to your parents myself." Jeremy who hadn't expected such an offer, replied, "Oh wow—thanks!"

"Well, you're pretty talented, and we wouldn't want to lose you."

It was the first really positive feedback that Jeremy had gotten since starting college, and it brought tears to his eyes. He hurriedly wiped them away; meanwhile, the professor was taking a moment to rummage through some papers on his desk. Then he triumphantly held up a form and said, "Okay, then! Let's plan out your fall schedule. When you're ready to make the switch, I'll submit the paperwork and let your current advisor know that you're switching majors. And I'll be happy to be your new advisor."

As Jeremy and his professor planned his fall courses—two art classes (including the second term of Digital Methods), a psychology class, and an English Literature class—Jeremy felt his spirits soar. It was like he was starting college fresh, only this time on the right path. Right after the meeting was over, he called Callie and told her everything that had happened. "I told you!" she said, and then added, with true sisterly fervor, "Of course they want you in the program—you're an artistic genius!"

That night after dinner, Jeremy told his parents that he wanted to switch majors to art and psychology. They listened solemnly as he talked about his unhappiness in pre-med and explained why switching majors would help. Then they took a few moments to look over the career pamphlets he had brought home. Although they expressed skepticism—"We have nothing against art, only it seems so insecure," his mother said—they were encouragingly less hostile to the idea of his switching than he had imagined.

Jeremy suggested his parents talk with his professor, which they did, a few days later—and that conversation did the trick. "That professor is a big fan of yours," his father said afterwards, with obvious pride. "He thinks you would have a good chance of succeeding. So I guess if you want to switch to art and psychology, that would be okay." His mother agreed, and added: "Your art has always been a big part of who you are, and a big part of what makes you special. Maybe we were wrong not to encourage you to continue with it."

Jeremy could hardly believe it: he was going to be an art major! He still had to get through the rest of his current semester, of course—but, to his surprise, that turned out to be not as difficult as he had expected. Just knowing that he wasn't "trapped" in the wrong major, and that, in a few months, he would be free to study what he truly wanted, was enough to lift his spirits and boost his motivation.

Jeremy wound up doing very well in his arts and psychology double-major. He was even able to develop "College: The Dream Versus the Reality" into a graphic novel, his first. (The major themes included the importance of being honest with yourself and finding your own path; also, the importance of taking action, even in the face of uncertainty.) It became his senior project and a major piece in what his arts professors assured him was an excellent portfolio.

And yes, he did get a good job after graduation.[37]

Solutions to Ambivalence

As Jeremy's situation shows, one solution to ambivalence is to **get clear on your relationship boundaries**—and, in particular, on your obligations and responsibilities to the various people in your life. (More on this in Chapter 48.)

Also, **work on your perfectionism**. Dichotomization is an obvious trigger for ambivalence, since it can cause you to reduce all of your options into two equally extreme and unappealing opposites—so that, for instance, you think you either have to spend all of your winter break with your parents, or none of it. Or, even worse, that you just have one unappealing option, like poor Jeremy thought he had. Perfectionism can also cause you to dismiss good, or even excellent, solutions that are right in front of you, while you carry on a quest for a mythical perfect solution with no negative aspects. Philosophers call this the "Ideal Solution Fallacy," and it's a close relative of the Nirvana Fallacy (where you compare things to an idealized version of themselves) that I discussed in Chapter 14—which, no surprise, can itself also cause ambivalence.

Find a mentor. Often we're ambivalent because we don't have enough information to make a decision. The person who hates their job, for instance, may not know how to go about finding another. (Or may erroneously think that they're not qualified for anything else, or that "all jobs are bad.") Because that lack of knowledge is often buried underneath layers of emotional turmoil and interpersonal strife, the ambivalent person may not actually be aware that that's the problem. So go ahead and do your obstacle-

---

[37] Just as this book was going to press, Pulitzer Prize-winning novelist Viet Thanh Nguyen published a great piece on issues similar to those discussed in this case study: https://www.nytimes.com/2021/07/08/opinion/culture/parents-expectations-writing-art.html.

resolution process (Chapter 9), and then discuss the situation with a mentor, counselor, or other expert.

Watch out for situations where you're having both halves of an important or difficult conversation in your own head. (As Jeremy was doing when he assumed that he knew how his parents would react to his changing majors.) It's a *very* common form of Quasiproductive Procrastination, and a recipe for ambivalence.

Finally, **learn to take the long view** (Chapter 16). It's always tempting to want to avoid the pain of dealing with the wrong major, a difficult relationship, a bad job, or some other problem. But ask yourself whether you really want to spend the next few months, years, or even decades dealing with it, especially knowing that it's only likely to get worse. Ask yourself, also, if you want to develop a habit of avoidance and denial, or one of problem-solving. Hopefully, it's the latter, because...wait for it!... you don't want to be ambivalent about tackling your ambivalence!

Exercise 15

Look back at an incident where you were ambivalent about something in your school, work, or personal life. List the ways that (a) perfectionism and (b) unclear interpersonal boundaries might have played a role. Also, think about how you responded to your ambivalence, and what might have been a better way to respond—and how you'd like to respond to future, similar episodes of ambivalence.

Okay, we're done with perfectionism! Thanks for hanging in there. In Part III, we'll discuss a non perfectionist work process called the Joyful Dance. It's as much fun as it sounds, and I can't wait to introduce you to it!

PART III
JOYFUL WORK

25. Introducing the Joyful Dance

The goal is easy, effective, and joyful productivity, which is really nonperfectionist productivity. To see why, let's look at the way many perfectionists tend to work. They're relentlessly linear, for one thing: always trying to do everything in what they consider to be the right order. When writing a paper, for instance, they try to do all the research before moving onto the outlining, all the outlining before starting to write, etc. And when they do, finally, start to write, they trudge through the manuscript from beginning to end, trying to perfect (red alert!) each sentence, paragraph, and page before moving onto the next.

Similarly, if a perfectionist has a problem set, they will do it rigidly in order, trying to complete the first problem before moving onto the second, the second before moving onto the third, etc.

Linearity isn't just boring, it's precarious. Get stuck, during a linear process, and you really are stuck, because the one direction you think you can move in is blocked off.

Linearity also invites a kind of do-or-die perfectionism. ("Okay, so I finished Section 3. Now it's time to start Section 4, AND I'D BETTER GET IT RIGHT!!!!!")

The fundamental problem is that linearity undermines your creativity. **Creativity is really a kind of conversation** between you (your knowledge, ideas, thoughts, beliefs, and perspectives) and your subject matter (including past and present experts), collaborators (including your professor, classmates, and others), materials, processes, and techniques. Like many conversations, these "creative conversations" go best when information can flow freely in many directions. This includes backward, by the way: because creativity is also fundamentally an act of discovery. The things you discover later in a creative conversation can, and probably will, illuminate some of the stuff you discovered earlier, making you want to go back and change it. As the poet May Sarton once helpfully observed, "Revision is not going back and fussing around, but going forward into the process of creation."

Creativity, in other words, is organic and holistic—pretty much the opposite of a linear process.

For all of these reasons, **nonperfectionists work *non*linearly**—which means that they work on whichever parts of the project they feel like working on at the moment. Also, they work on whichever *stage* of the project they feel like working on. Organizing, writing, editing, etc.—they combine it all into one big jazzy jumble, switching among them with ease. (This includes sharing the work, as discussed in Chapter 16. Nonperfectionists share early and often.) There's just one stage you should leave out of your jumble, and that's research, which, as discussed in Chapter 5, is a common vehicle for Quasiproductive Procrastination (QP). It's okay—and desirable, as I'll be discussing in the next chapter—to write, outline, etc., while doing research, but you should avoid slipping into research when you're supposed to be working on the other stages. (More on how to handle research in Chapter 32.)

I call this jazzy, jumbly, nonlinear work process the Joyful Dance, because that's what it feels like when you use it: a joyful dance through your work. And I call the perfectionist way of working the Dreary Slog, because that's pretty much what it feels like. (Yup, I'm labeling and dichotomizing to get my point across. In real life, no one is 100% Dancer or Slogger.) The Joyful Dance supports and catalyzes your creative conversation, and so, when you use it, your work goes easier and faster, and is a lot more fun. You're also far less likely to get stuck when you're Joyfully Dancing, because "getting stuck," to a Dancer, simply means that it's time to switch over to another part of the project. (Which Dancers do without fuss or drama.)

Remember Chapter 4's point about how empowerment means having the best possible options? The Joyful Dance is all about that. When Dancing, you get to choose, at every moment, not just which part of your project you want to work on, but how you want to work on it. In contrast, the Dreary Slog only ever offers you the same bad choice: to keep working on whatever it is you're currently working on until you get it "right." Notice how your personal preferences and situation—not to mention, the specifics of the project itself—don't even enter into it.

Is the Joyful Dance actually joyful, though? Sometimes! Other times, it's "merely" interesting, satisfying, fulfilling, or fun. Don't knock it: those are excellent work experiences to have. What I can promise you is that **the Joyful Dance will maximize your odds of not just an easy and effective**

work process, but a good outcome. When you work nonlinearly, you're like a surfer on a beach with some great waves, each wave being a bit of inspiration comin' atcha. You see one, rush over to it, grab it, and ride it. Then, when it peters out, you look around and see another great wave, rush over, grab and ride *it*. Then another and another. You keep doing that throughout your whole work session. What fun! And look how much you're getting done!

Meanwhile, your poor Slogger friend is standing forlornly with their surfboard on the section of the beach where they think the next great wave is *supposed* to hit. Waiting...waiting...waiting...

Get Random!

Nonlinearity can feel weird if you're not used to it. But give it a whirl, and you should soon see the advantages. This randomizing technique should help:

Assign a number to every section of your project (assuming they're not already numbered, like in a problem set). Then roll some dice[38] and work on whichever numbered section you rolled. If you get bored or stuck, roll again and hop on over to the new section and work on that. Or, if you feel suddenly motivated to work on a section—say, because the current section gave you an idea for it—hop on over there and start working on it. Hop around as much as you like until you've completed your Timed Work Interval (Chapter 6), while resisting, as always, the temptation to judge your output.

Randomization works not just because it's fun, but because it subverts perfectionism. Instead of, "Now it's time to do Section 4, and I'D BETTER GET IT RIGHT!!!!!" you're all: "Hmmm, just rolled a '4.' Not sure what I want to do with that section, but I'll just play around with it and see what happens." And what often does happen is that you get a good creative conversation going.

Randomization also works well with another technique for avoiding perfectionism, **chunking.** That's when you break a big project down into manageable chunks, and then focus on one at a time. A chunk could be a page or a paragraph of a paper, or one part of a scientific or technical problem. Go ahead and assign numbers to your chunks, then roll those dice.

You probably won't need to keep using the dice forever, by the way. Soon you'll learn to ask yourself, when you sit down to work, "What do I

---

[38] Even fancy dice are pretty cheap (and fun): check out places that sell gamers' supplies. For free dice, ask a gamer friend for a set they're no longer using, or grab the dice from an old board game that no one's using. And, yes, I know that you can download a random number-generator app for your phone, but *puhlease* no phones while working.

feel like working on right now?" And, whatever it is, you'll start working on it. Then, when you feel like you're "tapped out" on that section, or simply have the urge to work on something else, you'll easily (without fuss or drama) switch over to the new section and start working on it. And you'll keep working, and switching over, and working some more, until you reach the end of your Timed Work Interval (Chapter 6).

But you should feel free to return to the dice if you ever feel yourself slipping back into linearity.

Exercise 16

This fun exercise, Rapid and Rowdy Randomization, will help you get looser and more flexible—a.k.a., less linear and perfectionist—with your work. It's even more fun to do with friends!

1. Number your project sections—for example, from 1 to 10.
2. Starting where you left off (e.g., 11), number all your project stages. For writing, for example, those would be: conceptualization (a.k.a. brainstorming), note taking, organizing/outlining, drafting, editing, and sharing all or part of the work.[39] (Please note that I am omitting research, which, as noted earlier, you shouldn't be doing during your writing intervals.)
3. For writing assignments, list a few alternative styles for your project (e.g., essay, fairy tale, fable, epic saga, hard-boiled detective novel, etc.) and number those as well, starting with where you left off in the previous step. (It's okay if a style doesn't make sense for your project: the silliness is part of the point.)
4. For both writing and nonwriting assignments, you could try varying your "props," e.g., your writing implement and paper type. Number those as well. (Ditto on the silliness!)
5. Write down all your numbers and their equivalents (section, stage, style, and prop) in a handy list. Also, get a timer.
6. You now have a lot of numbers! Either get a D20 die, or—if your numbers go higher than 20—a pair of D10 dice, one of which will be your "tens" digit, and the other your "ones."
7. Do a series of super-fast (e.g., two-minute-long) intervals. At the start of each interval, roll dice and spend the next minute doing the instruction corresponding with the number you rolled. (Have fun with it!)

---

[39] We commonly say "submitting the work" instead of "sharing the work," but I try not to use the verb "submit" in this context as it implies a profound disempowerment.

8. Do at least five intervals.

There's nothing like randomly switching among the pieces and phases and styles and props of your project to really shake things up and liberate you from Oh-So-Serious Perfectionism.

26. Speed It Up!

We all want to work faster, but make sure you're aiming for the right kind of speed: not the frantic and stressful kind that depletes you (and triggers procrastination), but the cool and steady kind that you can maintain for long periods without getting bored or tired. (What marathoners call their "stride.") The kind of speed, in other words, that helps you get a lot of work done while also supporting your learning and other objectives.

Pretty much every technique in this book will help you to achieve some of that speed, but to reach your personal maximum, you'll need to do what the marathoners do and organize your life and work around that goal. Below are some tips for doing that:

Do your time management (Part V) to make sure that: (a) you're getting enough sleep, exercise, and other self-care, and (b) you have lots of high-quality time in which to do your work. ("High quality" means time when you're alert, energetic, and relatively free from interruptions: see Chapter 49 for more on this.)

Eliminate interruptions. As discussed in Chapter 5, they're more "expensive," time-wise, than we realize. (Breaks are okay and necessary: see Chapter 33.)

Get comfortable, not just because that helps with speed, but also because, as discussed in Chapter 9, a lot of procrastination begins in the body.

Optimize your workspace. If you need quiet, find quiet. If you need the room to be at a certain temperature, find that. And if you need a window, or no window, find that. Don't settle for a space that's not a great fit, because that will be just one more obstacle to doing your work.

Work alongside other focused workers. Many of us work faster when we're among others who are themselves focused on their work. So, find yourself a library or café full of quiet and industrious people, and enjoy the boost you get from working alongside them. (The more you overcome perfectionism, however, the easier you should find it to work alone—and if solo work becomes your preference, you shouldn't hesitate to do that.)

Do some preemptive obstacle work (Chapter 9) before starting projects, so that you can eliminate obstacles while they're still small—or, better yet, prevent them from occurring in the first place.

Plan your large or complex projects. It doesn't have to be a super-detailed plan. (And shouldn't be: don't turn your planning into Quasiproductive Procrastination.) Just write down a few milestones and deadlines. Planning not only helps you stay on track, it helps you visualize your project as a whole, which further boosts your productivity.

Reduce your project's scope. As discussed in the "What to Do If You've Got an Urgent Deadline" section at the front of this book, and also in the "Cut it Out" section of Chapter 28.

Stick to "process" goals. As discussed in Chapter 7, even some seemingly benign goals, such as "to do a great job" or "get a great grade" are perfectionist. The only goals you should be working toward are *process* goals, and these two goals, specifically: "to do the best that I can *right now*" and "to finish." The first goal ("to do the best that I can right now") reminds you that creativity is an organic process that takes time, so you shouldn't get bogged down trying to perfect a bit of work in the moment. The most effective and efficient work method, generally speaking, is to do the best you can on a bit *without pushing it*; then let it "rest" and "marinate" in the back of your mind while you work on other things; and then come back to it when you're ready. (See, also, the discussions of trial-and-error in Chapter 28, the importance of not forcing/controlling the work in Chapter 29, and Quick-Drafting in Chapter 30.)

A related process-related maxim to bear in mind is, **"I don't have to fix this problem right now. I'll have time to fix it later."** This really is one of the most calming things you can tell yourself when you're in the midst of a difficult project.

The second process-related goal, "to finish," can alternatively be expressed like this: "to get this project done and off my desk." Keeping this goal prominent while you're working reminds you not to overwork/hoard your projects in an attempt to perfect every little detail. (See Chapter 7's discussion of quantity versus quality, Chapter 16's point about how nonperfectionists don't give themselves permission to miss deadlines, and Chapter 31's discussion of the importance of finishing one's work.)

Pilot/Prototype your scientific, technical, and artistic projects. When doing a science experiment, for instance, collect and analyze a small amount of data first, just to make sure your setup is working as planned (as Aisha does in the next chapter). Or, if you're writing a computer program, first create a "bare bones" version, without any fancy bells and whistles, just to make sure it does the basic things it's supposed to do. Or, if you're doing an art or writing project, start with a storyboard, outline, or sketch.

Do at least some of your work on the day you get the assignment. Your creativity and enthusiasm are often at their peak right after you're given an assignment, so don't waste that valuable time.

Alas, many students not only don't do this, they do the exact opposite and wait till the last minute to start their work, either because they're procrastinating, aren't managing their time well, or both. This almost certainly means that they'll wind up rushing through their work and having a miserable time. (And getting a mediocre result.) Waiting until the last minute is also, I'm reliably informed, one of the student behaviors that most upsets professors, both because they know you're capable of doing better work, and because it creates more work for them when you miss your deadlines.

Do a bit of work on all your subjects (or projects) most days. Productivity-wise, there's nothing worse than a "cold start," where you return to a difficult project after days or weeks or months of neglecting it. While you should do most of your work in stretches of half an hour or more—that's both efficient and often needed for concentration (more on this in Chapter 49)—in between those stretches, do some short intervals of around five or 10 minutes on any projects that you're not focusing on that day. This will not only help you keep the material fresh, it will leave you with much less work to do during your final push. (Because the intervals, although small, do add up!)

While working, **keep a light touch and a light heart**, even if the work itself is serious. You may have difficult problems to solve, and serious points to make, and intense scenarios to explore, but try to do it all while keeping at least some emotional distance. This can be difficult, so if, despite your best intentions, you find yourself getting caught up emotionally, try journaling about the situation or discussing it with a friend, your professor, or a counselor.

Above all, you want to **resist the perfectionist stereotype of the tortured creator or scholar**. Like a lot of perfectionist stereotypes, it has some superficial dramatic appeal, and is therefore widely promoted in the media. But it is a *terrible* model to follow, for productivity and other reasons.[40] The

---

[40] See, for instance: https://www.minnpost.com/second-opinion/2016/02/tortured-artist-meme-lacks-good-evidence-says-british-psychologist/ and https://www.independent.co.uk/voices/world-mental-health-day-tortured-artist-dangerous-myth-pain-art-depression-suicide-a8576971.html.

goal is to be able to, as much as possible, stay light and playful even when working on your "serious" stuff. (And please watch the labeling!)

The above techniques are humane and effective alternatives to trying to shame yourself into working faster—which, in any case, is only likely to backfire. But let's take a deeper, more philosophical look at the whole "speed" question.

Make Haste, Slowly

Perhaps you've heard of the global Slow Movement, which urges that, in an age of technological speedup, we all become more deliberate and mindful about our various activities. The movement has spawned several sub-movements, including Slow Food, Slow Schooling, Slow Travel, and Slow Parenting.

Let's talk about Slow Work. Over the years, I've spoken with teachers in many fields, including science, the arts, engineering, the building trades, and automobile mechanics. They've all said the same thing: that one of their major challenges is getting their students to slow down enough to focus on the details of their work. Students tend to rush, in large part because they don't realize how long it takes to do good work. The truth is, it can take a shockingly long time, especially when you're still learning, but also even when you're more experienced. (I *still* can't believe how long it can take me to write a "simple" blog post.) A physics professor I know gives his students time estimates for their homework (e.g., "1–2 hours per problem"), and also suggests that if the work takes much longer, they consult him to make sure they're using their time well. If your professors aren't offering similar guidance, you should ask them for it.

Working too fast yields not just sloppy work, but a difficult and joyless process. Plus, it's an obstacle to learning. You need to slow down enough to not only get the details right, but understand why they're right. In fact, **whenever you sit down to do your work, it should be with the attitude that, "I have an infinite amount of time to get this done."** This will slow you down to your natural, relaxed, unhurried speed—the speed at which you can focus on the details. Now, of course, I know that you don't actually have infinite time. But in yet another one of those happy productivity paradoxes, pretending that you do can actually speed your work, because it minimizes perfectionism and procrastination, thus liberating your creativity. As Carl Honoré says in his book *In Praise of Slowness*, an overview of the Slow Movement, "Performing a task in a Slow manner often yields faster results."

I can't emphasize this enough! There have been countless times, during the writing of this book, when I caught myself thinking, "This bit of writing is taking too long! If I spend this much time on every page [or paragraph, or sentence], the entire book is going to take *forever!*" Whenever I caught myself thinking that way, however, I intentionally adopted the opposing view: "I have unlimited time to work on this." And at the very moment I did that, the stress and pressure would melt away, leaving me relaxed and eager to do my work—which then invariably went much faster than it had before. This example also shows that **you must always counter perfectionism with a strong opposing stand**. Weak neutrality isn't sufficient! If I had responded to my internal pressures by saying, "I'll give myself a day to write this paragraph. That's a generous amount of time." I still would have felt pressured and constrained. (This is an experiment you can try for yourself.)

This "infinite time" trick also aligns with Anne Lamott's technique, from her writing guide *Bird by Bird*, of viewing your work as if through a "one-inch picture frame"—meaning that you focus on just the tiny bit of it that's in front of you, without worrying at all about the rest.

To recap: you want to work with focus and intentionality and commitment, but *not* with any sense of urgency. Obviously, there will be times when you're facing an urgent deadline and need to step on the gas. But the more you learn to, as one of my mentors put it, "make haste, slowly," the better and faster you should be able to work, and the fewer of those kinds of urgent deadlines you should encounter.

At the same time you're doing your Slow Work, be sure to choose relatively short and simple projects. That's especially important when you're a student and/or working to overcome your perfectionism, for five reasons:

1. All projects are harder than they seem. Even a seemingly "simple" project will probably be hard enough.
2. Keeping things simple will allow you to focus on the details while still completing your project on time.
3. As already noted, novices tend to overstuff their projects, so keeping things simple will help to counteract that.
4. As noted in Chapter 7, quantity (i.e., finishing lots of small/simple stuff) will help you build your quality.
5. "Finishing" is a vital skill, and working on smaller/simpler projects will allow you to practice it more often. (More on this in Chapter 31.)

What if you want to do longer and more complicated work projects? No problem! Just build up to them gradually. Every new project can be as long and complicated as you like—*until* you start feeling scared, pressured, under-resourced, or otherwise perfectionist.

If, while you're keeping it small, a critical internal voice pops up saying stuff like, "Wow, you're really unambitious! Step it up!" I believe you now know exactly who that voice is, and how you should handle their advice.

27. Get Fresh!

Ideas are like cookies: better when fresh. A fresh idea is rich with meanings, associations, connotations, and other "flavors." It's also soft and malleable, so you can use it in different ways. But old ideas, like old cookies, go stale, losing a lot of their flavor and becoming stiff and brittle. When a Slogger uses a linear process that involves "doing all the research and organizing first, and only then starting to write," they're doing the intellectual equivalent of constantly eating stale cookies. (Yech! No wonder they procrastinate.)

So use your ideas when they're fresh. You do that by doing your **writing and other "output" work *in parallel with* your planning, research, and other preparatory ("input") steps**. Let's say you're researching a paper and find a useful nugget of information. Don't write it on an index card or in a notes file with the idea of later transferring it into your manuscript. Just plunk it right down into your manuscript, in the spot you think it best fits. Then start writing and editing around it. (Obviously, never plagiarize and always be sure to use proper citations.) Then, when you run out of steam with it, go back and do some more research until you find your next useful nugget.

As noted in Chapter 5, however, you shouldn't do the opposite and research when you're supposed to be writing or doing other output work, because research is a prime vehicle for Quasiproductive Procrastination.

Aisha's story demonstrates how you can use this "parallelism" technique even for scientific and other work that would seem to require a linear approach:

For her senior chemistry capstone project, **Aisha** is investigating the process of nucleation, in which the addition of a tiny amount of an impurity (e.g., clay or talc) can cause a supersaturated solution to crystallize. It's a dramatic and beautiful effect—and, by the way, without the impurity, the solution would just sit there unchanging, forever boring in its static perfection.

Her initial ambitious plan is to use nucleation to create several types of organic and inorganic crystals, measuring both the speed and thoroughness of the crystallization process. Her professor, however, says STOP! Her project, he says, is too ambitious, and she's unlikely to finish it in time. He instead encourages her to build her experiment around just one type of crystal, testing its growth rate, purity, etc., under conditions of varying temperature and pressure. This way, every phase of her experiment—preliminary literature review, hypothesis formation, experimental design, apparatus setup, data collection and analysis, comprehensive literature review, and writing up her results—will be *much* simpler, and she'll have plenty of time to get it all right.

She agrees—and is relieved, actually, because she had suspected that her plan was too ambitious. (Hopefully, in the future, she'll listen a bit better when her Inner Compassionately Objective Adult whispers such wisdom to her.)

After she runs her experiment, Aisha is required to produce a research paper and a 20-minute slide presentation summarizing her work. Her professor suggests she start working on both of those immediately so that she doesn't get stuck starting them from scratch near the end of the semester. She follows this advice, and because she's using all the Joyful Dance techniques we've been discussing, the work goes pretty easily and is fun.

Her professor also suggests she do a small pilot project, just to make sure her experimental design is solid and her apparatus is working as intended. This advice she's *not* so enthusiastic about, since she's short on time and absolutely certain that everything works. Still, she follows it—and it's a good thing she does, because it turns out that her solution doesn't nucleate (probably because of some contamination that's getting in). Once she recovers from her shock, she rebuilds everything from scratch, this time working much more slowly and carefully. Then, with some trepidation, she repeats her pilot.

This time she gets a great crystal! And so, in a happily confident frame of mind, she continues on with the rest of her experiment.

Thanks to her parallel work process, by the time Aisha's finished her data collection and analysis, her paper and presentation are already largely done.

She feels great about that, and, in particular, relieved not to be facing a mound of disorganized notes and possibly questionable data, like some of the other students. Later on, she's happy to get a great grade on her project, but her gratification mostly comes from her deeper understanding of, and appreciation for, the scientific process in general, and nucleation in particular. She's looking forward to doing more experiments—and will *always*, she promises herself, work slowly and carefully, especially when designing her experiments and setting up her apparatus.

And she'll also always run a pilot.

28. Wizard-Level Problem-Solving

The problem, often, is problems. We can be happily chugging along doing our work and then be stopped cold by one. Our tendency, at such times, is to sit there and ponder, á la Rodin's sculpture, "The Thinker." Most of us aren't that great at abstract thought, however, and so our efforts don't yield much—at which point, there is a strong temptation to flee via procrastination.

To do better, you need to first understand that most of what you're doing, when you're working, is making decisions. It doesn't matter whether you call those decisions, "physics," "anthropology," "music theory," or something else: it's still just decisions. Even a "small" project can require hundreds: a few large, some small, many tiny. Some you make consciously, while others are automatic. (But weren't always! While you can now write simple sentences and do simple math automatically, those tasks would have involved some very big decisions back in elementary school.)

In between the decisions is the time we spend "implementing," or doing what we decided to do. But decision-making is usually a much bigger part of our projects than we realize, and even when we're implementing, we're still usually making some decisions.

The next thing you need to understand is that **what we refer to as a "problem" is just a set of decisions that requires more time and effort than most**. (Again, watch the labeling.)

So, a key to working fast is to make efficient decisions—and a key to that is, again, nonperfectionism. Dichotomizing, pathologizing, rigidity, impatience, etc. are all obvious barriers to decision-making. Perfectionism can also convince you that none of your solutions are any good, thus getting you stuck on looking for "the right one."

143

One of the saddest things about perfectionism is how it can suck the joy out of a potentially fun process. Think about it: many people solve problems for fun via crossword puzzles, sudoku games, mystery novels, and "brain teaser" puzzles. Why should the problems you solve for your schoolwork be any different? This may sound silly if you're used to viewing "work" and "fun" as opposites, but, as I've discussed at various points in this book, you absolutely do want to approach your work as play.

The foundational solution for speeding up your decision-making, and hence your problem-solving and overall productivity, is nonperfectionism. Here are some others:

Trial and Error. Instead of sitting there and pondering, go ahead and try out some solutions. This gets you out of the realm of abstract thought, and into the far more productive (and fun) one of using your skills. (You're "thinking by doing," in other words.) Sooner or later—and probably sooner—you'll come up with a solution that works.

The key to successful trial and error is to not censor yourself. The whole point is to give yourself the freedom to experiment and play. But if you start preemptively shooting your ideas down—say, as "unlikely to work" or even "silly"—that defeats the whole purpose. (I guess I don't need to tell you which part of yourself is likely to do that.) Also, "unlikely" or "silly" ideas often turn out, with just a little tweaking, to be winners.

Trial and error is another example of Chapter 7's idea that quantity yields quality. Generally speaking, the harder your problem is to solve, the more trials it will take to solve it. But solutions can often come surprisingly quickly. Or, to put it another way: our problems often aren't as tough as our inner perfectionist would have us believe.

To be clear, **trial and error isn't just a problem-solving technique, but your main work method**. It's what writers do when they Quickdraft, for instance (see Chapter 30), and what coders do when they use iterative development techniques. Architects and engineers often develop their ideas by creating multiple virtual or physical models, and many visual artists and performers work by adding and subtracting bits until their vision emerges. Trial and error is the main "format" of your creative conversation, in other words—and it's no coincidence that it also provides you with lots of empowering options (Chapter 4) for proceeding with your work.

Write for Help. Write an email to someone summarizing the problem and asking for help. Doing this gives you some emotional distance from the problem, while at the same time allowing you to look at it from a fresh angle. The amazing thing is that, often, you don't even have to send the email: just writing it is enough to get you "unstuck." (As discussed in Chapter 10, asking for help, all by itself and regardless of any response that you receive, is empowering.) But if you want to go ahead and send it, feel free.

Cut it Out! As noted earlier, novice scholars and creators, and even experienced ones who are perfectionist, tend to overstuff their projects. And guess what? It's often that excess that clutters up your argument and otherwise causes problems. So try removing the problem bit. (Possibly saving it for another project.) This advice applies not just to entire sections of your work, but to individual sentences, phrases, and even words. Even a tiny bit of excess can cause problems, so if a sentence, phrase, or word is bedeviling you, try deleting it.

It's amazing how often this trivial-seeming action of cutting works, and how good it feels. There's something deeply satisfying about giving a troublesome part of your project the boot. One caveat, however: don't cut out of fear. Some of the most valuable work happens when you arrive at a mess, take a deep breath, and then dive in and really try to work it out. A general guideline for when to cut content is: if there's a problem with your central thesis or theme, try working it out. But if the problem is a tangential bit, go ahead and cut. (Obviously, keep a backup in case you change your mind.)

The worry, when you cut, is that the project is going to wind up too short. This is often both a perfectionist worry—because perfectionists mistrust "easy" success—and a pragmatic one: if the assignment is for 10 pages, you can't hand in eight. Sometimes you can gather the more interesting cut bits into a new paragraph or section devoted to "secondary issues" or "topics for further research and discussion." Even when you can't, however, there's probably some part of the work that you can expand, which brings us to...

Expand It. Often a bit of work won't come together because we're trying to cram too much information into too few words. So another technique is to expand the troublesome bit. First, copy it into a new window so you have lots of room to experiment and play, then let your creativity take charge. Often, the piece will open up in interesting and fun directions. Finally, for very tough problems that are resisting any solution...

Start Over. This time letting the work find its own way. Impatient and rigid perfectionists are often horror-struck when I suggest this—and I do agree that it does sound very inefficient—but productive people do it all the time. And you know what? The new version usually goes way faster. That's often because: (a) after all your prior attempts, you finally do know what it is that you're trying to do or say, and (b) you're less controlling this time around. (See the next chapter to learn why trying to control the outcome isn't helpful.) Please note, however, that **there's a difference between occasionally starting a difficult project over from scratch and constantly**

starting *all* of your projects over from scratch because you're afraid to finish. The former is great while the latter is a seriously self-sabotaging perfectionist behavior that I discuss in Chapter 13.

29. How to Get, and Stay, Inspired

Poets, philosophers, and others have been pondering the "mystery of inspiration" for thousands of years, but all "being inspired" means is that you're ready and motivated to do the work. And all "being uninspired" means is that you're not—yet. So what does it take to be ready? A few things, including an understanding of the process you need to follow, confidence, a detailed knowledge of how to do the next couple of steps, and abundant preparation. Let's discuss each individually.

An Understanding of the Process. This may seem like a no-brainer, but many people who think they know what they're doing actually don't. They're operating from a mix of hunches and guesswork, perhaps with a dash of shallow media advice (e.g., "10 Tips for Writing Your Thesis" or "How to Succeed as a Musician") mixed in. What often happens, in such cases, is that the person gets mired in a lot of Quasiproductive Procrastination—e.g., busy work, redoing the same work over and over, over-researching, etc.—that gives them the illusion that they're making progress. On some level, though, they know they're stuck—and their doubts keep growing until, one day, they're tipped over the edge by a "failure," harsh criticism, or other crisis. Then they quit—and maybe not just the project, but also their class, major, school, or even career.

You need to think very carefully about whether you're in this situation if you're: (a) working in isolation, and especially without mentors, or (b) not using a plan with deadlines.

Confidence. Even if you understand your process, it's easy to get discouraged if you don't feel confident. You obviously need confidence in your skills, but it's even more important to have confidence in the availability of help. Most of all, you need confidence that, if you make a reasonable effort, you have a reasonable chance of success. (As mentioned in Chapter 4, futility may be *the* most disempowering emotion.) Of course, some goals are harder to achieve than others—and it always helps, if you're going after one of the tough ones, to maintain an expansive and holistic, otherwise known as nonperfectionist, view of success. For example: "Even if I don't achieve my primary goal, I still will have learned many useful things, and had a great time doing this project, so my efforts weren't wasted."

Detailed Steps. Along with understanding and confidence, you also need to know **how to do the next couple of steps *in detail*.** Otherwise, you might get stuck on one of them, or on your current step. (Because you're aware, at least subconsciously, that you don't know how to proceed, and are afraid of failure.) Good ways to test whether you know enough are to: (1) write the steps down in detail, and (2) try explaining the steps to someone else—even your dog or cat. Any holes in your knowledge should quickly become apparent. (If you're working without a mentor you should assume you don't have all the information you need to proceed.)

One of the benefits of being in school is that, in theory at least, you should always understand your assignments, have confidence that they're doable, and have a detailed knowledge of the next couple of steps. But people make mistakes, miscommunicate, and fail to communicate. Especially when working on important or complex assignments, please check in frequently with your professor, and be honest and specific about the difficulties you're facing.

Abundant Preparation. Finally, to be inspired, you need to have done **Abundant Preparation**. Here, again, are the typical steps of a writing project: conceptualization (a.k.a., brainstorming or idea generation), research, organization/outlining, first draft, revisions, and sharing the work. **Notice how the step most people think happens first, "first draft," actually happens more than halfway through.** It takes a lot of work even to be able to do a first draft! If you get stuck, therefore, try going back and spending more time on the conceptualization, organization, and research stages, and you should regain your inspiration. Similar advice applies to science, math, and engineering: if you're stuck, go back and review the fundamentals. When you do that, it often turns out that you don't understand them as well as you think you do, and that, once you correct that problem, your work goes much more easily.

The word "inspiration" literally means "breathing in," and that's exactly what you're doing during the early stages of your project: "breathing in" the work of experts past and present, which you then combine with your own ideas and insights in your creative conversation. But if you rush through those early stages, as many students do because they don't know any better and are in a hurry to get to what they consider "the real work," you starve yourself of the inputs needed for inspiration, pretty much ensuring that your work will be a grind.

Know Thyself and Thy Motivations

Even if you do have the understanding, confidence, detailed knowledge, and preparation needed to proceed, you can still find yourself getting stuck. In such cases, try answering these four questions:

(1) Am I being perfectionist? I know, I know: *again* with the perfectionism! But it will rob you of your inspiration faster than just about anything. Ask yourself, especially, whether you're overfocusing on outcomes, or being overidentified, grandiose, impatient, mistrustful of success, and/or rigid. If the answer is yes, then use your reframing, dialoguing, and other solutions to overcome that.

(2) Am I doing this project for the right reasons? Especially, ask yourself if you're doing it to try to impress others. That's a sign of overidentification, among other possible problems. I can usually tell when someone is in this bind because their project will be overserious, overcomplicated, and overintellectualized—e.g., "My paper is about death as a metaphysical protest and ecstatic reaction, as interpreted by Tolstoy and Dostoevsky, with supplementary analytical comparisons using Gogol and Chekhov." Also, it's pretty clear, usually, that the person's heart really isn't in the topic. (Also see Chapter 13's discussion of overambitious projects.)

(3) Am I ambivalent for other reasons? Perhaps your project revisits some difficult personal or family history, or explores challenging issues such as war, genocide, domestic violence, or animal cruelty. (All real-life examples from people I've worked with.) If so, try the solutions in Chapter 24, and always remember that empowerment means creating more good options for yourself—including the option to *not* work on a project, or with a topic, if you don't feel fully ready to do so.

(4) Am I trying to force the work? Imagine that you're having a fun conversation with friends. Then, all of a sudden, someone starts to talk over everyone else, and insist that the discussion be held in a certain way, and arrive at a specific conclusion.

Not so fun or productive anymore, is it?

It works the same way with creativity: the moment you try to control it, you shut it down. Often, when we do this, it's because we're aiming for a certain quality standard like "excellence" or "comprehensiveness" or "originality." That's admirable, but repeat after me: You Can't Force the Work.

As the French novelist Gustave Flaubert put it, "Success is a consequence and must not be a goal."

Therefore, a final thing to ask, and answer, when you're feeling stuck or uninspired is, "Am I trying to force the work? Or, alternatively: **"Am I trying to control the outcome?"** or "Am I trying to dominate the creative conversation?" Any of these can stop your creativity cold.

If this turns out to be the problem—and it often does—then politely ask your Inner Perfectionist (and ego) to step aside and stop trying to dominate, so that your creative process can take its natural, organic course. The only potential problem with doing that is that the work might start going beyond the bounds of what your professor assigned. If that happens, go ahead and talk with them. Hopefully, they'll be understanding, because what you have here is an honest-to-gosh case of creativity. But if they aren't—and they may have their legitimate reasons—then you get to practice another valuable life skill: working on something you don't particularly want to be working on. (The "boredom" discussion in Chapter 32 offers some tips for that.)

30. How to Write Like a Pro

Writing is a paradox. On the one hand, it's an incredibly common activity that many of us feel like we mastered way back in elementary school. On the other, it's really easy to get stuck when doing it.

Clearly, there's a lot more to the "simple" act of writing than many of us think. The main problem is that, along with the intellectual and creative challenges we expect, writing presents a whole other set of challenges that we don't expect: challenges of solitude, sedentariness, and—let's face it—monotony. (All those endless rounds of putting down words and taking them out again.) Add to all that, the fact that it often takes a lot more work than we expect to create a good piece of writing, and it's no wonder that many people struggle.

Fortunately, there are some groups of professional writers who are taught how to deal with all that, and whom we can learn from. They include journalists—who often must make weekly or even daily deadlines—and the "genre" writers of science fiction, fantasy, romance, mystery, etc., many of whom write a book (or more!) a year. Below is a suggested writing process that incorporates many of the techniques used by these highly productive writers. Even if you're not a self-described "writer," but simply someone who is expected to write a lot for class—and, later, on the job—they should work for you.

(1) Stay grounded. Some people approach their writing like it's some kind of holy mission: an overidentified and grandiose approach which, needless to say, isn't helpful. In his memoir *On Writing*, Stephen King suggests you view your writing as, "Just another job like laying pipe or driving long-haul trucks." It's good advice!

(2) Stay playful, even when writing serious stuff. Writing, like all creativity, demands freedom and a light touch—and that's true even when what you're working on is highly serious and/or intellectual. That doesn't mean that you should be all ha-ha jokey when writing about, say, climate change or genocide, but only that you shouldn't fall into the trap of thinking that you're supposed to be actively depressed while doing so. A little emotional distance from your subject matter is usually a good thing, especially if the subject matter is emotionally challenging.

All that said, however, it can be difficult to maintain that distance. If you do find yourself getting depressed or otherwise affected by what you're working on, talk to your professor, a friend, or a counselor. And don't feel obligated to tackle a subject if it seems too emotionally challenging: your mental health should be your top priority.

(3) Daydream productively. Recalling the last chapter's discussion of "abundant preparation," another secret of prolific writers is that they invest heavily in the foundational "conceptualization" step of the writing process. Charles Dickens, for instance, would often take, "a vigorous three-hour walk through the countryside or the streets of London… 'searching for some pictures [he] wanted to build upon.'"[41] I imagine him, while walking, pondering the next scene in *Oliver Twist* or *Great Expectations*, then coming upon a real-life scenario that helped him put everything in focus.

Ursula K. LeGuin once told an interviewer that, after waking up, she spent around 45 minutes lying in bed and thinking, before having "lots of" breakfast, and then sitting down to write for around five hours.[42] We can assume that she used her early-morning thinking time to fuel her ideas for her writing, just as she used the big breakfasts to fuel her physical energy.

I'm guessing that Dickens kept a notepad handy while he was walking, so that he could jot down his inspirations. And perhaps LeGuin kept one by her bedside. (One way you know you're in a creative person's home is that there are notepads and/or piles of scratch paper everywhere.) I similarly recommend that you carry a notepad, or use your phone's voice recorder, when daydreaming away from your desk. But also try daydreaming *at* your desk, by journaling about what you're working on and the specific problems you're trying to solve. You can do that either via freewriting, a Q&A format (e.g., "Q: Why is this section of my paper so confused?" "A: Maybe it's because I'm trying to say too many things at once…"), or even in the form of a letter to someone (which you don't have to send). Like all forms of

---

[41] From Mason Currey's book *Daily Rituals*, which includes lots of fun descriptions of how famous creative people work, or worked.

[42] https://www.openculture.com/2019/01/ursula-k-le-guins-daily-routine-the-discipline-that-fueled-her-imagination.html

thinking-by-doing (Chapter 28), thinking-by-writing accelerates your creativity and problem-solving. The seemingly random stuff you write often turns out to be surprisingly useful for your project.

(4) Use props. Some writers work to a music playlist that's thematically related to whatever it is they're writing. Others create mindmaps, flowcharts, or timelines. And still others create posters, scrapbooks, maps, collages, and even faux book covers. Props can be fun to create, and very inspiring and motivating. So have fun creating some! Only *don't* do it when you're supposed to be writing, because that would be Quasiproductive Procrastination.

(5) Create your "shitty first draft". The idea of a shitty first draft was popularized by Anne Lamott in her book, *Bird by Bird*. She describes it as follows: "The first draft is the child's draft, where you let it all pour out and then let it romp all over the place, knowing that no one is going to see it and that you can shape it later. You just let this childlike part of you channel whatever voices and visions come through and onto the page."

Lamott also describes shitty first drafts as self-indulgent, boring, stupefying, incoherent, hideous, and, "almost just typing, just making my fingers move." She also notes how perfectionism—which she calls "the voice of the oppressor"—is the main obstacle keeping you from completing your shitty first draft, because you can't tolerate the shittiness. Interestingly enough, when I ask perfectionists to describe what a shitty first draft looks like, they typically say something like this: "Well, it's rough in places, but it's mostly organized and the major points are there..." Perfectionists' shitty first drafts, in other words, are like nonperfectionists' almost-final drafts! For the record, most shitty first drafts, including my own, are pretty self-indulgent, boring, stupefying, incoherent, and disorganized. So make sure you're comfortable creating truly shitty, shitty first drafts.

Once you've written your shitty first draft, it's time to move onto my favorite part of the writing process...

(6) Quickdraft. During writing productivity classes, I sometimes ask the trick question, "How many drafts should you do of a paper or other piece of writing?" The students who are creative, academic, or business writers usually answer something like, "three" or "five" or "10." But the journalists always answer, correctly, "As many as it takes." But you need to know what they mean by a "draft": *not* a slow, linear slog through your paper (or chunk), but a kind of nimble dance through it, during which you stop to make only the easiest and most obvious edits.

The goal, in other words, is to do lots and lots of fast drafts. Now, sooner or later, while you're doing that, you're going to come across a bit you feel like focusing on, and you absolutely should do that! That feeling is called "inspiration," and you don't want to waste it. When it passes—meaning you've written or edited as much as you can, at that moment, on that bit—simply return to your nimble dance.

Your writing process, then, consists of alternating fast and slow work, with you shifting as desired between those two modes without hesitation, fuss, or drama. Then, when you reach the end of the paper (or chunk), you return to the beginning and start over.

You keep doing all that until you finish your Timed Work Interval (Chapter 6).

I call this process **Quickdrafting** and it offers some terrific advantages, including that it's:

- Nonlinear and fresh. You can start anywhere within your piece that you want, and are also free to stop and focus on whichever bits you'd like.
- An active, easy, interesting, and fun way to write, so you don't get bored.
- Preserving of your energy, so that you can work longer without getting tired.
- Generative. Each time you do a Quickdraft, you gain ideas and insights that fuel the next.
- Accelerative! Meaning that, the more Quickdrafts you do, the faster the remaining ones should go. (In contrast to linear work, which tends to, first, slow down, and then bog down.)

Quickdrafting is particularly useful for big projects because it helps you to comprehend your project as a whole, leading to more speed and a better, more integrated product. Quickdrafting also helps you to avoid the kinds of rabbit holes, tangents, and other time-wasters (see Chapters 31 and 32) that are easy to fall into when you overfocus on one part of a big project. Your early Quickdrafts will, in effect, be "sketches" for your final written product. Just as visual artists do preliminary sketches to make sure they've got their overall composition right before starting work on the details, writers can also benefit from doing that, and Quickdrafting will help.

How many Quickdrafts does it take to complete a paper or other piece of writing? (*Not* a trick question, this time.) The answer varies, depending on the project. It could be as high 10, 20, or even more—but don't panic! A nonperfectionist can do dozens of Quickdrafts faster than a perfectionist can do even one "Slowdraft." (Assuming that they even finish that one.)

You can sometimes Quickdraft your way right through a shorter piece, from the beginning to the end, without any major problems. But if you get stuck—and, at some point, in most projects, you probably will—then use the techniques in Chapters 28 through 32 to get unstuck and resume your Quickdrafting. Especially, don't forget to show your drafts early and often, to avoid hoarding (Chapter 32).

(7) Be extra patient when handling feedback and criticism. The moment when you get some comments back on your piece, from a professor, classmate, friend, editor, or someone else, is one of the most fraught in the entire writing process.

The first pitfall is emotional. Obviously, you want to set your perfectionist ego aside and evaluate those criticisms and suggestions nondefensively, with an open and objective mind.

After you decide what changes you want to make in your work, there's another challenge, which is that it can take a surprising amount of work to integrate even small changes into an existing text. Sometimes that's because you have to do a lot of writing and editing around a change, or because a change triggers more changes, and then more, etc., in a kind of domino effect. And sometimes it's because a change requires that you view your text in new and unfamiliar ways. In all cases, the key is not to panic. Start just by recording, right in your manuscript, notes about the changes you want to make. (I often list the changes in bullet point format.) Then start Quickdrafting around those notes, working with even more patience than usual.

(8) Remember the goals. As discussed in Chapter 26, those are: (a) to do the best you can at the moment, and (b) to finish.

(9) Remember the rewards. It's noteworthy that, despite writing's many inconveniences, so many people are drawn to it. That's probably because it offers numerous and profound rewards, including meaning, growth, transcendence, transformation, and joy. As Flaubert famously put it, "Writing is a dog's life, but the only life worth living." And Toni Morrison once said that, while she didn't particularly enjoy the act of writing, "Without it, you're stuck with life."[43] (The same can be said, really, of all creative and intellectual pursuits, of course.)

Staying mindful of the personal rewards of writing (and other creative/intellectual pursuits) can help you stay motivated throughout the course of your projects. And if you use the techniques in this chapter, the writing itself should go much more easily. Casey's story, below, shows how you can combine these techniques with nonlinearity and parallelism to wind up with

---

[43] Quoted by writer Fran Lebowitz in this interview: https://freshairarchive.org/segments/humorist-fran-lebowitz-writing-and-not-writing-0.

not just a great paper that is written efficiently, but an enhanced understanding of, and appreciation for, a vivid aspect of the human experience.

For their comparative religion class, **Casey** is writing a paper on the Japanese concept of *wabi-sabi* (finding beauty in the imperfect and transient), which is closely associated with Buddhism. They start by doing some research, and then lay out their ideas in a very rough—a.k.a., "shitty"—first draft.

Then, they start Quickdrafting, gradually improving upon that draft.

After doing some more research, they find this exciting quotation from Kakuzo Okakura's classic work, *The Book of Tea*: "Perfection is everywhere if we only choose to recognize it." They copy it, with attribution of course, right into the relevant section of their manuscript; then start writing and revising around it.

The Okakura quote inspires some other ideas, so Casey starts writing about those, too. Eventually, they decide that all the Okakura-related material would work best gathered into one section, and so, without hesitating, they create that section and do some bold reorganizing. (They save their current version as a backup, just in case.)

Casey keeps Quickdrafting. Whenever they encounter a problem, they resist the urge to ponder, and instead do some trial and error; and so, all the problems get resolved relatively quickly. Still, for what seems like a scarily long time, their paper resembles a giant mishmash, and they worry that they're not making enough progress. They keep the faith, however—and, in particular, are careful to resist the temptation to try to force the work in any particular direction. Sure enough, the compelling themes soon start to emerge.

The more Casey focuses on those themes, the more their paper gels. Pretty soon—and with some judicious cutting of some sections and expanding of others—all of the paper's major problems have been resolved, and it starts to resemble a coherent whole. After that, it's pretty much mostly smooth sailing—or, more accurately, smooth QuickDrafting—until the end of the project.

When it's time to hand their paper in, Casey does so with satisfaction and a confidence that they've done their best. Not surprisingly, their professor gives them a great grade, and also praises their "depth of analysis" and "ability to capture the subtleties of the concept." Casey's happy about all that, but even happier to have engaged meaningfully with such a fascinating topic. They're eager to learn more about Buddhism and Japanese culture, and to one day visit Japan.

31. Navigating the Project Life Cycle

Just as humans go through life stages—infancy, childhood, adolescence, adulthood, etc.—projects also go through life stages. In this section, I discuss each stage individually, so that you can anticipate its characteristic challenges and prevent them from stalling your projects.

The **Honeymoon** is the very beginning of your project—literally, the first few minutes or hours, or (for bigger projects) days or weeks. At this stage, the project exists mainly as a glorious golden vision in your head—and what you are probably envisioning is not the product itself, but how amazed and impressed others will be when they see it. Even when you do envision the process, it's probably all smooth sailing, with few, if any, serious problems.

This golden vision is super motivational, and so, for a while at least, you work like gangbusters. But then, inevitably, the vision starts to crack and tarnish as you realize that:

The work you've done so far isn't great. In fact, it's pretty bad. (Shitty first drafts and other early attempts always are.)

The project's got some serious problems that you don't know how to solve, or even if you can solve them. And even if you can...

The project is going to turn out very different from, and not nearly as good as, the golden vision. (Because nothing could possibly turn out that well.) And, finally,

You still have an enormous amount of work to do.

Welcome to the **Anti-Honeymoon**, the stage of peak disappointment, disillusionment, and demotivation. It's the stage at which many people abandon not just projects, but classes, jobs, careers, relationships, etc. English Literature majors will recognize it as the "Slough of Despond" from John

Bunyan's classic 17[h] century allegory, *The Pilgrim's Progress*. And college students in all majors may experience it in the form of what is commonly called, "Sophomore Slump." (See Chapter 2.)

What's really going on is…you guessed it…perfectionism. The Honeymoon/Anti-Honeymoon cycle reeks of overemphasis on product, a narrow definition of success, overidentification, grandiosity, shortsightedness, impatience, pathologizing, and pretty much every other perfectionist characteristic. The key to coping, therefore, is to moderate your perfectionism and, especially, your expectations. Optimism at the start of a project is great, but avoid grandiose fantasies that will almost inevitably trigger a backlash of disappointment. And when the Anti-Honeymoon does arrive, keep cool and keep working, always keeping in mind that **the problem isn't your work, but your perfectionist attitude toward it.** (Just as, in *The Pilgrim's Progress*, the Slough consists of the Pilgrim's, "fears, and doubts, and discouraging apprehensions.")

Also, double down on your other solutions. Bunyan's protagonist, the pilgrim Christian, finally escapes from the Slough with the assistance of, "a man whose name was Help," hint, hint.

Get past the Anti-Honeymoon, and you'll soon enter the **Vast Middle.** If the Honeymoon/Anti-Honeymoon combination and Home Stretch (see below) each represent around 10% of your project, that leaves 80% for the Vast Middle. (That's vast!) The real problem, however, isn't the Vast Middle's vastness, but the fact that, much of the time when you're in it, you don't feel like you're making progress. In the midst of what can feel like endless rounds of trial and error that seem to be going nowhere, it's easy to get discouraged.

The solution, again, is to keep your cool and keep working—keeping in mind that the **"Vast Middle" is simply another name for "doing the work."** Joyful Dancers and process-focused people in general don't actually mind the Vast Middle: it's only those who are overfocused on product—or, I guess, late on their deadlines—who see it as something to be rushed though.

Hang out long enough in the Vast Middle, and eventually something great happens: you start to see the faint outlines of where you're going. (As Casey, from the last chapter, did while writing their paper.) Other ways of describing this exciting moment are: you start to "discover" what it is you're trying to say; your creative conversation starts to home in on a conclusion; your project starts to "gel"; and your meaning starts to emerge from all the chaos. Your work will probably get easier at this point, and it should continue to get easier, until you eventually arrive at…

...the **Home Stretch**, where what's mostly left to do is formatting, proofreading, and other relatively easy "polishing." Many people enjoy this stage: just be sure not to enjoy it too much and get stuck there, because that's a common form of Quasiproductive Procrastination. (Also see the discussion of Fear of Finishing in the next chapter.) Avoid that trap, however, and you soon should experience...

The Finale. A mere moment in time, but a deeply satisfying one. Take a moment to acknowledge and celebrate your achievement before moving promptly onto...

Sharing a.k.a., handing the work in. After you do, don't sit around and wait for the grade or other outcome: start working on your next project. (As discussed in Chapter 15.)

Later on, of course, comes **handling the feedback**. As discussed in previous chapters, remember not to take it too much to heart. Enjoy your "successes," learn from your "failures," and move on.

How to Handle "The Question"

Sooner or later, someone's going to ask you about the progress of one of your projects. If you're lucky, the inquiry will be phrased something like this: "So, how's it going?" If you're not so lucky, it will probably be more along the lines of one of these: "Still working on that thing?" "Haven't you finished it yet?" And, worst of all, "What's taking so long?"

Let's agree that, regardless of the form of the inquiry, the asker probably means well. But the last three phrasings are all perfectionist. (Not to mention, rude!) So how to handle them?

First, **be nonperfectionist**. Obviously, if you yourself are impatiently overfocused on product, or are devaluing the progress you've made (an example of negativity), then having someone ask about your progress is bound to be painful. So, keep your focus on your process, and remember that many projects that seem to be "not going well" or "going too slowly" really aren't: they're just in their Anti-Honeymoon or Vast Middle stage.

Next, **instead of trying to justify or defend yourself, educate**. For instance: "Actually, senior projects usually *do* take this long." Or, "My advisor says I'm right on track." Or, "I'm still collecting my data, and when that's done, I've got to do some analysis before I start writing. But things are going great, actually. Thanks for asking!"

Often, however, before we can educate others, we have to educate ourselves—and here, once more, mentors can really help. Acclaimed writer of massive biographies, Robert A. Caro, tells this story in his autobiography *Working*:

I was bothered, too, by the length not only of the manuscript [of his book *The Power Broker*, about New York City "master builder" Robert Moses], but also of the time I had been working on it.

That was the thing that made me doubt the most. When I had started, I had firmly believed that I would be done in a year, a naive but perhaps not unnatural belief for someone whose longest previous deadline had been measured in weeks. As year followed year, and I was still not nearly done, I became convinced that I had gone terribly astray. This feeling was fed by the people Ina and I did know. I was still in the first year of research when friends and acquaintances began to ask if I was "still doing that book." Later I would be asked, "How long have you been working on it now?" When I said three years, or four, or five, they would quickly disguise their look of incredulity, but not quickly enough to keep me from seeing it. I came to dread that question...

Skip forward a few years: Caro has been given desk privileges in the New York Public Library's prestigious Frederick Lewis Allen Room, where he finds himself working alongside, among others, two of the 20th century's most celebrated biographers: James Flexner (author of a multivolume biography of George Washington) and Joseph Lash (author of *Eleanor and Franklin*, a big biography of the Roosevelts). One day, Caro looks up from his work:

The expression on [Flexner's] face was friendly, but after he had asked what I was writing about, the next question was the question I had come to dread: "How long have you been working on it?" This time, however, when I replied, "Five years," the response was not an incredulous stare.

"Oh," Jim Flexner said, "That's not so long. I've been working on my Washington for nine years."

I could have jumped up and kissed him [...] as, the next day, I could have jumped up and kissed Joe Lash...when he asked me the same question, and, after hearing my answer, said in his quiet way, "*Eleanor and Franklin* took me seven years." In a couple of sentences, these two men—idols of mine—had wiped away five years of doubt.

This anecdote also illustrates why it's important to have mentors who have accomplished the same type of thing you are trying to accomplish. None of Caro's journalist friends—who were also writers, but of a very different type, and used to quick deadlines—could give him the specific information and perspective he needed. It had to be biographers—and not just any biographers, but those whose goals, in terms of scope, quality, and ambition, were similar to his own. And in case you're wondering, not even fame and acclaim will put a stop to the perfectionist inquiries. Caro reports that he is still, "constantly being asked why it takes me so long."

Finally, keep in mind that **how you say something often communicates as much as, or even more than, what you actually say.** So, try to answer the difficult inquiries with confidence and optimism, even if you don't actually feel that way. (The first person you convince may be yourself.)

How do you ask after the status of someone's project without putting pressure on them? It's usually fine to ask, "How's the work going?" in a neutral tone. But don't ask it if you're not prepared to really listen to the answer, and respond with understanding and compassion.

It's even better to ask, "Is there anything I can do to help?" Or, better still, "How about if we work together on our papers Saturday night? If you want, I can proofread for you. And I'll bring pizza!"

Exercise 17

Think back on some of your projects that have gone past deadline, or otherwise taken longer than they should have. Did you spend too much time on one or more of the project stages? More generally, is there a stage that you particularly enjoy—like research or revision—and tend to get stuck at? If so, then recognizing the problem will hopefully help you avoid it in the future.

32. Avoiding the "Big Four" Project Derailments

Along with the project stage-related challenges I discussed in the last chapter, there are four other very common project derailments that you need to watch out for. They are "Beginning Bias" (and other forms of avoidance), Reckless Research, Fear of Finishing, and Boredom. I discuss each individually below.

Banish "Beginning Bias" and Other Avoidance-Related Problems

Beginning Bias is what I call the tendency some of us have to overwork the beginnings of our projects relative to, and usually at the expense of, the middles and ends. (Quasiproductive Procrastination in action!) Years ago, a professional book reviewer told me that she could always tell when an author had this problem because the beginning of their book would be much more polished than the rest, which obviously got done in a hurry after their editor told them to, "hand it in or else."

Running out of time before you finish a test is also often at least partly a Beginning Bias problem, with the test-taker spending too much time on the first part of the test, thus leaving themselves too little time for the rest.

Beginning Bias is actually a subset of a bigger problem with the Joyful Dance, which is that, by giving yourself "permission" to nonlinearly work on any part of your project, you're also giving yourself "permission" to *not* work on any part. Especially, we tend to avoid those parts that are difficult, tedious, scary (e.g., a presentation), or collaborative (e.g., if you're shy, or

162

your collaborators are hard to work with). Even worse, the more we avoid a piece of work, the scarier it gets, and the more we want to avoid it.

Chapter 25's Randomization technique can help with mild cases of Beginning Bias and other avoidance problems. You can also use a "semi-random" technique that ensures that you do at least some work on every part of your project. When writing this book, for instance, I made sure to devote at least some Timed Work Intervals to each of the five main sections every week.

For stronger cases of avoidance, I recommend a technique I call **Microintervals**. Every hour or so while you're working on the easier stuff, switch over to the scary bit and work on it for a very brief amount of time, like a minute or even 30 seconds. You might edit a sentence, research a math or science problem, or send out a quick email for a collaborative project. As always, don't judge your work. (Obviously, you shouldn't be expecting to accomplish much in a minute, anyway.) Then, return to what you were doing.

After a few Microintervals, the scary bit won't seem so scary anymore. You'll be able to do longer Microintervals, and then even longer ones. Then, eventually, the scary bit will become just another *un*scary part of the project.

Rein in Reckless Research

Research is a common vehicle for Quasiproductive Procrastination because:

- It can be endless. You can take even many "small" topics in dozens of directions. Plus, new source materials are constantly being created.
- Many people enjoy it. Rooting around in archives, or falling down an Internet "rabbit hole," is fun!
- Every project is different, and so it's hard to come up with general guidelines for what, and how much, research you should do.
- You learn how to research your topic partly by actually researching it—which is why so many scholars, after finishing their research, wish they could start over from scratch. (Some do just that, starting over and over and over, and never finishing.)

Perfectionism, as usual, makes everything worse, because, along with the usual types of fear of failure, you now have the additional, research-related fear of, "leaving something out." One solution to over-researching, therefore, is to build your nonperfectionism. Another, as discussed in Chapters 5 and 25, is to not do research during your writing and other "output" work intervals.

If you think you're slipping into Reckless Research, use your Obstacle Analysis, Timed Work Intervals, Microintervals, and other techniques to get back on track. And, as always, ask your professor. In fact, it's a great idea to ask your professors, at the beginning of projects, what kinds of research you should be doing, and how much. Rest assured that these are not naive questions, but pretty savvy ones that they themselves probably still occasionally ask their own mentors.

Finish Off "Fear of Finishing"

Finishing your work is important, and not just for the obvious reasons. You gain confidence from finishing, and also learn valuable lessons, like how to persevere through the Vast Middle or at other times you're feeling unmotivated. Finishing lots of projects will also help you build your skills and knowledge—Chapter 7's "quantity yielding quality," again—and gain a sense of who you are as a creator, and what specialties you'd like to develop (Chapter 46).

Finishing is a skill. You learn it the same way you learn other skills: by practicing. Start by finishing small and easy stuff, then work your way up to bigger and more difficult stuff. All the obstacles and barriers discussed in this book can cause you to quit your projects before they're finished, but developing a commitment to finishing, and a self-image as a "finisher," will help you to persevere through them. One way to do that is to learn to recognize and celebrate your finishes as you would any success (Chapter 23).

Being a finisher doesn't mean you have to finish every single thing you start. (Even professionals experience the occasional false start.) But you should finish most of them—and also have a really good reason for not finishing something. Above all else, you want to avoid becoming the poor shortsighted perfectionist (Chapter 13) who abandons projects because they can't see past ordinary obstacles and "bumps."

Give Boredom the Boot

As discussed in the last chapter, the Vast Middle of projects can be boring; and your job, when there, is to maintain perspective and keep working. But there are two other common causes of boredom: (1) you're just not that interested in a topic (or project), and (2) the work is too simple, repetitive, or otherwise tedious.

Let's discuss those one at a time.

Nearly all college courses examine some fundamental aspect of the human experience, so, in theory, at least, no college course should be boring. As the Roman/Berber playwright Terence said, "I consider nothing human alien to me." Strive, therefore, to have as wide a range of interests as possible.

Sometimes the boredom is a reflection of another problem, such as:

- perfectionism (it destroys all fun).
- bad teaching (Chapter 35).
- bad study habits (you're not paying attention, not doing the work, etc., see Chapters 8 and 36) or poor time management (Part V).
- lack of commitment (e.g., the only reason you're taking the class is to fulfill a requirement).
- personal problems. (If you're feeling bored, tired, or unmotivated a lot, that could be a sign of depression, so please see a counselor.)

Resolve these and other obstacles, and you should find yourself getting more interested.

Select classes based on the quality of the professor. As discussed in Chapter 8. An excellent teacher can make even "boring" material exciting, while a not-so-great teacher—like the "droners" who recite endlessly from their notes or the textbook—can turn even the most fascinating topic into a snooze.[44]

See the big picture. Students often overfocus on details, but you usually have to connect the dots to have a subject come alive.

Don't dichotomize between "fun" and "boring" classes. Just like there's no such thing as a complete failure or success, there's also no such thing as a completely boring class (or professor). Try focusing on the interesting parts.

Don't make snap judgments about your classes. If the first session of a class isn't to your liking, hang in there for another session or two. Sometimes professors have to convey a lot of information at the very beginning of the course, but then, after that, things get more interesting and interactive.

Connect the subject to your own experience. Admittedly, this is easier with some classes, such as history and psychology, than others, such as math and physics. But be open-minded and creative! Many common activities,

---

[44] Apparently Tolkien—yes, *that* Tolkien—was the ultimate droner. A professor of medieval philology at Oxford University, he not only spent the entire class lecturing, but did so with his back to the students while writing on the blackboard! I guess he saved all the excitement for his books.

including music, cooking, crafts, and sports, have a fun science or math component.

Go Slow. (As discussed in Chapter 26.) When we encounter boring stuff, our tendency is to try to blitz through it and finish as quickly as possible. Unfortunately, this pretty much guarantees a miserable work experience and an inferior result. Instead, try slowing down and savoring the details, and you'll probably wind up having more fun *and* getting a better result. You might even finish sooner, since attempts to "blitz it" often lead to procrastination.

Now for the second type of boredom: when the work is too simple, repetitive, or otherwise tedious. Please note that there are two types of this repetitive work:

1. The practice work you do to build your skills, like when a musician practices scales or a basketball player shooting and dribbling. This work is important, and if you do it mindfully and with proper coaching and other support, it shouldn't be too boring. (If it is, try slowing down.)

2. Any task, chore, or other work that you're either not learning anything from, or that is wholly outside your mission. Mostly, you'll encounter these kinds of tedious tasks at a job or in your personal life. In the former case, the boring task could be one that you once found interesting but have since outgrown. (You see this a lot in people stuck in a job rut.) In the latter case, it could be something you're doing because it's "normal" or because other people expect it. (You see this a lot in people caught in a rut of perfectionist housekeeping or overgiving; for solutions to the latter, see Chapter 48.) In both cases, your boredom is actually a kind of rebellion against using your time unrewardingly, and is thus a good thing. The first rule of coping with this kind of "truly boring" work, therefore, is to do as little of it as possible. (Section V will help.) Intellectually, creatively, and otherwise, always strive to follow your passions, and to live and work as much as possible among others who are following theirs.

Even if you're terrific at all of the above techniques, you'll probably never entirely get rid of the boring stuff. When you find yourself stuck working on something you'd rather not be working on, try working alongside a Study Buddy or two. Working in community can be fun, even when the project you're working on isn't. (And don't forget to slow down!)

Exercise 18

The next time you're stuck on a project, use journaling to answer these questions:

1. Which part of the project life cycle (from Chapter 31) is your project is at? Does your answer add any clarity to the situation, or suggest any solutions?
2. Are any of the derailments listed in this chapter present? If so, which of the solutions offered will help?

33. How to Take Excellent Breaks

Breaks are the productive person's secret weapon. They're essential from both a health standpoint (especially if you're doing a lot of sitting and screen work) and from the standpoint of avoiding fatigue, stiffness, restlessness, and other mental and physical triggers for procrastination.

They're also great for problem-solving. Many people have had the experience of struggling with a tough problem, only to have the answer "magically" pop into their head while taking a coffee break or walking the dog.

Your Inner Perfectionist probably disagrees. For them, breaks are just so much wasted time. "If you *must* take one, *at least* make it productive," they drawl, with supreme condescension. You know: by doing some other schoolwork, or learning a musical instrument, or aerobically running up and down five flights of stairs. (All real-life examples people have shared with me.) Important Reminder: as per Chapter 19, you should empathize with your Inner Perfectionist but *never* take their advice.

Your breaks should be easy and enjoyable. Sure, pick out a few guitar chords *if you want*. Or do a few dishes or fetch the mail. Or, even do some push-ups or pull-ups, if that's your thing. But no strenuousness, unpleasantness, intensity, depletion, deprivation, coercion, etc.

Unfortunately, many who avoid the trap of a productive break fall right into the trap of a screen break. (Social media, Web videos, gaming, television, etc.) Screen breaks have two very serious problems, the first being that you're still sitting and using a screen. (So: not healthy, and mentally and physically it still feels like work.) The second is that most screen activities are engrossing and distracting *by design*, so once you start one you're at serious risk for getting sucked in. (And even if you do manage to avoid that, your 10- or 15-minute break will fly by, and you won't feel rested.) An easy way to resist the lure of a screen break is to keep your phone off while you're working, and also to work on a disconnected computer, as discussed in Chapter 6.

A final type of problematic break is the social break. A bit of casual conversation while waiting for your chai is okay. An intense online or in-real-life (IRL) interaction that can suck you in, and maybe leave you upset or otherwise distracted afterwards, isn't.

The best breaks tend to be enjoyable, active, low-stress, and not intensely interactive or otherwise distracting. A walk, some stretches, a romp with an animal companion, some dancing (assuming you work at home, but if public dancing is your thing, then go for it), or some meditation are all great choices. As always, do what works for you.

As for the interesting question of how long your breaks should be, I recommend tracking your "Break Percentage": the percentage of time, out of your entire work interval, that you devote to breaks. While you're still working on overcoming your perfectionism, your Break Percentage might be 50% (equal time spent working and on break) or even higher (more time breaking than actually working). That's probably not a number you're happy with, but keep the faith: as you get more and more nonperfectionist, your work should flow more easily, and your Break Percentage should drop. A good goal to aim for is around 20% (12 minutes of break time out of each work hour, perhaps divided into two or three chunks). But again: do what works for you.

Finally, **learn to distinguish a true break from disempowerment and procrastination.** Many people, when they encounter a problem with their work, zip through the entire Disempowerment Cascade in an instant and then "decide" to take a break. They're not breaking, they're derailed! Instead, stay calm and either use your obstacle-resolution (Chapters 9 and 10) and problem-solving (Chapters 28 through 32) techniques to resolve the problem, or switch—as always, without drama or fuss—to an easier bit of work. (While letting the problem "marinate" for a while.)

So that's the Joyful Dance. Use it, and you'll create, finish, and share more work than ever before—perhaps more than you ever thought possible. And you'll also enjoy your work more than perhaps you ever thought possible. But there are even bigger yields than that, because **once we learn how to easily work on the things that are truly important to us, we become more free to develop into our truest self, and to help others to do the same.**

The Joyful Dance, it turns out, is not just a tool for productivity, but for liberation and love.

Finish and share more of your work, and you'll start getting more feedback. Some of it will probably be positive, but some will probably be critical, judgmental, or even rejecting. Part IV tells you how to handle that.

PART IV
RESILIENCE

34. The Many Forms of Criticism and Rejection

Criticism and rejection can take many forms. There's "classic" criticism: when someone has something negative to say about you or your work. And "classic" rejection, or denial of a request or opportunity.

Then there's all of these: bias, callousness, carelessness, contempt, deprecation, devaluation, dismissal, disparagement, labeling, marginalization, mockery, neglect, ostracism, ridicule, sarcasm, shaming, and tokenism.

And these: passive-aggressive withholding of information, time, or other support, and non-accommodation of reasonable requests.

(Throughout the rest of Part IV, except where specifically indicated, I use the words "criticism" and "rejection" interchangeably to refer to all of the above.)

Constructive criticism—meaning criticism that's useful, appropriate, proportionate, and sensitively delivered—is essential to learning and growth. Painful as it can be, it's a sign that others are taking you seriously. (This includes being graded, by the way.)

But harsh, arbitrary, or otherwise *un*constructive criticism can be really destructive. You know how an oyster responds to an irritant, like a grain of sand, by coating it with layers of nacre, eventually creating a smooth and non-irritating pearl? We often do something similar with harsh criticism: "coat it" with denial and procrastination to protect ourselves from present and future hurt. (Denial is when you bury the hurt and pretend it's not there. Procrastination, as discussed in Chapters 2 and 14, "protects" you by making you and your work invisible.) This process continues until you have, not a lovely pearl, but an unlovely block—and I know that this happens a lot because frequently, in classes, after I mention a specific type of harsh criticism or rejection, a student will get one of those *Whoa!* looks and say, "I just realized that that happened to me and afterwards I never wrote another poem."

Or "...I dropped the class and switched majors."

Or "...I stopped applying for internships."

Of course, it can work the same way in our personal lives: after someone rejects us cruelly, we may stop approaching others for friendship or love.

I call any criticism or rejection that leaves you feeling ashamed, unfit, fearful, hopeless, and/or otherwise diminished, "traumatic." I'll discuss the different types of traumatic rejections, and how to cope with them, throughout the rest of Part IV. First, however, let's discuss a piece of advice that's commonly given to those hurting from a rejection that *isn't* at all useful: the suggestion that they "toughen up" or "grow a thicker skin." It's lousy advice for at least three reasons:

First, it's vague. How, exactly, do you do that?

Second, it implies you're being weak, and is therefore shaming. In fact, it *literally* adds insult to injury. (Recall Chapter 15's story about the "soccer dad" who unintentionally wounded his daughter with a similar comment.) And third...

We—meaning society—don't need any more thick-skinned people. Thick-skinned people go around stomping on others' feelings and generally causing trouble. And it's simply not true that they don't feel the hurt of a criticism or rejection. They might be in denial about it, but the pain is there, causing them to suffer and, often, mistreat others.

The goal, in other words, isn't toughness, but resilience. You want to be open, alive, caring, and sensitive, but also capable of coping with the inevitable hurts and disappointments. To achieve that resilience, it's helpful to understand why criticisms hurt, and why some hurt more than others.

Why It Hurts

If your adored but somewhat-out-of-touch parents tell you that they dislike your new hairstyle, you probably won't get too upset, and might even take it as a good sign. But if your fashion-forward friend says the same thing, it can really hurt. The same criticism (or rejection) will hurt more or less, in other words, depending on who's delivering it.

It will also hurt more or less depending on a few other factors, including:

- How much you care about the thing being criticized.
- How hard you worked on it.

- Whether the criticism occurs publicly (for instance, in front of a class or on social media).
- If you're criticized at a time when you're also coping with other difficulties.

The content of a criticism will also (obviously) determine its hurtfulness. The most hurtful criticisms tend to be harsh, cruel, and/or shaming. And the very worst tend to be personal attacks, such as, "Do you really believe those things you wrote in your essay?" or "What makes you think *you* can be a [fill in the blank]?" People sometimes say these kinds of harsh things in a caring or reasonable tone of voice, which can be confusing. But the pain is real—and, as usual, it's often the best and most caring people who tend to be the most vulnerable.

Bigoted or biased criticisms and rejections are also extremely hurtful—not to mention, violations of basic principles of social justice, *and*, in some cases, illegal (if they cross the line into discrimination or harassment). Bias can also lead to internalized oppression, which is when you start to believe the bigoted view, thus limiting your sense of yourself and your potential.

Callousness is another common offense. It's when someone criticizes or rejects you without making a reasonable effort to minimize the hurt. Along with the pain of the criticism itself, it sends the additional painful message that you don't merit ordinary consideration and respect. Form letter rejections, especially for opportunities you were personally encouraged to apply for, or had to do a lot of work to apply for, are a common type of callousness.

Don't be fooled if a harsh or callous criticism comes labeled as "tough love" or "fun ribbing." It's still hurtful and irresponsible, especially if coming from either someone who says they care about you, or a professor or other educational professional with a responsibility for your welfare.

Finally, we have **blindsiding**, which happens when we either don't expect a criticism, or don't expect it to be as harsh as it is. Because your defenses are down, blindsiding can be *very* painful, and take a long time to heal. A common form of blindsiding is when someone whom you would reasonably expect to be on your side—like a parent, professor, lover, or friend—attacks or betrays you. But you can also blindside *yourself* by expecting a success that doesn't happen. (Recall Chapter 13's discussion about how expectations are always risky.) Even when—especially when—all indications are that a project will succeed, always be prepared for the unexpected possibility.

As Luke Skywalker warned the evil Emperor Palpatine in *Return of the Jedi*, "Your overconfidence is your weakness."

How to Be One of the Good Ones

I hope this discussion will help you better understand, and cope with, any criticisms and rejections you may have received, or might receive in the future. I also hope it inspires you to be a kind and competent critic (and "rejector") yourself. You achieve that by doing pretty much the opposite of everything I've been discussing—i.e., delivering your criticisms as kindly, fairly, privately, etc., as possible—and by not criticizing too much. Criticism is a *very* strong spice, and so in most cases just a pinch or two is fine—and only after getting the person's explicit or implicit permission for such feedback. ("Implicit" permission, by the way, is what we give professors and others with a professional mandate to teach us.) Also:

- Always follow through when you offer to critique someone's work, and do so in a timely way. If you don't, it can be not just inconveniencing, but hurtful, to the person who trusted you. A corollary to this is: think carefully before agreeing to critique someone's work, especially if it is outside your specialty. I've gotten stuck a few times by agreeing to critique someone's work, only to realize, later on, that I really didn't know enough to do so. The ensuing conversations were, to say the least, awkward. (An exception would be if they explicitly want your opinion as a non-specialist in their field.)

- Always find something good to say. If you don't like the work itself, then find something to praise in the person's process or approach. (As discussed in Chapter 14, praising their process is a good idea in any case.)

- Get specific. As Joni B. Cole writes in her book *Toxic Feedback*, "Writers... can handle specifics. It's the generalities that bring them to their knees. 'Your story didn't work for me.' 'I don't get it.' 'This isn't my thing.' Those [...] only serve to leave writers feeling more at a loss than usual."

- Be generous. You don't have to write (or speak) pages, but going into detail about two or three specific points will be helpful, and also show that you care.

- Before passing judgment, ask questions. Example:
  Person A: "Before I give you my feedback on your paper, can you tell me what the main points are that you want to communicate?"
  Person B: "I want to communicate X, Y, and Z."
  Person A: "How well do you think you did that?"
  Person B: "Pretty good on X, okay on Y, and not great on Z, for

these reasons..."

Person A: "Okay, based on all that, here's what I think..."

- Notice how, like conflict resolution (Chapter 10), offering great feedback is more about listening than talking.
- Use the "sandwich" technique: put a criticism in between two compliments. It's kind of obvious, but still helps.
- Critique the project on its own terms, instead of comparing it to the project you would have done. Granted, this sometimes is difficult— and if you sense that it's going to be *really* difficult, then you should probably decline the request to critique.
- If your opinion is mostly negative, do your best to deliver it either in person or via phone or videocall. Email and text don't allow for much emotion and nuance.

Everyone should learn how to deliver compassionate and constructive criticism, especially if they desire to mentor or teach others. And it also goes without saying (or should) that you should be an effective *receiver* of constructive criticism. Don't be one of those who gets defensive or angry when someone is legitimately trying to help. (Especially if you asked for the help!)

Exercise 19

1. Journal about some criticisms and rejections you've experienced, both in and out of school. See if you can link them to any procrastination, perfectionism, or blocks you might have experienced, or may still be experiencing.
2. For each incident, list any elements of context (e.g., the critic's identity, or the time or place of the incident) or content (e.g., harshness or callousness) that increased the hurtfulness. Hopefully, identifying these amplifying factors will help you to further "process" the event, and defuse any lingering pain. If it's still painful, however, you might want to talk to a counselor.

Exercise 20

Can you think of any times when you criticized or rejected someone in a needlessly hurtful way? What could you have done differently, and what will you do differently in the future? (It may not be too late to apologize and make amends.)

35. When Professors Screw Up

I think professors[45] are the bomb. (Okay, I'm a bit biased, being the partner of one!) Many are fascinating people who do interesting and important work, and also work hard to support their students. But it's also true that some professors aren't great at their job, just as some people in every field aren't great. Bad professors waste students' precious time and money, worse professors can kill your love for a subject, and the very worst can derail careers and even lives.

Professors are human and are thus capable of screwing up in all the ways listed in the last chapter. And they can also screw up by being...

- Unprofessional: unskilled, unknowledgeable, arbitrary, or unprepared.
- Uncaring: negligent, neglectful, unsupportive, or unresponsive.
- Rigid: "There's only one way to approach this material," "My way or the highway," etc.
- Biased against you and/or your ideas. We all have biases, but a professional educator has a special responsibility to not let theirs interfere with their job. This is not to say that all ideas are worth defending or discussing, however. A biology professor has a professional responsibility to refuse to discuss ignorant creationism or evil "race science" in their classes, except perhaps as cautionary tales.

---

[45] As per the Vocabulary Note at the front of the book, when I use the word "professor," in this chapter and elsewhere, I am referring to all teaching professionals.

- Negative, fatalistic, and/or cynical. A professor should be candid about their field's drawbacks, such as a lack of jobs, but shouldn't exaggerate them.
- Arrogant, aggressive, condescending, or patronizing.

You should also watch out for professors who:

- Prioritize their own needs (e.g., for friendship or a "fan") over their professional relationship with, and obligations to, you.
- Play favorites. (Bad for the favorite *and* the rest of the class.)
- Exploit you as free professional or personal labor. If you must take on an unpaid research assistantship or similar gig, make sure that you're at least getting "paid" in quality mentoring.
- Target you sexually.

If a professor is mistreating you, *don't* blame yourself. Instead, talk with your advisor (or a department head, counselor, or provost) immediately. This can be a difficult step, but, as Leslie's story, below, shows, it can help you to reclaim your power. (Content warning: sexual harassment.)

Leslie, an ambitious and confident biochemistry major, was thrilled when she was offered a part-time laboratory assistant job with Dr. Patrician, a world-famous biochemist at her university. It was a great opportunity that would also look terrific on her graduate school applications. Maybe, she thought excitedly, Dr. Patrician himself would be so impressed with her work that he would write her a letter of recommendation! That would certainly open doors.

Feeling both lucky and honored, she accepted the position enthusiastically. But her enthusiasm was somewhat diminished when, later that day, she told her news to a graduate teaching assistant for one of her classes. His reaction was, at best, mixed. "Congratulations," he said. "They don't take just anyone. But be careful. Some people have had problems working in that laboratory." When Leslie pressed him for specifics, he said, simply, "I've heard they can be a little sexist." Then he added, about Dr. Patrician himself: "He's a genius, but not the easiest guy to work for."

The conversation was a bit of a downer, but Leslie never seriously considered not taking the job. It was too great an opportunity—and, besides, she saw herself as a strong person, capable of handling anything, including, if necessary, a little workplace sexism. So, she took the job, and the first few weeks went great. Everyone was friendly and welcoming, and she quickly got up to speed on the procedures for washing and sterilizing glassware, organizing and restocking the supplies closet, preparing batches of simple reagents, and her other duties. The lab comprised more than 20 researchers at all levels, from other undergrads to graduate students to Ph.D.s and visiting researchers, so she was kept pretty busy. People seemed appreciative of her efforts, however—and that included even the supposedly hard-to-please Dr. Patrician. He always greeted her cordially when they passed each other in the laboratory or hallway, and once he had even complimented her on her reliability and attention to detail. Leslie felt proud, but also relieved, because by then it was evident that the teaching assistant had been right: Dr. Patrician wasn't easy to work for. He was impatient and often harshly critical, and didn't refrain from criticizing people publicly. People tended to "tiptoe" around him.

As for sexism, Leslie couldn't help but notice that nearly all of the laboratory's senior positions were filled by men, and that even the most senior women in the laboratory were doing a lot of support work for the men, versus running their own experiments. They were also doing a lot of emotional labor, including comforting people after Dr. Patrician had yelled at them.

It all made for a weird, and occasionally unpleasant, work situation. Leslie decided that she would just stay in the job for a year, or maybe six months. "You can put up with anything for six months," she thought. She would learn that this was not true, however, when one of the senior researchers, Bill, started interacting with her in ways that made her uncomfortable. He would stand just a bit too close to her during conversations, and sometimes touch her on the shoulder or arm. If she moved away a bit—sending a clear signal that she didn't want the physical contact, she thought—he would just move closer to her and continue with the touching. She spent a lot of time wondering whether this behavior was deliberate, but when he escalated to touching her on the back or waist whenever he walked past her in the laboratory, she no longer had any doubts. He always murmured an apology, as if the space between the benches was too narrow and he had no choice. But no one else needed to touch her.

At times, Leslie would look up from her work and see him staring at her from across the laboratory. He always held her eye for a couple of moments, a slight smile on his face, before, deliberately and without haste, turning away.

Soon she was going out of her way to avoid Bill and was also constantly on the alert lest he approach her. Not surprisingly, her work began to suffer. Once, distracted, she dropped a whole tray of glassware: the crash echoed throughout the entire laboratory, bringing all activity to a halt. It was mortifying. Another time, she screwed up ordering some chemicals—in part because she had been reluctant to check the order over with Bill—costing the laboratory money and delaying some research.

After these incidents, Dr. Patrician's attitude toward her was no longer gracious. When they passed each other in the laboratory, he would nod curtly, or simply stare at her coldly for a moment.

Leslie started to wonder whether she was on the verge of being fired. That would be incredibly humiliating—not to mention, a blot on her record—so she resolved to "suck it up" and be more focused at work. Then, Bill started asking invasive questions about her personal life, such as what she did on the weekends, what clubs she liked to go to, and what her relationship was with the woman he sometimes saw stopping by to pick her up after work. Leslie jokingly told him to mind his own business, but he persisted.

She knew she had to talk to someone, and chose Rosemary, a senior scientist who had often presented herself as a mentor to Leslie and the other young women in the laboratory. Rosemary's reaction, when Leslie told her what was happening, was less than helpful, however. "Bill? Really?" she said, in obvious disbelief. "I mean, I know he can be a bit touchy-feely, but he really doesn't mean anything by it." And about the staring: "I don't understand...he's looking at you?" And the invasive questions: "People talk about their weekends and social lives all the time."

Rosemary was obviously seeing Leslie, and not Bill, as the problem. Frustrated, and not knowing what else to say, Leslie just stood there and stared at Rosemary, who finally said, "Okay, I'll talk to Bill."

That night, Leslie called her parents and told them what had been happening. They were outraged, and told her to quit immediately. "Don't even go back there!" her mother implored. But Leslie balked at the idea of quitting without notice, which she felt would be unprofessional. (Even though, by now, she had given up on the possibility of a recommendation letter from Dr. Patrician.) She decided to give the standard two weeks' notice.

It was a decision she would soon regret. When she returned to the laboratory, the next afternoon, it was clear that Rosemary had spoken to Bill, who was now keeping his distance from her. That was great, but the laboratory itself now felt full of bad associations. She hated every minute of being there...and was it her imagination, or were others besides Bill also now avoiding her?

She gritted her teeth and focused on getting through the next two weeks.

Then, late on the Friday afternoon after she had spoken with Rosemary, Dr. Patrician called her into his office and berated her for, "making accusations against people in my laboratory!" Clearly, Rosemary had told him about their supposedly "confidential" conversation. He then went on to attack, in vehement terms, her supposed "bad attitude," "poor attention to detail," "lack of teamwork," and other deficiencies. Caught totally off guard, Leslie didn't even try to defend herself, but just repeatedly apologized.

Dr. Patrician ended the conversation with an abrupt, "Your services are no longer needed." In a daze—and conscious of everyone's eyes on her—Leslie returned to her bench to pick up her coat and backpack. Then she left, never to return.

Over the next week, Leslie was assailed by doubts about her own behavior. Had she somehow misconstrued Bill's actions? Or overreacted to minor offenses? Should she have handled the conversation with Rosemary differently? She debated these and other questions endlessly with herself, to the point where she couldn't concentrate on her schoolwork or anything else. She also suffered from headaches and insomnia, and spent her days in a kind of exhausted and demoralized fog.

Her parents, girlfriend, and friends all repeatedly assured her that, not only had she *not* screwed up, she had done as well as anyone could have hoped to, given the toxic environment. She understood their point, but couldn't see past her sense of humiliation and failure. Her loved ones also urged her to talk to her advisor or a school counselor, but she resisted doing this. She was too buried in confusion and shame to even think of talking to a school authority, and she was also afraid that doing so would trigger a mandatory sexual harassment (Title IX) investigation that she wasn't sure she'd be able to handle.

A couple of weeks later, however, she knew she had to talk to someone. She was still very distracted and unhappy, and her schoolwork was continuing to suffer. She realized that, if she didn't do something, she was in danger of compromising everything she had worked so hard to achieve. And so, with her family and friends solidly behind her, she made an "emergency" appointment with her advisor.

Sitting in his office, the next day, Leslie felt a turmoil of shame and anger and confusion as she told her story. But her advisor didn't seem confused at all. As he listened to her, his normally easy-going expression turned serious; and when it was his turn to speak, his voice was also serious. "I'm really sorry that that happened to you," he said. "It was *completely* unacceptable." Hearing those unambiguous words of support from an "official" college representative, Leslie felt a huge weight lift. He believed her! She wasn't overreacting!

They discussed the incident some more, and then her advisor reminded her that he was mandated to report the harassment to the school's Title IX Coordinator, who was in charge of setting and enforcing campus policies against harassment and discrimination. "She'll call you to set up a meeting to discuss your options," he said, adding: "Whatever you decide, I'll fully support you."

That night, Leslie was able to focus better on her schoolwork than she had in weeks, and she also felt physically better. Seeing these positive changes, her girlfriend noted, "You're taking your power back."

During their meeting, later in the week, the Title IX Coordinator told Leslie that she would assist her in submitting a complaint, meaning a document outlining the events in question. After that, the school would start a formal grievance process, which would include an investigation into what had happened, followed by a statement of the investigator's findings submitted to an Adjudication Committee. The Committee would make the final determination on whether a Title IX violation had occurred, and also decide which penalties to impose.[46]

Leslie, who was eager for justice, welcomed the grievance process, but had two worries. The first was that Bill, Rosemary, and Patrician were likely to defend themselves by attacking her work and character, which wouldn't be pleasant. The Title IX Coordinator assured her that, while their statements were likely to be critical of her, the experience typically wasn't as bad as people anticipated, and the investigator would also disregard any inappropriate statements they might make.

Leslie's other big worry was the possibility of getting a reputation as a "troublemaker" that could hurt her chances of getting into graduate school. (The Title IX Coordinator told her she would be identified only as "complainant" on the public documents, but she was pretty sure that, sooner or later, her identity would get out.) Her advisor assured her, however, that such repercussions were unlikely. "People outside the campus probably won't know who you are," he said. "Besides your academic record is strong, your GRE scores will probably also be strong, and you'll also get strong letters from me and others. Those are what really count."

The whole process took several months, and yes: Bill, Rosemary, and Patrician did attempt to defend themselves by attacking Leslie. At times, it was hard, but Leslie, with the full support of her family, partner, friends, and

---

[46] The Title IX statute mandates certain general procedures for dealing with sexual harassment and related complaints, but the specific processes, penalties, etc., can (within the bounds of the law) differ from school to school. Also, had an actual crime, like sexual assault, been committed, Leslie would have had the option of filing a criminal charge with the police.

advisor, hung in there. When the Adjudication Committee eventually relayed its decisions—that:

1. Bill had indeed violated her Title IX rights,
2. both Rosemary and Dr. Patrician had violated school policy by not reporting the possible violation when they learned of it, and
3. Dr. Patrician had engaged in illegal "retaliatory behavior" when he fired Leslie

—it was a moment of triumph.

Perhaps because of Dr. Patrician's institutional status and power, however, the announced penalties were disappointingly small. Bill was put on probation for five years, with a warning that any additional episodes of harassment could lead to his firing. (That "could," especially, irked Leslie.) Rosemary and Dr. Patrician were given no penalties at all, just warnings. And the entire laboratory was mandated to take Title IX training.

The investigation was written up in the local press, and even in the science press, which pleased Leslie. As she had predicted, even though her name hadn't appeared in those accounts, some people in the biochemistry department guessed that she was the student involved. Several people approached her and expressed their support and appreciation for her having taken action, a positive response she hadn't expected. Even better, a student from another department wrote to her, saying that, because of her brave example, she herself was filing a Title IX complaint of her own against one of her professors.

These were all good outcomes. But for the rest of her time at college, Leslie avoided going into the building that housed Dr. Patrician's laboratory. That meant that she missed some seminars and other events that could have been useful to her. And the few times she happened to see Bill, Rosemary, or Dr. Patrician out on campus, it was awkward. At the Title IX Coordinator's suggestion, she got some counseling, which helped some, but wasn't (obviously) a "fix" for those problems.

Happily, however, Leslie's advisor had been right, and the grievance process did not prevent her from getting into a good graduate school. She breathed easier at her new school, although she couldn't help anticipating the uncomfortable day when she would run into Bill or Rosemary or Dr. Patrician at a scientific meeting.

Leslie was never again harassed, partly because she had made a strong pledge to herself to never again work in a known toxic work environment, or with a known toxic person, no matter how great the opportunity seemed. As she progressed in her career, Leslie also made a second pledge: to always do her best to believe and support anyone who came to her for help with harassment or other workplace problems.

Both professionally and personally, always seek out the kind ones, the competent ones, the fair ones: those who hold themselves to a high bar, in terms of their personal behavior, and who are invested in others' success along with their own. You'll not only save yourself lots of pain, but find more pleasure, ease, and success in both your life and work.

Exercise 21

Think of some difficult interactions you've had with professors. Did they behave in any of the ways described in this chapter? If so, did you recognize the problem at the time? Did you blame yourself or feel guilty for problems you didn't cause or weren't responsible for? If the answer to any of these questions is "yes," then journal about the situation to understand it better, and hopefully neutralize any remaining guilt or shame. If necessary, discuss what happened with a friend or counselor.

36. When Students Screw Up

While some professors go around saying stuff like "some people can't do math," or "creative writing can't be taught: you've either got talent or you haven't," I strongly believe that, **if a student is really trying, then any learning failures are the professor's or institution's responsibility.** First, because those kinds of sentiments are flat-out wrong. (I've already mentioned the deficiencies in U.S. math education, and also how abstractions like "talent" are pointless.) Also, helping students identify and overcome their barriers to learning happens to be one of the major responsibilities of professors and other university staff. Even in the relatively uncommon cases where a student is simply not up to doing the work, it's those professionals' job to identify the problem early and help the student to find an alternative course or major that's a better fit.

Note, however, that "if a student is really trying." Students also have responsibilities, including:

- Doing your work.
- Using effective study habits (see Chapter 8).
- Working to overcome, as much as possible, internal barriers including procrastination, perfectionism, and poor time management.
- Asking for help early and often, as discussed in Chapter 10.
- Showing up early for meetings. (The paradox of time management is that you can either be early or late, but never exactly on time. So be early.)
- If you must cancel a meeting, not doing so at the last minute.

- Responding promptly to professors' emails. (I.e., either the same day or first thing the next day.)
- Reaching out when there's a problem. Unfortunately, that's the opposite of what many students do, which is to hide. That's a totally understandable reaction, but again: isolation and invisibility aren't your friends.
- Not being perfectionist! For instance, not harping on the one thing your professor does badly—or that you think they do badly—while ignoring all the other things they do well.

It's a short list, and very reasonable, yet many students don't do one or more of those things. Students can also be pretty callous: for instance, by not paying attention during lectures, or acting bored or sullen during office meetings.

I get that college is a busy and stressful time. But the way to cope with that is to do the stuff in this book. Don't take your frustrations out on others, especially if they are trying to help you.

Exercise 22

Think back on incidents where you might have mistreated a professor. What happened and why? What might have been a better way to behave, and what steps can you take in the future to ensure that you do better? (If this exercise is making you feel bad—don't! As discussed in Chapter 22, regret is useless. Learn from the experience, apologize and make amends if appropriate, then move on.)

37. How to Cope

The goal, as stated in Chapter 34, is resilience—and, fortunately, you already know much of what you need to achieve that, because **90% of resilience is nonperfectionism.** Perfectionists are like burn victims: sensitive to even the slightest "touch." That's partly because they're already suffering under a barrage of constant self-criticism, which the external criticism only reinforces, and partly because their overidentification, pathologizing, distrust of success, and other perfectionist characteristics make them vulnerable.

So, to be more resilient, work on overcoming your perfectionism.

Here are some other tips:

Share with care. While you want input from many sources, there is zero benefit to getting it from someone informationally, temperamentally, or otherwise unqualified to give it. So, share your work, thoughts, feelings, ideas, personal struggles, etc., only with those capable of offering a wise and compassionate response. This also applies to your family, by the way: they don't get a free pass to criticize you harshly, neglect you, marginalize you, etc. (More on coping with family in the next two chapters.)

Take the long view. Just as most "failures" turn out to be unimportant (Chapter 22), so, too, do most criticisms and rejections. Therefore, remind yourself, when you're hurting, that "this too shall pass."

Work to positively reframe your rejections. Here's a fun example from writer Chris Offutt:

> The notion of submitting anything to a magazine filled me with terror.
> A stranger would read my precious words, judge them deficient, and
> reject them, which meant I was worthless... My goal, however, was
> not publication, which was still too scary a thought. My goal was a
> hundred rejections in a year.

I mailed my stories in multiple submissions and waited eagerly for their return, which they promptly did. Each rejection brought me that much closer to my goal—a cause for celebration, rather than depression. Eventually disaster struck. *The Coe Review* published my first story in spring 1990.[47]

Notice how empowering the positive reframing is, especially when combined with Offutt's playful approach. (Also, notice the overfocus on outcomes, overidentification, and other perfectionist characteristics that probably contributed to his being so scared of rejection to start with.)

Prioritize healing/cope lavishly. When you do experience a painful criticism or rejection, resist the temptation to minimize it or ignore your hurt. (In other words, ignore those who tell you to, "Get over it.") If you need to have a crying jag or a sulk—or a few—do that. BUT...

Don't isolate yourself. Sure, hide out for a little while, if you want. But after that, discuss the situation with a trusted friend, advisor, or therapist.

Speak truth to power, judiciously. Speaking truth to power can be a healing and empowering act that can also lead to changes that prevent others from being harmed the way you were. There's always a risk, however, that the person you're speaking to will respond negatively. So think carefully before doing it, perhaps asking yourself whether the offender is a good person who simply made a mistake, or someone who is often harsh or callous. The former may be worth having a discussion with, while the latter may not be. (This is yet another area where it's probably best to err on the side of caution.) All of which brings us to the most important coping strategy of all...

Minimize the stuff you need to cope with. You do this by avoiding classes, projects, personal relationships, and other prolonged interactions with known harsh people, exploiters, and other problematic types. (Personally, I do my best to avoid even brief interactions with these kinds of people, as some can do an amazing amount of harm in a short time.) This rule is usually easy to follow...until it isn't. Sooner or later, you'll probably be tempted by, for instance:

A research gig with a famous professor with great connections but also a reputation for harshness.

A job at a prestigious company known for burning out its employees.

A romantic relationship with someone who is sexy and glamorous, but also mean and self-centered. Or,

Some other opportunity that sets off your warning bells.

Just. Say. No. Relationships with toxic people and organizations rarely work out the way we hope they will, and frequently leave us worse off.

---

[47] Chris Offutt, "The Eleventh Draft." In Frank Conroy (ed.), *The Eleventh Draft*.

Dealing With Professional Stereotypes...

I've been talking, mostly, about serious rejection and criticism, but what about the smaller offenses? You know: the comments and questions that sound a bit judgmental or callous, but are really mostly clueless. They're not the worst thing in the world, but because our goal is to address, as much as possible, every obstacle to productivity, it's a good idea to learn how to recognize and be prepared for them.

Let's start with the **negative professional stereotypes**. Engineering majors are geeks (or nerds), math and physics majors are eccentric, art majors are broke and tortured, English majors will correct your spelling and grammar, and psychology majors are "shrinks" who can see into your innermost soul. These kinds of stereotypes get tiresome, after the hundredth or so time you've heard them.

Even the compliments can be problematic. Art majors are told that they "must be creative," often with the implication that that's their defining, or only, virtue. Business and economics majors are told that they "must be good with numbers," often with the same implication. And social work and education majors are told that they "must be nurturing," often with gender stereotypes coming into play. The offenders can include your family, friends, acquaintances, and even strangers you meet at the laundromat or bus stop. In fact, you'll even hear these tired old stereotypes from people within your field. (Who really ought to know better!)

If you're on the receiving end of a tiresome comment, don't assume ill intent. The speaker is likely trying to show interest, make a connection, or even show some respect. But they don't know how, and may be intimidated, besides. If it's an occasional problem, it's probably best to ignore it. But if someone is frequently making the same tiresome comment, you should ask them to stop.

It's also helpful to compile a list of professional truths about your major and its practitioners. Far from being "nerds," for instance, many engineers tend to be technical, precise, skilled, playful, versatile, quantitative, curious, creative, clever, detailed-oriented, systems-oriented, analytical, innovative, and good with technology—and that's just for starters. Make it an expansive list! (It's not like every single engineer has to have every single one of those attributes. We're generalizing.) This is a great exercise to do with friends in your major, and I actually think that all college departments should assign it as an exercise in one of their introductory courses.

After you compile your list, review it every so often to neutralize the stereotypes and build pride in your field and yourself.

...and Tricky Inquiries

Then there are the **tricky inquiries**. I already discussed one type—the product-focused, "Is it finished yet? What's taking so long?"—in Chapter 31. But there are others. Liberal arts majors often get asked, about their major and/or intended career, "Can you make any money doing that?" And graduates in all fields can get peppered with questions about their employment status, as in: "Got a job yet? Why not?"

Or, about the pay-the-rent job you're holding onto while you look for better opportunities: "That's not what you went to college for, is it?"

These types of questions can be especially galling coming from older people who started their own career during more prosperous times and have no idea what you're up against.

Again, be nonperfectionist and don't assume ill intent. Also:

Remember the goal. It's not to convince the other person—you have no control over that—but to share as much of your truth as you want to share, in an empowered way.

Speak and act with confidence. Contrary to widespread belief, it hasn't actually been proven that acting confident can help you feel more confident. But if a confident voice and body language help you to feel better in the moment, then I would use those. A confident appearance can also discourage others from persisting with an unwanted discussion. So, practice saying your most uncomfortable answers—"No job yet, still looking!"—in a confident voice, and also practice looking confident by making eye contact and smiling while you reply. (Acknowledging that this advice might be more difficult to apply for some who are on the autism spectrum, or whose cultures discourage eye contact.)

Educate, instead of defending or justifying (as discussed in Chapter 31). Example: "Yup, I'm still living at home. I've sent out lots of resumes, but no one seems to be hiring right now." Bonus points: "I'm looking to get a job with a union, or to do some other form of community organizing. Do you happen to know anyone in those fields whom I could talk to?"

Argue from authority (also discussed in Chapter 31). Example: "My advisor says it typically takes a few years to break into the field. She advised me to do some volunteer work with the national association to build my connections, and that's what I'm doing."

Set boundaries. You do not have to answer every question put to you. So think about what you're comfortable sharing, and with whom, and practice gracefully pivoting away from unwanted requests for information. Example:

Questioner: How's the job search going? Found anything yet?

You: Nope, still looking! [Resists the temptation to offer further details.] How are things with you?

Questioner (persisting): The job market's pretty tough, eh?

You: Let's talk about something else, okay? How are the Phillies doing this year?

Boomerang the focus back on the listener. Example: "Did *you* ever go through a period where you had a hard time finding work? What did you do?"

Humor is a risky tactic because it's easy to screw up, and if you do screw it up, you risk sounding not just unfunny, but bitter or condescending. But give it a try, if you want. Example: "Why don't I get another job? Great idea! Maybe I'll stop by the job store on my way home and pick one up." By the way, professional comedians are able to get the jokes right because they spend lots of time refining and practicing their routines. Which brings us to...

Plan ahead and practice. Especially if you know a challenging encounter is coming up, plan out your answers to difficult questions and practice saying those answers with confidence. Each time you practice, you should hear yourself improve; and knowing that you've practiced will, in itself, aid your confidence.

The ability to respond to even challenging inquiries with ease and confidence is a great skill to have and a sign of some excellent empowerment.

38. About Your Family I: Empathy is Empowering

Note: This chapter and the next are about how to handle situations where your values and/or lifestyle are in conflict with those of your parents or other family members. They're *not* about how to handle racism, homophobia, transphobia, or other bigotry directed at you personally. Although there can obviously be some overlap between these two types of problems, the latter is a potentially much more serious one that is beyond the scope of this book. If you are subject to bias, from your family or anyone else, I urge you to get the best help and support you can from friends, counselors, and groups that specialize in helping your community.

For many years, I lived in and around Boston, earning my living teaching productivity and entrepreneurship classes at nonprofit organizations around town. Boston, as you may know, is a city filled with cool people, many of whom are artists, activists, academics, entrepreneurs, musicians, organizers, social workers, teachers, and other creative and caring types. After a while, I couldn't help noticing a pattern: many of my cool friends and students would visit their families for the holidays, then return depressed, exhausted, and, in some cases, crushed. When I asked what was wrong, the inevitable reply was that the Bostonian's family members were more conventional than they themselves were, and so, during the visit, there were ongoing conflicts in values, ideas, politics, and, usually, wealth. (Social workers and activists and artists tending to earn less than software developers and financial executives.) There would also often be conflicts in other areas, such as when an atheist was expected to participate in their family's religious practices, or a vegan to eat nonvegan food.

No doubt about it: it can be tough even for like-minded family members to get along. Add some social, ethical, political, or class differences to the mix, however, and things can get way more complicated and intense. Unfortunately, the advantage, in these types of conflicts, tends to be with the more conventional family members, both because theirs is usually the majority opinion, and because they have the whole power of the status quo behind them—so that, for instance, the morning headlines are more likely to support their views.

No wonder so many of my friends and students came back from their trips home exhausted, or worse.

And things have only worsened in recent years. The world's on fire, both figuratively and literally, and many of our relatives have fallen into the abyss of authoritarianism.[48] Even many families that weren't previously in conflict now are—and the conflicts seem more ingrained and intractable than ever.

If you don't have this kind of conflict with your family, either because your views happen to coincide with theirs, or because you have all learned to disagree without too much conflict, congratulations: you're one of the lucky few. For those who aren't so lucky, I offer some ways of coping below and in the next chapter. First, however, let's look at some of the intolerant things our relatives and others can say or do. Mockery is prevalent, for instance:

- "Here he goes again...," or an eye-roll, when you point out an injustice.
- "We can't all be saints like you," when you suggest a behavioral change. A tricky type of comment in which an insincere compliment ("saint") is used passive-aggressively to dismiss your valid concerns.
- "She always takes things *so* seriously." This was said mockingly about *me*, after I casually mentioned, during an event that was held on Columbus Day but wasn't about Christopher Columbus, that he had committed genocide and shouldn't be honored. (I think the person who said it was embarrassed that I had even brought up the topic.)

There can also be conflict when you return home with different vocabularies, values, ideas, and friends from those you grew up with. "Oh, so now you think you're better than us?" and, "Oh, so now you think you know everything?" are questions that many students in this situation hear from

---

[48] Like Jen Senko's father: http://www.thebrainwashingofmydad.com.

their parents or others. (I heard them, too.) Anthony Abraham Jack, whom I quoted in Chapter 10 on the importance of interacting with faculty and administrators, says that first-generation students often have to do "a lot of translational work" for their families, and that, "Sometimes you have to forgive family for maybe feeling a little resentment that you are doing the exact thing that they are most proud of and wanted you to do in the first place."[49]

Later on, in your creative or helping or social justice career, you can be subject to these kinds of put-downs:

- "When are you going to settle down and get a *real* job?"
- "Aren't you embarrassed to be driving around in that old car?"
- "I don't know why you'd want to do something so depressing." (This was said to a friend of mine by one of her siblings, about her work helping refugees. And, by the way, her work was *amazing*.)

In college and beyond, **condescension**—e.g., "You'll grow out of it."— is prevalent, since conservatives have always sought to reframe progressives' caring and concern as naive and childish. Ditto for accusations of **oversensitivity**, as in: "Snowflake!" "Bleeding heart!" "Tree-hugger!" etc. Don't fall for any of it! Your caring and concern are wonderful qualities.

Accusations of **hypocrisy** are another common "gotcha," since none of us can lead a 100% ethical life. Matt Bors skewered this one in his famous "Mr. Gotcha" cartoon.[50]

Marginalization can likewise be a problem. It's when your values, concerns, and/or achievements are trivialized, dismissed, treated as an afterthought, or ignored. It's often done passive-aggressively—meaning, your relatives wound you by *not* acting or speaking—which makes it even harder to identify and deal with. Some examples are when your family:

- Doesn't take your needs or values into account. For instance, when they refuse to serve a vegan dish (except, maybe, a side salad) at dinner. Or, when someone says, "There's just a little bit of meat in the sauce, what's the big deal?"
- Refuses to consider easy alternatives to objectionable practices. (Like when they insist on shopping at a store, or dining at a restaurant, with bad labor practices or political affiliations.)

---

[49] https://www.gse.harvard.edu/news/uk/19/04/real-advice-first-gens
[50] https://thenib.com/mister-gotcha/

- Says nothing/asks nothing/does nothing about an important project you're working on, or about a recent success or failure you experienced.

Make no mistake: the above behaviors can hurt, especially coming from people you love, and especially if they happen repeatedly.[51] In situations like these, you're often caught between either sticking up for yourself and your values (and being seen as an irritant or source of conflict), or staying quiet and not advocating for yourself. Or worse, you're caught between either putting up with the mistreatment, or not seeing your family much, if at all. In both cases, the phrase "caught between" indicates your disempowerment and lack of good options—and I'm not even talking about the situations where you are *literally* stuck because you're dependent on others for transportation, as many students are when they return home for the holidays.

Meanwhile, if you do speak up, you're at risk for getting DARVO'd. DARVO is a useful acronym coined by psychologist Jennifer J. Freyd to describe a common response to accusations of abuse: the abuser Denies, Attacks, and Reverses Victim and Offender.[52] An example would be when you get upset because a family member is being hurtful, and they turn it around and say that *you're* the unreasonable one and are victimizing *them*.

I won't lie, I personally experienced a lot of the above types of family problems, and they were hard to deal with. But there are solutions. Below, I talk about the main solution, and in Chapter 39, some others.

To Be Understood, First Seek to Understand

I never reached any kind of great resolution with my parents, who are now both deceased. But I'm happy to say that my sisters and I stuck with it, worked it out, and now get along pretty well. **My first piece of advice if you're struggling with your family, therefore, is to keep trying.** People can, and frequently do, surprise us. This assumes that: (a) your relatives aren't toxic, and (b) both you and they are committed to the sometimes-difficult work of listening, sharing, and self-examination. If you all are, then you can start the process by discussing a couple of concerns using Chapter 10's Cooperative Problem-Solving approach. Counseling can also be helpful, and you might also consider taking a class in either assertiveness or

---

[51] Research by psychologist Naomi I. Eisenberg and colleagues found that rejection and other forms of "social pain" activate the same brain areas as physical pain. See: https://ncbi.nlm.nih.gov/pmc/articles/PMC3273616/.

[52] https://dynamic.uoregon.edu/jjf/defineDARVO.html

nonviolent communication. (Your school's counseling center may offer these, or can direct you to local organizations that do.)

Even if everyone is on board and well-meaning, however, these types of situations can be incredibly complicated. It can be hard when those around us seem not to care about others' suffering, or imminent catastrophes like environmental collapse. Or, when they say they care about those things, but aren't willing to take even small steps to mitigate harm. You may even be right that their failure to act constitutes a moral failing. But don't be so quick to judge. We all have our strengths and weaknesses, including morally.

Never forget that capitalism excels at distracting people, lulling them,[53] exhausting them (e.g., by forcing them to work long hours at difficult jobs for little pay), frightening them (e.g., with scarcity or an invented external threat), and limiting their view of themselves and their options so that, for instance, they see their civic responsibilities as limited to voting.[54] Also, don't forget that the oligarchical capitalism we're all suffering under right now is especially good at extolling and promoting some of the very worst behaviors, including greed, selfishness, self-centeredness ("My only responsibility is to take care of me and mine"), technocratic paternalism, deflection ("Look! The next bright and shiny thing!"), and coming up with fake solutions to serious problems (like privatization, or the self-interested philanthropy many oligarchs engage in).[55] Any of our family members could fall prey to one or more of these behaviors.

Other things can also contribute to family conflict. Your relatives might not like talking about politics. Or, they might feel guilt, regret, or insecurity about some of their choices, and have a sense that the topics you want to raise are only going to make them feel worse. When people sense that their actions don't match their beliefs, they often experience cognitive dissonance, an uncomfortable feeling that can cause them to lash out.

Always strive for empathy and understanding. A wise friend reminded me, while I was writing this chapter, that people's worst behaviors often develop, "as the residue of strategies that empowered their survival," and also that, "not everyone has the luxury of interrogating their own experience." This is not to excuse someone's bad behavior! But it can be a survival strategy for *you* to at least understand where that behavior is coming from. With that in mind, I did an **Empathy Exercise** in which I wrote a

---

[53] Like K.C. Green's famous "This is Fine" cartoon dog: see https://knowyourmeme.com/memes/this-is-fine.

[54] Edward Herman and Noam Chomsky famously called the media's role in getting people to accept an unequal and unjust status quo, "manufacturing consent." Here's a great explanation of it: https://youtu.be/34LGPIXvU5M.

[55] See Anand Giridharadas's excellent book, *Winners Take All.*

narrative about my parents, with whom I had many conflicts, trying to see them through the lens of their own experience. Here's what I came up with:

Despite all our fighting, my parents and I actually had a lot in common. They were both solidly pro-union, my father was very creative, and my mother passionately loved animals and the environment. In different circumstances, he could have been an artist, she an animal activist or eco-warrior. But, as I mentioned in the Introduction, they both grew up the children of struggling and not-entirely-acculturated immigrant parents during the 1930s Great Depression—a situation that would have constrained anyone's opportunities and sense of self. Both started working right out of high school, with no opportunity to attend college. And they kept working for decades, often at jobs they didn't like.

My parents also lived through decades of war and lost extended family in the Holocaust. (My family is Jewish.) They survived vicious anti-Semitism in the United States, much more pernicious sexism than we have now, and some especially nasty 1950s-era reactionary politics. (When, at that time, my dad told a coworker at the post office that he wanted to take classes at New York City's leftist New School for Social Research, the coworker said that doing so would damage his career.) Furthermore, they suffered many personal and familial losses and traumas, including the death from cancer of my father's younger brother, Harry, when he was just 16, at a time when there were far fewer options for treatment and pain remediation.

Given everything they lived through, it's perhaps not surprising that both of my parents struggled with anger, addiction, low self-esteem, and other problems. Throughout most of their lives, solutions such as therapy, trauma work, addiction recovery, and self-care were far more limited and rudimentary than they are now. (Not that they were likely to have encountered them, or think of them as something that they could use.)

After doing this exercise, I felt more understanding of, and empathy for, my late parents. You can do it, too—hopefully for loved ones who are still around, and with whom you have a chance of relationship repair (see Exercise 23 for instructions). Empathy is very empowering, giving both you and the person you're empathizing with additional options and potential outcomes.

The Empathy Exercise can help you deal with loved ones who are politically, religiously, or otherwise more conservative than you are. You can even use it to try to better understand and relate to those who have fallen into terrible white supremacist or other antisocial views. As Ian Danskin discusses in his animated film, *The Alt-Right Playbook: How to Radicalize a Normie*,[56] many white supremacists start out as lonely, depressed, traumatized, and/or alienated men (and some women) who get sucked into racist groups through social media algorithms that send someone searching for "cures for depression," for example, to an alt-right gateway video or site. From there, it's only a few short steps to joining an outright racist group, and once the victim is in the group, they get psychologically groomed, primed, pressured, bullied, and otherwise coerced into staying.

So, there's plenty to feel compassion for. You may even wish to go farther and do the work of trying to persuade your relative to give up their hateful views. That's admirable, but proceed with caution, because while their racism may have indeed begun as the "residue of strategies that empowered their survival," after years of consuming racist media and hanging out with other racists, it may be entrenched. "Deprogramming" a racist is often a big job akin to cult deprogramming.[57] Danskin advises:

> I want to state plainly that Gabe [his film's fictional main character, who becomes a white supremacist] went off the deep end because he found a community willing to tell him that, because he is a cishet white man, the world revolves around him. Do not treat him like this is true. If a fraction of the energy spent having debates with America's Gabes were spent instead on voter re-enfranchisement, prisoners' rights, protection for immigrants, statehood for DC, and redistricting, Gabe's opinions, in the societal sense, wouldn't matter.
>
> If you think you can get through to him, it is worthwhile to try. But [anti-fascism] is a fight with many fronts, and deradicalization is only one of them. It sends an awful message when we spend more time trying to get bigots back on our side than we do on the people they are bigoted against.

Even if you decide you don't want to take on such a "deprogramming" project, doing the Empathy Exercise will help you in your attempts to deal with the Gabes in your life. And in the happy event that they one day start to rethink their choices, your increased empathy will have left the door open for discussion.

---

[56] https://www.youtube.com/watch?v=4xGawJIseNY
[57] https://www.lifeafterhate.org/ and https://www.freeradicals.org/ are two groups that may be able to help.

Exercise 23

Interview your parents (or other family members) about their lives, paying special attention to the time and place they grew up, the challenges they faced, and the choices and opportunities they had or didn't have. Do this as if you were a journalist or biographer without a personal stake in the information, and be as impartial and nonjudgmental as you can. Proceed chronologically, starting with their childhoods—or even earlier, with their parents' lives—and when you're done, write a narrative similar to the one that I wrote about my own parents in this chapter.

Some notes on the exercise:

1. Many people love the opportunity to tell their stories to an empathetic listener. But some don't. This could be for many reasons, including trauma. *Never* pressure someone to talk who doesn't want to, or to talk about something they don't want to talk about. In the worst-case scenario, you can piece together your narrative from what you already know—as I did with my parents—and still achieve your goal of increasing your understanding and empathy.

2. It also sometimes works better to ask your questions casually, and over a period of time, instead of trying to do a formal sit-down interview.

3. In your narrative, and at other times, don't compare the person to others who lived through similar or worse circumstances and made what you consider better choices. Such comparisons are perfectionist and judgmental, not to mention reductive.

4. I suggest you *not* share your narrative with your parents or anyone else, because that will put pressure on you, and possibly influence the way you write it. Keep it private. If you want to write a separate document for your parents—perhaps using more of a "family history" approach—that's fine.

39. About Your Family II: Time is on Your Side

Here are some additional techniques you can use to repair and improve relationships with loved ones:

(1) Look at how your own behavior might be contributing to any conflicts. We do this not just because it's the responsible thing to do, and not as a way of excusing the other person's bad behavior, but because, in the end, our own behavior is the only thing we have any control over. Besides, it's true that, when we change ourselves, others often (although not always!) change in response.

Anger is a tricky subject. There are some who feel it's never productive, but it can be difficult to set it aside in social justice contexts, especially when you or others are being oppressed. C. Daniel Batson and colleagues have written about how, "moral outrage—anger at the violation of a moral standard—should be distinguished from personal anger at being harmed and empathetic anger at seeing another for whom one cares harmed."[58] And David Pilgrim, curator of the Jim Crow Museum, advises:

> There will, undoubtedly, be times when you are justly angered. How can anyone look at the infant mortality rates of poor people in the United States and not get angry? That is justified, righteous anger—and so is the anger directed against the patterns of sexual assault in this country. Direct your anger against systems and patterns of injustice, not against individuals. That is hard, I know. Whenever possible, try to replace anger with focused passion and a zeal to address the

---

58 https://www.onlinelibrary.wiley.com/doi/pdf/10.1002/ejsp.434

injustice. And, finally, as much as is possible within you, avoid the anger that simmers, paralyzes, and morphs into hatred.[59]

The reference to paralysis in the last sentence reminds us that anger can be disempowering. Anger that you don't take positive action on can fester, which doesn't do you *or* your cause any good. Look, for instance, at the many people whose "activism" consists solely of ineffectual raging on social media. No, I'm not saying that social media is a waste of time. But the ultimate test of whether your activism is working is whether you're influencing people to change their attitudes and behaviors. Many social media ragers—especially if they're mostly raging either at allies who already agree with them, or opponents who are raging back at them—aren't. (This risk of paralysis, incidentally, is yet another reason why, in Part V, I urge you to include some activism in your weekly schedule.)

Keep in mind that your reactions can actually feed the behavior you're objecting to. Psychologists tell us that *any* response to an unwanted behavior, including a negative one, can reinforce that behavior. But a total lack of response can cause the behavior to fade away, a phenomenon called behavioral extinction. The trick is that you can't respond *at all*—not even with the teensiest eye-roll or annoyed sigh. You. Give. Them. Nothing. Even if the behavior doesn't entirely fade away, or fade away at all, training yourself to be less reactive is a good way to preserve your own energy, equanimity, and power. Speaking of which...

(2) Choose Your Battles. This is probably a good place to address the complaints that some of my older manuscript readers had about this chapter and some other parts of this book: complaints that can be best summed up as, "But young people today are so entitled! They're all about cancel culture, call-out culture, trigger warnings, and the weaponization of identity politics and social justice! And they grew up getting participation trophies, so if they don't get constant rewards, they feel mistreated! All your talk of compassion, self-acceptance, etc. just encourages all that!"

Whew! Leaving aside the points that: (a) bashing the young is probably history's oldest and most boring hobby, (b) elders should be understanding and supportive of youth and its occasional foibles, and (c) today's elders should be *especially* understanding and supportive, given the environmental, economic, political, and other messes they're leaving behind—yes, there probably are instances where members of your generation have been entitled or overreactive. (Just as I'm sure there have been incidents where members of your critics' generations were, and, in some cases, still are.)

---

[59] https://www.ferris.edu/htmls/news/jimcrow/question/2009/june.htm

Canceling, callouts, safe spaces, content warnings, etc., are all excellent and useful, but any tool or strategy can be misused or overused. So, choose your battles, keeping in mind Chapter 34's point about how a criticism hurts more or less depending on how much we respect the person delivering it. Maybe, just maybe, Great Aunt Grumpypants's ignorant political jabs aren't worth getting that steamed up about. (Although if you interview her for Exercise 23, she might be thrilled, the result will likely be revelatory, and it could transform your relationship.)[60]

(3) Plan Ahead/Set Boundaries. If your family is likely to fight about politics, maybe suggest that some topics be off-limits during the holiday dinner. (Or your whole visit.) If your family isn't going to accommodate your veganism, then bring your own food. (They'll probably object to that too— but hey, they had their chance!)

If you know a racist or otherwise problematic relative is going to ruin an upcoming holiday meal, then maybe you could skip that meal, or sit at the other end of the table, or just show up for dessert. (Notice how you're creating some better options for yourself, as recommended in Chapter 4.) Or maybe you and some other family members can have a discussion with the racist person and get them to agree to keep their noxious opinions to themselves. Or, if they won't do that, maybe you can convince your family to not invite them to this or future events. These options aren't perfect, but they are far better than not dealing with the problem, a.k.a., procrastinating.

(4) Make sure you're comfortable with your own values and choices. Remember Chapter 24's point about how we're often ambivalent because we at least partly share the other person's view? If, post-college, you truly think that a humbler lifestyle is a good trade-off for getting to do work you love and feel is important, then it shouldn't bother you too much if others disagree. Yeah, it's tedious if they keep harping on it, and you should definitely ask them to stop. But the occasional ill-chosen comment in an otherwise caring relationship can be forgiven and forgotten.

What if, however, you actually do want both the meaningful career and to make more money? That's okay, too! Problem-solve around that and do your best to create some good options for yourself.

---

[60] Conservatives often use term "cancel culture" cynically to shut down any questioning of the status quo. But some on the left have raised legitimate concerns about online shaming and pile-ups. Here are three excellent discussions of the topic: https://www.youtube.com/watch?v=OjMPJVmXxV8 (Natalie Wynn in her "ContraPoints" podcast), https://www.buzzsprout.com/1112270/8656464 (Michael Hobbes and Sarah Marshall in their "You're Wrong About" podcast), and https://lee-mandelo.com/f/that-twitter-thread-on-criticism?s=09 (Lee Mandelo in their blog).

(5) Create your own "family". Meaning, back on campus and, later on, in your chosen community, create your own "family" of loving people who share your values, and can provide the kinds of support that your family of origin can't. You can find these people online, of course, but it's best to have at least a small supportive community in real life.

(6) If persuasion is a goal, then learn how to do it. Persuasion is a skill: you can't wing it. (Hint: it's not about nagging, hassling, harassing, judging, shaming, nitpicking, or name-calling.) Once again, I recommend Faber and Mazlish's *How to Talk So Kids Will Listen and Listen So Kids Will Talk*, from which Chapter 10's Cooperative Problem-Solving technique is adapted. If your college offers a course in negotiation or sales, you might consider taking it. You'll mostly likely find it in the business or communications department; and, regardless of your major or future plans, it could well wind up being one of the more valuable courses you take.

The Appendices lists some books that will be useful for those who want to do serious activism or community organizing. Keep in mind, however, that your family may not actually be the best target for such work. In my book *The Lifelong Activist*, I wrote about how, often, "your ideas are held in lower regard by the people who watched you grow up, and who in some cases diapered you, than by the general population." Save your efforts at persuasion, in other words, for those most likely to be convinced, whether or not they happen to be related to you. And always remember that **how we say something is at least as important as what we say**, and that happiness and pride in your choices can be just as persuasive as logical appeals, if not more so. (And I have two words for you vegans out there: fabulous desserts.)

(7) Finally, and especially if all else fails, **patiently await your eventual vindication.** Martin Luther King, Jr. famously said, paraphrasing the abolitionist Theodore Parker, "the arc of the moral universe is long, but it bends toward justice." Some of the difficulties you're experiencing are intrinsic to being a caring person and a visionary, both of which are good things to be. Later on, hopefully, you'll experience the pleasure of having the mainstream catch up with you. (I'm happy to report that, less than a decade after my Columbus Day episode, that holiday is well on its way to being replaced by Indigenous Peoples' Day.) Time, in other words, is on your side.

If your relatives are gracious, as some of mine were, you may even experience the pleasure of them admitting that you were right all along. You might even wind up being some young person's "cool" parent, aunt, uncle, friend, mentor, teacher, or boss, which is one of the best gigs around.

Exercise 24

Before your next call or visit home, journal about any anticipated problems or conflicts, then make a plan for avoiding or minimizing them. Your plan could include using Cooperative Problem Solving to set some ground rules, scheduling more "alone time" and self-care during a visit, and/or shortening your visit.

40. How to Stay Safe and Sane on Social Media

Although the various social media platforms are amazing, game-changing, society-evolving technologies, they are also cauldrons of abuse and dysfunction where you'll find every single perfectionist characteristic discussed in Part II, and every form of criticism and rejection discussed in this section, in abundance. So it's no surprise that, as discussed in Chapter 17, social media has been linked to depression and anxiety in college students and others.

Of course, you'll also find rampant sexism, racism, religious bias, homophobia, transphobia, ableism, classism, and nativism online.

Then there's the whole set of *other* problems intrinsic to social media, including reductiveness (from the often terse communications); a lack of body language, vocal tone, and other cues; a lack of privacy; a lack of boundaries (so that your family and boss can read stuff you'd normally just show your friends); and the pressure to post frequently. Plus, all the usual writing and editorial quandaries. As renowned blogger Jason Kottke put it:

> Doing kottke.org is this constant battle with myself: staying in my comfort zone vs. finding opportunities for growth, posting what I like or find interesting vs. attempting to suss out what "the reader" might want, celebrating the popular vs. highlighting the obscure, balancing the desire to define what it is I do here vs. appreciating that no one really knows (myself included), posting clickable things vs. important things I know will be unpopular, protecting myself against criticism vs. accepting it as a gift, deciding when to provoke & challenge vs. when to comfort & entertain, feeling like this is frivolous vs. knowing this site is important to me & others, being right vs. accepting I'll

make mistakes, and saying something vs. letting the content and its creators speak for themselves.[61]

Kottke has been blogging for more than 20 years and is considered a master at it: if he still finds it challenging, I guess we can all be forgiven for feeling the same way. In any case, you probably do want and need to be on social media, at least to some degree. As discussed in the Appendices, proficiency on at least one platform is a requirement for many entry-level jobs. Also, we—meaning society—need you to be on social media, to the extent that you're comfortable being there. We need as many voices and visions as possible, and yours are especially important if you're a member of a marginalized or otherwise oppressed community. With all that in mind, here are some steps you can take to stay safe and sane on social media, and even have some fun:

Prioritize safety. Don't pressure yourself to participate more than you'd like, or in ways you don't like, and don't let anyone else pressure you either.

Work on your nonperfectionism. Remember: it's the foundation of resilience.

Be strategic. Figure out your goal(s) for participation and tailor your online presence accordingly. If your primary goal is to communicate with family and friends, for instance, then tighten up your privacy settings. If it's to advance your career, then keep things professional. If it's to promote a political viewpoint, you might want to engage more broadly—but still, not with everyone.

Consider having two accounts. A private one just for close friends, and a public one for everyone else. That way, you have at least one account where you don't feel the need to censor yourself.

Find role models whose online success you'd like to emulate. Look for those who are relatable—i.e., ordinary people, not celebrities—and two to 10 years further along the path than you.

Block the troublemakers. If someone is causing you stress or pain, block them, even if they happen to be related to you. Do it sooner rather than later.

Don't feed the trolls! If someone is playing devil's advocate, or sealioning, or being a "reply guy," or otherwise posting in bad faith, don't feel obligated to respond.[62] You don't owe them your time and attention.

---

[61] https://kottke.org/20/07/a-moment-of-reflection-on-the-paradox-of-individual-creative-work

[62] Citations for this sentence: https://www.reddit.com/r/Feminism/comments/dry3dn/let_me_play_devils_advocate/ (devil's advocate), https://en.wikipedia.org/wiki/Sealioning (sealioning),

(Alexandria Ocasio-Cortez wisely compared one right-winger's incessant demands that she debate him to street harassment.[63]) Ignore them, and they'll probably get bored and go away.

Trust your gut. If you're not mostly enjoying your time spent on social media, something's wrong.

If you're being harassed, stalked, or threatened, get help *immediately*. Keep records of all incidents, including not just a timeline, but printouts of messages, texts, posts, etc. https://www.fightcyberstalking.org offers downloadable forms for recording incidents, and also information for dealing with harassers on different platforms. Other useful resources include: http://www.cyberbullying.org/resources/, http://1800victims.org/crime-type/cybercrimes/, and https://www.gameshotline.org (for harassment on gaming platforms or in gaming communities). Also, consult your college's campus safety department, department of student life, and Title IX Office.

For Those Posting Political Content

A few more steps, specifically for those posting political or otherwise controversial content:

Know what you're doing. Persuasion, as noted in the previous chapter, is a skill.

Expect pushback. Remember that your goal is to (choose one or all): shake up the status quo, speak truth to power (or take that power down!), "Comfort the afflicted and afflict the comfortable," in the words of journalist Finley Peter Dunne, and/or, "Go where you are least wanted, because that is where you are most needed," as per abolitionist Abigail Kelley Foster. You obviously can't do those things without making at least some people mad, so be prepared for pushback, and learn to see it as a sign you're having an impact.

Remember your silent audience. Even if some people are responding negatively or obnoxiously to your posts, there are probably many more who are quietly appreciating them (and see the obnoxious bullies for who they are). Speaking of which...

Support others. If you see someone being picked on online, support them with a public comment or private message.

Educate yourself on your online rights, and use technologies appropriate to your values and situation. These sites will help:

---

https://twitter.com/i/events/1041376202391343104?lang=en (reply guy),
https://meta.wikimedia.org/wiki/What_is_a_troll (bad faith).
[63] https://twitter.com/aoc/status/1027729430137827328

https://www.eff.org/pages/tools/, https://www.fsf.org/,
https://www.aclu.org/issues/privacy-technology#current, and
https://electronicintifada.net/content/guide-online-security-activ-
ists/17536.

One of the major problems with social media is that it can eat up so much of our time. If only there were a tool that could help us keep everything in balance... Oh wait—there is! It's called "time management," and I discuss it in the next section. See you there!

PART V

ABUNDANCE

41. An Awesome Liberation

The big reason to practice time management is that **there's no such thing as unmanaged time.** If you're not managing your time, someone else is managing it for you. That could be your family, friends, professors, classmates, employer, and/or coworkers. Or it could be corporations trying to sell you a particular product or lifestyle. Bad enough to let those who truly care about you rule your time—but corporations?

The capitalist/consumerist lifestyle common in the U.S. and some other countries emphasizes long workdays (often with additional long commutes), with much of the rest of your time spent on chores. "Free time," after all those obligations, is often limited to television, Web surfing, gaming, and other passive and/or isolating activities, both because those are the major options available and because you're too tired to do anything else. Meanwhile, relationships, socializing, self-care, caregiving, civic work, and activism—all the major contributors to a happy and healthy life and society, in other words—are given short shrift.[64] Is it any wonder that, in such societies, so many are stressed, unhealthy, and unhappy? That there are so many troubled relationships? And so many unraveling communities?

Our time use is also hugely gendered, with women almost always on the losing end of the equation. Globally, we women remain hugely disproportionately responsible not just for caregiving for children and others, but for

---

[64] Notice how many of the countries that provide workers with the most paid time off (https://en.wikipedia.org/wiki/List_of_minimum_annual_leave_by_country) also top the World Happiness Report's list of happiest countries (https://en.wikipedia.org/wiki/World_Happiness_Report#2019_report). Also note that many of those same countries also provide strong health, housing, and educational benefits, thus further improving individuals' lives while simultaneously freeing their time by easing their caregiving and other obligations.

household chores and maintenance work. At the same time, far less of our labor is paid than men's.[65] Furthermore, women are still frequently encouraged to stay quiet and subjugate their needs to those of others, and so over-giving (Chapter 48) remains a problem.

I teach—and, in this book, will be discussing—what I call **Values-Based Time Management (VBTM)**. Unlike some other time-management systems that focus narrowly on maximizing your work output, VBTM's goal is more holistic: to help you to align, as much as possible, your actions with your values. VBTM also concerns itself with both your professional (in this case, school) and personal lives. That's not just because it doesn't make sense to only manage half your time, but because your personal life is important.

Like most time-management systems, VBTM involves budgeting, scheduling, and tracking your time, all of which I'll be discussing. But the core is organizing your time as much as possible around the activities that are truly important to you.

VBTM, in other words, maximizes the chances that you'll achieve a happy, healthy, and productive life—however *you* define that. And here are some other reasons to do it:

Success makes you busier. (As discussed in Chapter 23.) Developing a time-management practice today will help you to cope with the flood of opportunities we're all hoping you'll be deluged with tomorrow. This also applies to your personal life, by the way. Many people, post-college, aspire to not just a great career, but a great family life, a comfortable home, and to do good work in their community. Despite perfectionist media that implies that such a life is easily attainable, it's actually a lot to handle. But time management can help.

Society promotes unhealthy ideas of time use. Many people still believe, for instance, that the busier you are, the more successful and/or important you must be. Or that multitasking is a good idea. (Chapter 5 debunked that one.) Or that they work best under pressure. Speaking of which…

No one works best under pressure. And those who say they do are deluding themselves. Sure, pressure may terrify you into finally overcoming your procrastination and focusing on your work. But there's no way that that work will ever equal the quantity or quality of work done under conditions of abundant time and attention, such as time management can provide.

---

[65] See, for example: https://www.bls.gov/news.release/atus.nr0.html. (Scroll down to the discussion of childcare.) And https://unstats.un.org/unsd/gender/chapter4/chapter4.html.

Besides, as discussed earlier, using pressure and other punishments as motivators will only make it harder for you to do your work in the future.

Last but not least...

Your professors will love you. Believe me, they can tell when you've waited till the last minute to do your work, and they hate that! (Partly because they know you're capable of doing better, and partly because the missed deadlines create more work for them.)

Here's the good news: for all its liberating potential, **time management often comes down to making just a few simple changes** in your life and habits. This chapter, as well as Chapters 42 through 48, will discuss the fundamental ideas underlying VBTM. Then, Chapters 49 and 50 will tell you how to use those ideas to create the values-driven time budget and schedule that work best for you.

First, however, let's take a closer look at the difference VBTM can make in a student's life.

A Tale of Two Students

The alarm goes off at 8:00 a.m. **Ray**, however, just dives deeper under the covers. He stayed up late finishing a history paper and now needs to sleep in.

He finally wakes up at 10:00, which means he's already missed his calculus class. It's the second time in two weeks, and he's disappointed in himself. (And knows his professor won't be happy.)

He's also going to be late for his next class, Biology.

It's a lousy way to start the day.

He drags himself out of bed, quickly showers and dresses, then heads out. He doesn't have time for breakfast, so as he walks he munches a dry-as-dust protein bar and reviews his schedule:

8:00 – 9:00 a.m.	Wake up, shower, dress, breakfast (missed!)
9:00 – 10:00	Calculus class (missed!)
10:30 – 11:45	Biology class (late!)
11:45 – 1:00 p.m.	Study (also includes 1/2-hour lunch with Carla)
1:30 – 2:30	Sociology class (test)
3:00 – 4:00	Calculus study session
4:30 – 5:30	Workout
5:45 – 6:45	Dinner

7:00 – 8:30	Orchestra rehearsal
9:00 – midnight	Study (do calculus problems, review history chapter)
Midnight – 1:00 a.m	Relax, get ready for bed
1:00	Go to bed

There's no way he can get it all done—especially since he hasn't even begun to study for his sociology test. He takes a deep breath, then texts his girlfriend Carla to cancel their lunch date.

The seconds crawl by as he nervously awaits her response.

Finally, it arrives: *Again?*

Yeah. Really sorry.

It's OK, Carla texts. *Know you have to study.*

Relieved, he texts back, *Thanks for understanding. Love you.*

Carla replies: *Love you too. But we have to talk.*

The words send a chill through him. "She's going to break up with me!" he thinks, panicking. He wants to call her and beg for another chance. But now he's on the verge of missing his second class, so all he can do is text a quick *OK* before dashing into the classroom.

The rest of the day goes about the same—which is to say, not well. Ray rushes from commitment to commitment, frazzled and unprepared. Even the hour and a half he reclaimed for studying for his test isn't well used, since he's exhausted (despite his two lattes) and distracted by the impending breakup.

That afternoon, while he's rushing to get to the test, he's stopped by a person puzzling over a campus map. "Can you help me find the admissions building?" he asks.

Inwardly Ray groans: dude is hopelessly lost. "It's over there," he says, pointing. "Go through the main quad, down the stairs past the Student Center, then take a left. You'll see it, okay?" Then he rushes off.

"Uh, okay, thanks," the lost dude calls uncertainly after him.

Ray feels bad about not having been more helpful, but those regrets are soon swamped by an even worse feeling: his test is a disaster. After it's over, he's so demoralized he goes home and crawls into bed, skipping both the calculus study session and his workout.

At dinner, he has a heartfelt conversation with Carla, who agrees to give him another chance. The conversation is a long one, however, so he winds up missing orchestra rehearsal. (Still more people he's disappointed...)

Ray's back home by 8:00, and in theory could get an early start on his evening's studying. But he's so stressed and depleted and depressed by the day's events that all he can do is watch television. "I'll do better tomorrow," he promises himself. Only, deep down, he knows he won't. That knowledge leaves him with a sense of hopelessness not just about his current semester, but his whole college career, and his whole life.

It's a lousy way to end the day.

The alarm goes off at 8:00 a.m. **Sophie** is already awake, having gotten her full seven hours of sleep. She gets out of bed, showers and dresses, and sits down for a healthy and sustaining bowl of oatmeal.

It's a nice way to start the day.

While eating, she reviews her schedule:

8:00 – 9:00 a.m.	Wake up, shower, dress, breakfast
9:30 – 10:30	Ethnic Studies class
11:15 – 1:45 p.m.	Study for Arabic test (eat lunch while studying)
2:00 – 3:00	English Literature class
3:30 – 4:30	Arabic class (test)
4:45 – 5:45	Workout
6:00 – 6:45	Dinner with Chelle
7:00 – 8:30	Orchestra rehearsal
9:00 – midnight	Study (read biology chapter, work on ethnic studies paper)
Midnight – 1:00 a.m.	Relax, get ready for bed
1:00	Go to bed

Like Ray, Sophie's taking four classes and participating in Orchestra. Unlike him, however, she knows not to schedule a social lunch right before a test. This almost trivial-seeming decision has a powerful effect on her day, giving her abundant time to do the things she needs to do, and eliminating the need to rush around. In fact, her schedule allows nearly 40% more study time than Ray's (5.5 hours versus four), with more of that time being earlier in the day, when she's more alert and focused. And because she's not stressed and depleted, she actually does use that time well.

As it happens, that afternoon Sophie encounters the same hopelessly lost dude that Ray met. Happily, she has the time to personally escort him over to the admissions building, and they have a nice conversation along the way.

That night, while preparing for bed, she feels good about her day, and particularly about having helped a stranger. She's looking forward to tomorrow, confident she'll be able to handle whatever school or other challenges arise.

It's a nice way to end the day.

42. What Makes a Good Time Manager

Sophie is clearly a **Good Time Manager (GTM).** GTMs make time management a priority, which means that they not only do their time budgeting and scheduling and tracking (Chapters 49 and 50), but are also **optimizers**. They're always asking themselves questions like, "Did I do this task as efficiently as I could have?", "Was this event a good use of my time?", and "Is this [personal or professional] relationship working for me?" *And acting on the answers.* Please note that this "inner Q&A" is *always* supportive and encouraging, and *never* perfectionistically harsh. Always be your own best coach!

Professionally and personally, GTMs are busy but not frantic. They meet their deadlines and do quality work. They show up on time, or a bit early, and prepared. They also prioritize sleep, nutrition, exercise, and other self-care. All of this means that they're as productive, healthy, and happy as possible, given their circumstances, and that they're not just great team members, but natural leaders and mentors. And so, interesting people and opportunities are always coming their way.

Are GTMs like this 100% of the time? Of course not: they have their "off" days like everyone else, and sometimes their "off" weeks, months, or even years. (And expecting someone to be doing well at anything "100% of the time" is perfectionist.) But even during difficult times, a GTM will function better than they would have without their time management skills, and those skills will also help them to get back on track as quickly as possible.

Unfortunately, judging by the frequent news stories about workaholism, "time poverty," and similar problems, there aren't a lot of GTMs out there. Most people, in fact, are probably **Poor Time Managers (PTMs)** who constantly overcommit themselves. (This obviously includes poor Ray.) As a result, they're constantly late, constantly missing deadlines, and constantly handing in poor-quality work. Also, most PTMs aren't exactly a picture of health and happiness. Mostly, they're walking around stressed, ill, fatigued, and depleted.

Needless to say, a PTM isn't anyone's idea of a good team member, much less a leader. Professionally and personally, GTMs tend to avoid relationships with PTMs, whose chronic unreliability not only creates a huge strain, but greatly lessens the chances of a successful outcome.

Unsurprisingly, there's a perfectionist angle to all this. Both overscheduling and expecting yourself to function without adequate self-care are classic grandiose behaviors.

PTMs aren't the worst-off people, however: those would be the **Wannabe Time Managers (WTMs)**. They're dabblers, trying a little time management here and there, but they won't commit. As a result, they often wind up experiencing all the inconveniences of the practice while getting few or none of the benefits. They also tend to be deluded about how much time management they're actually doing. Many think that they are "almost a GTM" or "halfway between a GTM and PTM." In reality, however, most are far closer to PTMs than GTMs. (From now on, whenever I mention PTMs, you can assume I also mean WTMs.)

Slow Down, You Move Too Fast

The signature behavior of PTMs is rushing around. People in time-dysfunctional cultures tend to see rushing as a sign of ambition or importance. ("Sorry! Gotta run! Three meetings this afternoon!") But rushing is *horrible*. We've already seen, in Chapter 26, how it impairs our ability to learn. But that's just one of the problems it causes. Rushing also impairs us physically and emotionally (all those stress hormones), intellectually (see Chapter 45's discussion of cognitive capacity), and even relationally (we treat both loved ones and strangers worse when we're in a rush).

Rushing even impairs our ethical functioning. This was demonstrated in a classic social psychology experiment by John M. Darley and C. Daniel Batson,[66] in which 40 Princeton seminarians were asked to write, and then later record, a sermon. Each was assigned one of two topics to write about: either, (1) the ethically instructive parable of the Good Samaritan, in which,

---

[66] John M. Darley and C. Daniel Batson, "'From Jerusalem to Jericho': A study of situational and dispositional variables in helping behavior." In Elliot Aronson (ed.), *Readings About the Social Animal*, 7th Ed. (This is the same C. Daniel Batson whom I quoted in Chapter 39 on the subject of anger, by the way.)

as you may recall, a king and a priest pass by a wounded man without stopping to help, but a "humble Samaritan" does the right thing and stops; or (2) the more ethically neutral topic of career paths for seminarians. After each seminarian had written his (they were all male) sermon, he was then told that either:

- He had plenty of time to get over to the recording studio (which was located in another building).
- He was on time, but shouldn't dawdle. Or,
- He was late! The recording staff was waiting for him, and he had to get to the studio *right now*!

Here's the twist: each seminarian, while en route to the studio, encountered a man lying in the street, seemingly ill and in distress. (He was actually an actor hired by the experimenters.) In other words, the seminarian was presented with the Good Samaritan scenario in real life!

What would he do? (What would YOU do?)

Not to leave you in suspense: the experimenters found that the seminarians in the third group, who were rushing to get to the studio, were far less likely to stop and help than the others—*and this was true even for those who had just written an entire sermon on the Good Samaritan.* All that thought and analysis—not to mention the basic helping orientation of most seminarians—flew right out the window, just because they were rushed.

Darley and Batson concluded that, "Ethics becomes a luxury as the speed of our daily lives increases." They also urged us not to be too hard on the "non-helpers," who, they said, were caught in a conflict between their obligation to help the needy person and their obligation to the experimenters. (Just as Ray really wanted to help the hopelessly lost dude, but also had to get to his test.)

The bottom line is that, **when you're rushing, you're not the person you're capable of being: not physically, intellectually, emotionally, relationally, or ethically. Moment by moment, you're only living up to a part of your potential.**

The opposite of rushing could be defined as presence, mindfulness, or the ability to "be here now," as Ram Dass famously put it. Also, the ability to devote abundant—or, as abundant as possible—time, energy, and attention to the people and things that are truly important to you. Values-Based Time Management will help you locate and focus on all those priorities, so that you can live a life filled not just with accomplishment but interest, meaning, love, and joy.

Exercise 25

Journal about how much rushing you do every day, how that rushing affects your schoolwork and life, and how things might improve if you could stop rushing.

43. Investing Your Time

Our time is valuable, and we should always strive to use it as well as we can. We should also value small amounts of it, both for their own sake and because they add up. Reclaim just 15 minutes of underutilized time a day and you'll gain more than 90 hours—the equivalent of more than two work weeks!—a year.

Now, a lot of people think they already understand all this. They go around saying stuff like, "Time is money." But watch them, and you'll see them squander their precious time in ways they never would their cash. Also, they're wrong, because time actually happens to be far more valuable than money. That's not just because it's finite, with even the richest person being limited to 24 hours a day; it's also because time can create outcomes that money can't, and those happen to be the most valuable outcomes.

Consider two students. One attends an expensive college, and also buys the best computer, textbooks, etc., but rarely studies. The other attends a cheaper school and makes do with cheaper supplies, but studies a few hours a day. Who will get educated?

Or, think of two people trying to get fit. One spends thousands on a gym membership and fancy workout clothes but never uses them. The other spends $100 on a decent pair of running shoes and some used weights, then runs or works out most days. Who will get fit?

Finally, think of two parents. One is always buying expensive gifts for their kids, but rarely spends any time with them. The other doesn't have a lot of money to spend, but tries their best to be present. Who will have the better relationship?

You get the idea—and it's not a new one. Around 2,000 years ago, the Stoic philosopher Seneca, in his powerful essay "On the Shortness of Life," said of those who misuse their time: "They are trifling with life's most precious commodity, being deceived because it is an intangible thing, not open to inspection and therefore reckoned very cheap."

I'm not saying, by the way, that money is unimportant. Of course it's important—and you should definitely take the time to learn some money management.[67] But research has shown that, after our basic material needs are met, the yields of time, including good health, good relationships, and a sense of personal fulfillment, become primary.[68] Also, people who value time over money tend to be happier in general.[69]

Time does have something important in common with money, however: you can invest it. You're probably familiar with financial investments, like stocks or real estate, that increase in value over time, thus earning you a "return." Buy $100 worth of stocks today, and if you've chosen well, you can sell them later for $200. (Or, sometimes, way more.) Personal financial experts tell us that anything that's not an investment is an expense, including not just your latest impulse purchase, but essentials like food, transportation, and clothing. All expenses, including the essential ones, lose value over time. (You can't resell that bag of groceries you just bought, or last month's train pass.) Experts therefore advise us to minimize even our essential expenses, so that can we put as much money as possible into investments.

Time investments work pretty much the same way—except that, as discussed, a time investment can yield not just money, but health, happiness, love, and even more time! So, as important as investing your money is, it's even more important to invest your time. The major categories of time investments are:

Self-care, including good nutrition, exercise, sleep, grooming, medical and therapy appointments and, for some, a meditation or spiritual practice. PTMs often stint on this and wind up going through their days exhausted and depleted. GTMs, in contrast, aim for abundant self-care, and they also understand that **the more ambitious your goals, or the tougher the barriers you face, the more self-care you need.**

Some activists and other good people mistakenly believe that self-care is an indulgence in a world beset with many urgent problems. But skimping on it makes you less effective, and is likely to lead to burnout. As the

---

[67] Recommended books: Thomas J. Stanley and William D. Danko's *The Millionaire Next Door* and Mark Bryan and Julia Cameron's *Money Drunk/Money Sober.*

[68] See, for instance, http://www.pewsocialtrends.org/2008/04/30/who-wants-to-be-rich/. Notice how, in the study, the most valued priority across all demographics, by a wide margin, is, "to have enough free time."

[69] https://www.nytimes.com/2016/09/11/opinion/sunday/what-should-you-choose-time-or-money.html

poet/activist Audre Lorde famously said, "Caring for myself is not self-indulgence, it is self-preservation, and that is an act of political warfare."

Relationships. You know: that thing that, at the end of their life, many people wish they had devoted more time to?

Values-driven work. Meaning work you do for love and not just a paycheck. (I also sometimes refer to this category as your "vocation" or "mission.") Since college is a time-intensive activity akin to having a job, I would include your college work in this category. Some caregiving, creative, spiritual, and other practices would also fit, if you devote serious hours and attention to them.

Education. By which I mean the lifelong education that you participate in after your college years. Some people continue to accrue degrees and certifications throughout their lives, while others skip the degrees but take whatever online or offline courses happen to strike their fancy, while still others do a lot of independent reading and study. It's all good. The important thing is that you never stop learning and growing.

Replenishing recreation. Activities that are fun and relaxing, and that also leave you healthier and happier (a.k.a., "replenished"). They tend to be active and engaging, and they also tend to connect you with others and/or nature and/or certain aspects of yourself, like your creativity, intellect, athleticism, or senses. Examples include socializing, sports, an art or craft, outdoor activities, and travel.

Activism/Community Organizing. This is perhaps the highest yielding of all the investment categories. Don't believe me? Well, consider the fact that you're able to attend college at all. A century ago, it might not have been possible, unless you happened to be rich, white, and male. Generations of activists and community organizers fighting for social justice on all fronts, including labor, education, race, gender, and disability, have granted you this precious opportunity—which, let's not forget, is still beyond the reach of many. So, pay it forward by investing a few hours a month on whichever social justice cause speaks most to your heart. Along with the good you'll be doing, you'll also find that activism yields some terrific personal benefits, including the opportunity to do meaningful (and resume-building) work alongside some of the best people you'll ever meet.

For more on activism, see my book *The Lifelong Activist*—and please note that I'm talking about activism/organizing and *not* volunteer work. Volunteering is good, but activism is better because it seeks to correct the conditions, such as poverty, that make the volunteering necessary to start with.

The final category of time investment is one that many forget, but it's actually the most important one because it underpins the success of all the rest:

Planning and Management. Success doesn't just happen: you have to plan for it, and then manage the process as it unfolds. You should, in fact, plan and manage all of the above investment categories, including those we typically don't think of as requiring planning and management, such as relationships. (Many people wing it in this crucial area, and then wind up with a failed marriage or alienated kids.) You should also plan and manage your resources, including your information, money, property, and (hello) time. All this planning and management may sound like a lot of work, but it really isn't, since a little goes a long way. Planning for a successful romantic relationship, for instance, might involve reading a few books on relationships, working with a counselor to overcome any relevant barriers, and then developing a set of principles (e.g., mutual support and open communication) and habits (e.g., weekly date nights and prompt resolution of conflicts) that you and your partner agree to moving forward. Career planning might involve more initial work, but the effort still remains small compared with the potential yield of a satisfying decades-long career. (See the Appendices for some career planning tips.)

Assuming you're not in the midst of actively planning your career or some other major life goal, two hours per week should be fine for all your planning and management activities.

Generally speaking, you want to put some time into each of your investment categories every week. Obviously, some weeks are busier than others, and you might want to skip, say, your activism and *some* recreation during midterms and finals weeks. But the goal is to maintain a balanced and healthy lifestyle where you address all of your priorities on a consistent basis.

So those are the time investments. All other activities are **time expenses,** including:

Chores, including housekeeping, errands, etc.

A **"day job"** you're doing just, or mostly, for money.

Your **commute**, an often time-consuming activity that is also often stressful. The average U.S. commute (round-trip) is 52 minutes/day.[70] However, a PTM's commute is likely to be longer than average.

Escapist recreation. In contrast to replenishing recreation, escapist activities tend to be sedentary, isolating, and disconnecting. Television is the obvious example, but social media and gaming can also qualify, despite their superficial social aspects. While small amounts of these activities are fine, too much is unhealthy, both in terms of sedentariness and content.

Procrastination is also a time expense. It may seem funny to think of it that way, since none of us really wants to procrastinate. But when you think

---

[70] https://www.census.gov/library/visualizations/interactive/travel-time.html

about it, that's true of all the other expenses, too! (Except, perhaps, for the escapism.)

The final category of time expense is: any activity you're doing just to **kill time**—and what a horrible expression that is—or out of **habit**, or because of **convention,** or because of a **reluctance to say no** (see Chapters 47 and 48).

Keep in mind that the line between time investments and expenses isn't hard and fast: an activity could be either, depending on who's doing it and why. **If you really enjoy something, and feel it enhances your life, then it's an investment.** If you love cooking and feel enhanced by it, for instance, then it's an investment for you. But if someone else finds it a tedious chore, then it's an expense for them.

It's also possible to overdo an investment, in which case it becomes an expense. We already know what that's called: Quasiproductive Procrastination (Chapter 5).

44. Shifting from Expenses to Investments

Similar to money management, a major goal of time management is to shift as much of your time as you can *out* of expenses and *into* investments. Doing this is arguably even more important for your time than your money, because everything we purchase winds up costing us twice, time-wise: once in the time it takes to earn the money to purchase it, and forever after in the time it takes to maintain it. "The things we own, own us," as the saying goes. (And, obviously, buying a lot of stuff is also not good for the environment.)

An investment-centered life offers some outstanding benefits, including not just increased productivity and achievement, but more health, happiness, fulfillment, and joy. You do the shift from expenses to investments systematically via budgeting, which I discuss in Chapter 49. But why not get started now? Here are a few easy suggestions for reducing expenses that you might want to implement immediately:

- Quit (responsibly—don't leave anyone in a lurch) any extracurricular activities that you aren't enjoying or that aren't accomplishing much.
- Quit (but not callously) any relationships that aren't working for you (for example, people you're seeing mainly out of habit or obligation).
- Work double shifts at your job to lower your commuting and preparation time.
- Set a time limit for household chores—say, half an hour of cleaning per room per week. (Without a limit, they have a way of

"expanding" to fill all your available time.) If you live with others, make sure that everyone in the household is doing their fair share.

- Buddy up with a roommate or friend for chores, so that, for instance, you do all the laundry or grocery shopping one week, and they do it all the next.
- Invest in great tools that make chores easier and quicker (e.g., great housecleaning supplies).
- Say "no" and delegate wherever possible. (See Chapter 47.)

A lot of these steps involve eliminating, or at least cutting down on, stuff you don't want to be doing anyway. In theory, that should be a no-brainer, but perfectionism, guilt, obligation, convention, peer pressure, and an over-giving habit can all get in the way. Be compassionate and patient with yourself while working to overcome these barriers, but definitely do work to overcome them.

As you eliminate expenses, start filling the liberated time with investments. Your choices will be based on your own particular values and goals, but a good rule of thumb is to put two-thirds of your liberated time into your work and one-third into self-care and replenishing recreation. Doing that should lead to a relatively quick improvement in both your productivity and your quality of life.

Reining in Your Escapist Activities

Probably the hardest expenses for many people to cut or trim are their escapist ones, such as social media, gaming, video watching, and television. These are so much fun and so stress-relieving! (And can be essential for some, including those who are disabled.) But they're also typically very sedentary and isolating. They also often promote terrible values: see, for instance, social media's ubiquitous perfectionism and some gaming communities' misogyny. Even when one of these activities has a social component, the socializing is often shallow or what psychologists call *parasocial*, which means that it is one-sided and unreciprocated. Psychologists have expressed many concerns about parasocial relationships, including that they reinforce unrealistic relationship models, erode people's ability to socialize in real life, and can render people vulnerable to advertising and other influences.[71]

In Chapter 49's sample budget I allocate 1.5 hours a day for escapist activities. That's actually a huge chunk of your precious time—around 10% of

---

[71] https://www.pbs.org/wgbh/nova/article/parasocial-relationships

your waking hours—but it isn't so huge that it's likely to sabotage your success. Still, if you're happy doing less, that's terrific. (Psychologist Melissa G. Hunt, whose research on social media harms I cited earlier, recommends limiting your use of social media to 30 minutes a day.) As with all Values-Based Time Management, the important thing is to be honest about your needs and preferences.

For those interested in reducing the amount of escapism they do, here are some suggestions:

- **Disconnect part-time**, as discussed in Chapter 6.
- **Use Clocks**. Remember, from Chapter 6, how removing clocks from your workspace can help you work longer? The obverse is also true: if you display a clock prominently while gaming or doing some other escapist activity, that can encourage you to limit that activity. It's best if the clock is either analog (non-digital)[72] or, if digital, a separate device from your phone or PC.
- **Use Timers**, as Gregory Ferenstein (Chapter 6) did. These can help to interrupt the trancelike ludic loop so you can get back to whatever it is you are supposed to be doing. Again, it's better to use either an analog timer or a standalone digital one (like the kitchen timer you're using for your Timed Work Intervals).
- **Have some low-stress and easy forms of replenishing recreation readily available**. It could be some light, fun reading, or a fun hobby like sketching, knitting, baking, beading, or gardening.
- **Be mindful of the opportunity costs**, meaning the more rewarding activities you could be doing if you weren't putting so much time into an escapist activity. (Try not to be one of those people who complains online about all the cool stuff they could be doing if they weren't online so much.)
- **Slow down/stop rushing.** As noted in Chapter 41, rushing is highly stressful, and the stress often increases our need for escapism.
- **Be mindful of apps' negative aspects.** I personally find social media engrossing, entertaining, and informative—but also, often, tedious, repetitive, shallow, stressful, and banal. Staying alert to, and

---

[72] https://www.sciencedirect.com/science/article/pii/S2352853215000140. I've been omitting the titles of the articles I'm citing for brevity's sake, but this one is too good not to share: "The Importance Of Analogue Zeitgebers To Reduce Digital Addictive Tendencies in the 21st Century." A *zeitgeber*, or "time giver" (another one of those great German words), is an environmental cue that helps you stay on a 24-hour cycle. Common ones are: sunlight, social cues (like meal times and bedtimes), watches, and alarm clocks.

mindful of, these kinds of downsides can make it easier for you to resist the temptation to overindulge.

- **Be mindful of apps' political and social context.** Fun as apps, games, videos, television shows, and other distractions are, they were created by corporations specifically to hijack and monetize your time and personal data. Many of the platforms have obvious and well-publicized problems, including privacy violations and an unwillingness to deal with racist, sexist, and otherwise harmful content. Staying mindful of these kinds of political and social concerns, along with those pertaining to your own personal welfare, can help you resist the temptation to overindulge. (Also highly recommended: taking a media studies course that explores issues like these.)

So far, I've been talking mostly about small and incremental changes. But there's one major change you can make that, all by itself, can help you shift a lot of your time into investments. It's called frugality, and I discuss it below.

Getting Frugal

Let's get one potential confusion out of the way immediately: **frugality isn't deprivation, it's intentionality.** Whether you think of your frugality as "living simply" or "minimalism" or "living below my means" or simply "being frugal," it all comes down to buying only what you truly need and want, and not what you don't: for example, the excellent wardrobe, cookware, art supplies, and/or vacations that truly enhance your life, but not the fancy car, furniture, gym membership, and/or electronics that don't. Again, these are just examples: you would make your choices based on your own values and goals—although a new car is literally *the* textbook financial expense, with most cars losing about 25% of their resale value the minute you drive them off the dealer's lot.

Frugality is, of course, a necessity in tough economies where wages are depressed, but it's a wise choice even in better economies. And while many people are frugal out of necessity in their 20s because of low starter salaries, I'm also talking about being frugal later in life when you actually do have some discretionary funds. This kind of "optional frugality" can be powerfully liberating, freeing you to be able to, for instance:

- Work at a job or career you truly want, even if doesn't happen to pay as well as some others.

- Work part time while also pursuing a cherished but low-paid or unpaid arts, activist, travel, caregiving, or other mission.
- Live in the community you really want to live in (because it's safer, more fun, less of a commute, etc.) instead of having to live where it's cheapest.

Frugality can also, obviously, help you to save money, and that, in turn, can help you achieve costly goals such as home ownership, parenthood, business ownership, and retirement.

So let's get frugal! It's good to pinch pennies where you can, but a Good Time Manager (GTM) will take this liberating step to the max using two techniques. The first is **living small**, by which I mean either living in a small space (thus reducing rent, utilities, furniture, cleaning, and other expenses), or sharing your big space with others. This can seem like a bold move if everyone around you is equating success with constantly moving into larger and fancier spaces. But it can really pay off in terms of freeing your time, money, and attention for the things you truly love.

True, it can be hard to find good housemates (if you're opting for that choice). But it helps if you are clear about your needs and desires. I once found two great housemates by posting an ad that included language like this: "Seeking housemates for a three-person household where we don't eat together every day because we're all busy and focused on our projects...a good apartment for someone who wants a nice companionable living situation where you have a lot of privacy and personal space, and that's also on the quiet side." Since all the other posts were for households with lots of communal meals and other socializing, I worried that my ad sounded unfriendly and unwelcoming. But it got me two housemates who were a perfect fit.

The other excellent frugality technique is **thrifting**. Find a good thrift store, resale shop, or consignment shop—meaning one in or near an affluent neighborhood, and that's also spacious, well-lit, and well-organized—and make a point of stopping by once or twice a month. Make a note of which days they put out new merchandise, and befriend the staff, who will sometimes let you know when a good shipment, or an item you need, has come in. Over time, you can acquire a great wardrobe (including jewelry and other accessories), or great kitchenware, sports gear, furniture, decorative pieces, etc., for pennies on the dollar.[73]

---

[73] Politician Cori Bush shares some great thrifting tips here: https://glamour.com/story/cori-bush-secrets-to-thrift-shopping-like-a-pro.

Obviously, you can thrift online, too—and many do that, with gusto. But it can be hard for even well-meaning and honest vendors to describe a used item accurately, and the shipping costs can also be prohibitive. So try to find at least one local store.

Although there are plenty of books, blogs, and other resources devoted to frugality, you really want to have some mentors who live in your community, because they'll be aware of local resources, including food co-ops, public transportation, shared housing opportunities, thrift stores, and inexpensive entertainments. You'll often find them in arts, activist, and co-housing communities. Chances are, in fact, that you already know someone who's rocking their frugality, so figure out who that is and ask them for advice.

45. The Only Thing More Precious Than Your Time

The only thing more precious than your time is your **cognitive capacity**, roughly defined as the amount of information you're able to work with at any given moment. We all have only a limited amount, and everything we are doing, thinking about, and emotionally dealing with uses up some. The goal is to maximize the amount you can devote to your important projects, including, of course, your schoolwork. (Also, your important personal "projects," such as your health and relationships.)

Happily, whenever you remove a time expense or other low-value activity from your schedule, you reclaim not just the time but the cognitive capacity you would have otherwise devoted to it. Free your time, in other words, and you also free your mind.

You also reclaim cognitive capacity when you overcome procrastination and perfectionism, because both, when present, tend to be ongoing sources of worry. Plus, many perfectionist characteristics, including the tendencies to overcomplicate your projects and work with inadequate resources, will also increase your projects' "cognitive overhead."

Excellent self-care, including good nutrition and abundant sleep and exercise, will also help you maximize your available cognitive capacity, and so can planning and routines. (For instance, going to the gym at the same time each day.) When Flaubert famously said, "Be regular and orderly in your life like a bourgeois so that you may be violent and original in your work," he meant that you should preserve your precious time, energy, and cognitive capacity for your important projects.

Recovering, even partially, from a physical or mental illness can help you reclaim some of your cognitive capacity, and so can coping (again, even partially) with a disability, learning difference, or constraining force such as poverty or bias.

Happily, the more cognitive capacity you reclaim, the more you're often able to reclaim. Every time you solve a problem, for instance, you reclaim the cognitive capacity (and time, money, energy, and other resources) you had been using to cope with it, which you can then apply to other problems or projects. This is even better news than it sounds, because **some of our most difficult problems are difficult mainly because we're not setting aside enough time and cognitive capacity to deal with them**. Many who struggle with health and fitness-related goals, for instance, underestimate how much work it takes to change your habits and maintain a healthy lifestyle. Changing your diet, for instance, might require that you read up on nutrition (or consult a nutritionist), figure out a meal plan, research shopping options, and become a more careful shopper and meal preparer. It could also involve seeing a therapist about the roots of any emotional eating you're doing, and changing your routines and even your relationships so that you're mostly hanging out in venues, and with people, that encourage healthy eating.

The first thing to do, therefore, if you have a seemingly intractable problem, is to set aside some time to think, research, and make a plan for solving it. Don't, in other words, make the common mistake of thinking that you should already have a plan before setting the time aside.

Another really excellent way to conserve cognitive capacity is to specialize, a technique I discuss in the next chapter.

Exercise 26

Is there a school, personal, family, or other problem that you've been trying to solve but haven't made much progress on? If so, consider whether you've actually invested sufficient time and cognitive capacity in solving it. ("Solving" means things like research, planning, discussions with mentors, etc., and *not* simply spending time worrying or feeling bad about it.) If you haven't invested sufficient resources, do so now.

Sometimes, when people do this exercise, they realize that the "problem" they've been feeling bad about isn't actually a priority. They haven't been procrastinating, in other words—they've been prioritizing. If that's what you've been doing, that's terrific! Keep in mind, however, that perfectionism can cause us to feel bad even about this. (It's grandiosity plus that whole "confuse success and failure" thing.) If that's the case for you, use Chapter 23's loss-acceptance work to neutralize any residual feelings of guilt or disappointment.

46. Specialize!

Everyone ought to have a specialty in every investment category.

In school, it might be history—and, more specifically, the history of China. (And, even more specifically: 19th-century Chinese history.)

Recreationally, it could be bicycling—and "century" rides rather than time trials or "ultras."

In self-care, it could be yoga or meditation, or even knowing how to dress well on a small budget. (Less spiritual than the first two, perhaps, but still pretty fun and useful!)

Your specialties don't just enhance your life and bring you joy, they're an important part of what defines you. When you specialize in something, you love it, look for reasons to do it, enjoy reading, listening, and talking about it, and seek out—or build—communities devoted to it. (One of the best things about specializing is that, once you start to do it, your supportive community often naturally and organically forms as you find others who share your interest.)

Productivity-wise, specialization is the bomb. It makes your work easier; saves you loads of time, energy, and cognitive capacity; helps you to develop your expertise; maximizes your enjoyment of your work; and makes you a desirable team member and a natural leader. (Because all that expertise and joy attracts others.) In other words, it's a key to both professional and personal success. Remember, from the Introduction, the advice I got from the multimillionaire to, "focus relentlessly on your unique value-add"? He was talking about developing a specialty.

Having a specialty doesn't mean you can't do other things. Our historian is perfectly free to delve into Brazilian history, our bicyclist to play tennis, and our discount fashion maven to meditate. And they'll all benefit from the diversity of experience. Specialization simply means that you make an activity a main focus of your professional or personal efforts and ambitions. Of course, you're free to change your specialties at any time—and you probably will change them over time, as you develop new interests and abilities.

When we specialize, we're usually leveraging our strengths, which is almost always a good idea. And we're also usually having fun! (Because we tend to enjoy what we're good at, and vice versa.) The Germans have yet another great word for the special kind of pleasure you get from doing something you're good at: *funktionslust*. Specialize, and you'll enjoy lots of it.

Sometimes others are better at spotting our specialties than we are. A wise student changed his entire research focus after a mentor heard him speaking about a different topic and pointed out, "You light up when you [talk about] that."[74] You should also take that kind of feedback seriously—and, obviously, it's also very helpful feedback to give someone else.

If you're having trouble choosing a specialty, you might be self-censoring. We sometimes do that when we're afraid of failing at our specialty, or think that others will oppose it. Self-censorship is a form of ambivalence, so see Chapter 24 for solutions. Or, you might be one of those naturally enthusiastic types with many interests—in which case, you'll probably need to make some tough choices and mourn the consequent losses, as discussed in Chapter 23. (Although if you journal about it, the choice might turn out not be so tough: "I can live, for now, without doing A, B, and C, but I *really* don't want to give up D, so I guess D's my specialty.")

Perhaps you're perfectionistically attached to the idea that you can, or should, be able to "do it all." Science fiction writer Robert Heinlein really went for the perfectionist gold with this passage from his novel *Time Enough for Love*:

A human being should be able to change a diaper, plan an invasion, butcher a hog, conn a ship, design a building, write a sonnet, balance accounts, build a wall, set a bone, comfort the dying, take orders, give orders, cooperate, act alone, solve equations, analyze a new problem, pitch manure, program a computer, cook a tasty meal, fight efficiently, die gallantly. Specialization is for insects.

Like most perfectionist harangues, it has a certain superficial appeal, but on closer examination makes no sense. Not only does almost no one need to know most of the things on Heinlein's list—plan an invasion? Really!?—we actually do want our bones set by, buildings designed by, and computers programmed by, specialists. To add to the general ridiculousness, Heinlein

---

[74] https://uvamagazine.org/articles/first_gens_first

gave that speech to his character Lazarus Long, a mutant human who lives thousands of years, and therefore has literally millennia to learn whatever useful and useless things he wants.

But we don't have those millennia: and so, I much prefer Jane Austen's sensible take in *Pride and Prejudice,* when her protagonist, Lizzie Bennet, after hearing the snobbish Mr. Darcy and Miss Bingley rattle off a voluminous list of things a woman must know to be "truly accomplished"—including "a thorough knowledge of music, singing, drawing, dancing, and the modern languages"—tells Darcy, "I'm no longer surprised at your knowing only six accomplished women. I rather wonder now at your knowing any."

You can also, and should, specialize in your personal life. For a life of vividness, intensity, joy, and true camaraderie, organize your free time around the (replenishing) recreational activities you love most, while at the same time investing in the best equipment, classes, excursions, etc. you can afford. If hiking is your passion, for instance, don't just settle for "okay" local hikes. Do your best to take wonderful hikes in amazing places, with excellent equipment, and in the company of other devoted hikers.

Also, specialize when it comes time to helping out friends and relatives. If a friend asks you to help them move, for instance, figure out which part of that process you're best at and help with that. (It could be the packing, the heavy lifting, or the unpacking and organizing of their new home. Or you could be the one who takes care of their dog or cat while it's all going on.) When assisting an ailing or homebound friend or relative, figure out how you can best use your time to support them. Don't trudge to the grocery store or pharmacy, for instance, if you can order online and have everything delivered. And don't mow their lawn or shovel their driveway if you can get a kid to do it cheap.[75] Instead, offer higher-value support, like escorting your loved one to a medical appointment or helping them with their insurance paperwork. Even a fun afternoon of lunch and Rummikub is a better use of your time and energy than running around doing a lot of chores that someone else could have easily handled.

Specialization's Fantastic Yields

Specializing can create many fantastic yields, as Ben's story illustrates:

---

[75] Some nonprofits offer grocery delivery and other services to homebound people— check with the local senior citizens' center and religious organizations, and also the city or county offices for the aged and/or disabled.

Ben's dorm is holding an antiracism event. He's eager to participate but knows the importance of specializing, and so he declines suggestions that he help set up the event, publicize it, or bring food. Instead, since he's a statistics major, he volunteers to create a display illustrating the health, economic, and other impacts of racism.[76]

Since the project is in his area of specialty, it goes pretty well, and he also has a great time doing it. (Or, as great a time as possible, given the depressing subject matter.) He's also very willing to ask for help, and so he winds up collaborating with four very cool people: a sociology-major friend who helps him with his research, a statistics professor who helps him improve his analysis, an artist friend who helps him design and create some really great displays, and an actor friend who helps him improve his verbal presentation. All this specialization and collaboration really pay off, with Ben's display and presentation turning out to be among the event's highlights. Several people tell him he's enhanced their understanding of racism, and the school newspaper even invites him to contribute an article explaining his project.

Beyond all this, Ben has also enhanced his skills in statistics, sociology, graphics, public speaking, and project management.

Afterwards, Ben is careful to follow up with, and thank, his collaborators. They're all happy to have helped, and they all express a willingness to work with him again on other projects. That's great, because Ben now realizes that this project could be expanded into an excellent senior project. (So he now has a head start on that!) Plus, his collaborators have themselves gained some new skills and experience.

So many great outcomes just from specializing! Imagine if, instead, Ben had agreed to do setup, publicity, or food. He would have wound up working much harder, and achieving much less.

Crucial to Ben's success were his abilities to both *decline* unwanted tasks and *delegate* some tasks that weren't his specialty, like the graphic design work. I discuss both of these crucial time-reclamation skills in the next chapter.

---

[76] It's okay, and an act of solidarity, to occasionally take on a non-specialist task, like setting up for, or cleaning up after, an event. But you shouldn't be doing that routinely. Needless to say, this problem, like many time-management problems, is gendered, with women disproportionately being asked to take on "support" tasks like food preparation, childcare, note-taking, and cleanup. Organizations with a sincere social justice mission will make sure that such tasks are distributed equitably along gender and other lines.

47. The Joys of Declining and Delegating

You mostly want to say no to (**"decline"**) any tasks, projects, and other opportunities that aren't your specialty. Even within your specialty, you'll want to decline most of them, keeping only the best—meaning, the most interesting, important, impactful, fun, relevant, strategic, etc.—for yourself. That way, your work itself will keep getting more interesting, important, impactful, fun, relevant, strategic, etc.

Unfortunately, many people have trouble saying no, either because they're afraid of disappointing others or grandiosely think that they should be able to "do it all." If you're one of them, now's the time to break the habit, because saying no isn't just a productivity skill, it's a profound form of self-care *and* one of life's great pleasures. (One of my favorite memes is the one with the woman snug in bed with her cat, both of them propped up on many pillows in television-watching position. Meanwhile, she's saying to someone on the phone, "Yeah, can't come out tonight. Super busy.")[77]

A reluctance to say no can also lead to overgiving, a seriously self-sabotaging behavior I discuss in the next chapter.

So practice saying no. Do it with small and easy requests at first, and then larger and tougher ones, until you're entirely comfortable saying it even to people who pressure you. Also **work on getting past needing a "good reason" to say no** (like a deadline or test). You want to get comfortable saying no for the simple reason that, "it's not a good fit for me."

Delegation, or getting someone else to do part of a task, is the other great time-reclamation skill. It's often thought of narrowly as something

---

[77] See https://anildash.com/2012/07/19/jomo/

bosses do "to" their subordinates, but you can do it more equitably by: (1) delegating tasks to those for whom they are a specialty (as Ben did), and (2) providing lots of support and mentoring while they're working. (Including of nonperfectionism, time management, and the other techniques in this book.)

You can also pay someone to help you. I'm actually a big fan of this if you can afford it. As discussed in Chapter 43, time is more valuable than money, and so it makes sense to use your money to "buy time." (It's also good to help a good person earn their living.) Also, since the person you're paying is hopefully an expert, paying is often the quickest and easiest way to get really great support. Paying someone to tutor you on a difficult subject for an hour or two each week, versus struggling for many more hours on your own, is a great investment, especially given that you're likely to learn more from the tutoring than your solitary struggles. Ditto for paying someone to fix your computer, versus spending days or weeks trying to fix it yourself. (Or worse, trying to live with the malfunction.)

Again, this is all contingent on your having enough cash. I know that many students don't, but I also know that some—and even more employed people—actually do have the ability to pay for services but are reluctant to do that. Please do not make that mistake.

Issues of payment aside, people often have lots of reasons why they "can't" delegate a particular task—or *any* task—including:

- "It's such a little thing that I might as well do it myself." (Nope! Your time is precious.)
- "I can do it better myself." (Even if that's true—and often it's not— it's usually better, from an overall efficiency standpoint, to delegate.)
- "I don't have anyone to delegate to." (Help is abundant. You may have to search a bit to find the right person, but believe me: that person is out there.)

Regardless of how compelling the justification sounds, you'll often find, at the root of a reluctance to delegate, a plain old reluctance to ask for help, as discussed in Chapter 10.

Another reason to embrace both declining and delegating is that, as noted in Chapter 41, success makes you busier. Each of your professional and personal accomplishments is likely to result in yet more invitations, ideas, projects, potential partnerships, and other opportunities arriving at your door. Don't get me wrong: this ongoing flood of opportunities is a great problem to have! But it's still a problem. Say "yes" to even just a few too many and you'll quickly run aground. So yeah: you want to get *entirely* comfortable declining and delegating all but the very best that's offered to you.

A good delegator must also be a good manager. Bad managers throw a task at someone and don't want to hear from them again until it's completed. Good managers, in contrast, take as much time as needed to explain things fully at the beginning of the project; then check in with their helper regularly while the work is underway. And after the project is done, they offer feedback.

Good delegators are also kind and patient and otherwise nonperfectionist.

So work to become a frequent decliner and delegator. Of course, if you do, then sooner or later you'll either decline a task you should have taken on, or delegate a task to the wrong person. These are almost inevitable mistakes, and are *not* a reason to stop declining and delegating, but rather to work on improving your process. (And also your ability to tolerate "failure," see Chapter 22.)

48. The Perils of Overgiving

Overgiving is when you frequently take on tasks, projects, relationships, and other commitments you should decline. At the very least, it's a pernicious form of Quasiproductive Procrastination. But often it's even worse than that. Here's what can happen when you overgive at your job, or to a group you belong to, or to a person:

- You're so busy doing their stuff that you don't have time to do your own.
- You're stressed, exhausted, and resentful.
- You're possibly also broke—because many overgivers are also too free with their money.
- Dangerously, you attract the wrong people: those looking, consciously or subconsciously, for someone to exploit.

While many overgivers are motivated by a sincere desire to help, the problem is also often rooted in perfectionism ("I should be able to do it all!") and an inability to say no. Some may also get an ego boost from being a "problem solver," "go-to person," or even—although they'd never say this word aloud—"savior." (Grandiose much?) Many fall into the trap of **workaholism**, which psychologists characterize as an addictive/escapist behavior linked to stress, depression, ill health, and impaired personal relationships. Workaholics may work long hours, but their accomplishments often fall short, both because their underlying motivation is escape (versus effectiveness or efficiency), and because their lack of life balance is sabotaging.

Sadly, many organizations encourage and exploit people's tendency to overgive. Many health, educational, and community organizations are seriously understaffed, thus forcing their employees to constantly have to choose between maintaining their own healthy boundaries, or meeting the legitimate, and often serious, needs of their patients, students, or clients. Many social justice organizations are likewise happy to exploit activists' guilt over taking any time off from fixing society's urgent problems. (It's especially shameful when organizations with a social justice mission exploit workers or volunteers.)

The solutions to overgiving are to work on your perfectionism, make sure you're doing things for the right motives, learn to say "no" and delegate, and consult a counselor if the problem persists. Also, find great mentors and learn from them. Many experienced health care workers, teachers, caregivers, and other helpers have learned how to best serve their clienteles while also maintaining healthy—or, as healthy as possible— boundaries, and many experienced activists, as noted in Chapter 43, see self-care and life balance as foundational. Finally, time budgeting (Chapter 49) and scheduling (Chapter 50) can also be a big help. Similar to chores, overgiving often expands to fill any available time, but a budget and schedule can help prevent that.

Operating Principles are also useful for overcoming overgiving, as well as for generally managing your time, relationships, and other priorities. An operating principle is a short, easily-remembered mantra or "rule to live by" that you use to make better decisions, especially under pressure. Here are three school-related examples:

- "Except for when someone is having a true emergency, classes and schoolwork *always* come first."
- "On weeknights I'm in bed by 1:00 a.m.—*no exceptions*."
- "I *always* shut off my phone while working."

And three more general ones:

- "Perfectionism is *always* a dead end, so I *never* go there."
- "With *very* limited exceptions, I *only* volunteer to help people when I can do so using my specialties."
- "When I'm in conflict with someone, I *always* respond with kindness."

The intensifiers—"always," "no exceptions," "never," "very," and "only"—are there to remind you to adhere to the operating principle even when you're tempted not to. It's not that you can never ignore an operating principle, it's just that you need a damn good reason for doing so. (You can also always revise or eliminate an operating principle if it's not working for you.)

You come up with your operating principles by researching your field's best practices, and also by observing your mentors and having discussions with them. You can also figure them out as you go along. Many Good Time Managers (GTMs), for instance, adopt the operating principle, "If someone I'm working with is unreliable or otherwise difficult, I end my work with them as soon as possible and *never* work with them again," after having gotten mired in a bad collaboration. And many performers adopt an operating principle similar to, "I *never* work for free, no matter how worthy or prominent the event is," after having been burned once too often by promises of "payment" in exposure or publicity that didn't pan out. (They might make an exception for one charity or cause that they especially care about.)

Overcoming Email/Collaborative Software Overload and Social Media Overload

> **Note:** You might mostly be sending texts now, so this discussion might not seem applicable. But you'll probably wind up sending more emails and participating in more collaborative discussions once you start your career.

Email and collaborative software are tricky, from a productivity standpoint, for several reasons:

- They combine the spontaneity of verbal communication with the permanence of written communication.
- The lack of nonverbal content, like vocal tone and body language, can cause confusion and misinterpretation.
- We email and message all kinds of people for all kinds of reasons, so it's hard to come up with a set of general principles.
- We get so many emails and messages that if we overwork each one even just a tiny bit, it can still add up to a lot of misused time.

Email/collaborative software overload can also be at least partly an overgiving problem, because many people spend too much time on their emails for fear of looking bad or disappointing others.

The solutions are the same as for general overgiving—reduce your perfectionism, understand your motives, and develop some operating principles. In addition:

- Reply tersely. Not every decision requires an explanation, and it's often when we're explaining, or trying to, that things get out of hand. Explanations can quickly turn into essays, and feeling like you have to write an essay—especially when you didn't mean to, don't need to, and don't want to—can lead to frustration and procrastination. Even if we do, finally, manage to get the email essay out, our long explanation can induce the other person to respond with an equally long explanation of their own, which adds still more unnecessary work.

  Instead of writing long explanations, therefore, try sending emails like this: "OK – thanks." and "Yes – please let me know if you have questions." And—as per the last chapter—"It's not a good fit for me, but thanks for asking." (In cases where you feel that an explanation is truly required, it's often quicker to communicate verbally.)

- Abstain from replying. Not every email requires a response.

- Learn from mentors. Many successful professionals have techniques for keeping their emails and messaging under control. They might, for instance, set a strict time limit on their daily email/collaborative software use, which encourages them to be efficient. Or they might affix a signature line to all their outgoing messages letting correspondents know that not all messages will be answered. Speaking of which...

- Let the technology do its thing. Autoresponders can be set up to automatically reply to routine queries. (This also helps ensure an accurate and consistent response.) Filters can be set up to separate out urgent from nonurgent emails—and maybe you only check the "nonurgent" folder once or twice a week. Customizing your email to boost your efficiency is an excellent time investment that can yield an incredible return over the years, so take as much time as you need to do it. (Get help if you need to.)

Overuse of **social media** is also often at least partly an overgiving problem. If you're sticking with a boring, stressful, or otherwise unproductive conversation (or platform) because others will be hurt or angry if you leave, that's overgiving. Ask yourself, therefore, whether you're giving too much of your precious time, energy, and cognitive capacity to online people, conversations, topics, groups, and platforms that aren't giving you much back. If the answer's yes, then leave as soon as you can.

About Boundaries

There are several things you need to know about interpersonal boundaries, from a time-management perspective:

(1) The important "boundary" isn't between you and the other person but within you. It's how you define your relationship with that person, and especially your obligations and responsibilities to them.

(2) You should make conscious choices about your boundaries. Do this even in relationships with a lot of personal and societal expectations, such as those with family members. Don't, in other words, automatically buy into clichés or traditions about how you're supposed to behave.

(3) It's your responsibility to state your needs. Often, others don't even know that there's a problem until we tell them—and when we do, they often surprise us with their supportiveness. ("Oh, so you need to skip some of the holiday events so you can finish your paper? No problem!") Sooner or later, however, you'll probably encounter someone who isn't so supportive, which brings us to...

(4) You should distance yourself from the unsupportive people. And give serious thought as to whether you even want them in your life. (If they're routinely unsupportive, you probably don't.)

These kinds of decisions—and the ensuing conversations—can be among the most difficult and unpleasant aspects of time management. But defending your boundaries isn't just an essential life skill, it's a profound form of self-care and self-preservation. If you find yourself struggling with this, it might also help to remember that, **in a world filled with Poor Time Managers (PTMs)—not to mention, the occasional clueless or callous person—disappointing people is a sign you're doing your time management right.**

Also remember that GTMs are problem-solvers and optimizers who don't settle for partial solutions. They also tend to be **clear on the long-term consequences of their actions**—or, perhaps more to the point, *in*-actions. So, while a PTM might be reluctant to disappoint someone by declining an offer, "impose" on them by delegating, or "upset" them by defending their boundaries, a GTM clearly sees the consequences of being reticent, and this motivates them to act.

Exercise 27

You've already sent out some fun Intentionally Erroneous Emails (Exercise 11) to help with your perfectionism. Now it's time to send out some **Intentionally Terse Emails** to help with your overgiving, as per the discussion in this chapter. So go ahead and do that!

Exercise 28

Start creating your lists of professional and personal operating principles. Write down a few you're already living by, and store the list somewhere convenient so that you can review and edit it frequently. Especially when something doesn't go as planned, think of what you might have done differently, and see if you can turn that insight into an operating principle.

Okay, we're done discussing the ideas underlying time management! On to the process itself...

49. Budgeting Your Time

As already noted, you need to budget, schedule, and (at least for a while) track your time. We discuss budgeting in this chapter, and scheduling and tracking in the next.

Budgeting is the act of defining your priorities, and determining how much time, each week, you'll devote to each. Sounds simple, but, as you will see, it can involve some tough choices and deep thought. Here's how you do it:

(1) Start by acknowledging that sleep deprivation isn't a valid time-management strategy.[78] Then, admit to how much sleep you truly need each night, and commit to getting that sleep. (For most of us, that will be around seven or eight hours.) Then, subtract your week's total sleep from 168, the total number of hours in a week. If you need seven hours of sleep a night, for instance, that's 49 hours of sleep a week, leaving 119 hours a week of "awake" time. That may sound like a lot, but just wait...

(2) Create your ideal weekly time budget. That's the budget you would use if you had unlimited time each week. We start with your ideal budget so that you can look at your time with fresh eyes, and make sure that the budget you come up with reflects your true priorities. This is the step in the time-management process where you go wild! If you dream of taking five classes, participating in three extracurricular activities each week, and going to the gym every day—all while partying every night *and* working a 20-hour-a-week job—here's the place to record it.

---

[78] If this article doesn't convince you to get enough sleep, I don't know what will: www.theguardian.com/lifeandstyle/2019/feb/09/best-thing-you-can-do-for-your-health-sleep-well. I especially like the author's call to, "**Reclaim our right** to a full night of sleep, without embarrassment or the terrible stigma of laziness." (Emphasis mine.)

Get detailed! List your classes, other major projects, and commitments individually. **Budget in 15-minute increments**—meaning that every activity should be allotted some multiple of 15 minutes. It's easiest to do all this on a spreadsheet template, and I provide one at www.hillaryrettig.com.

Some tips:

- Remember that in Values-Based Time Management we manage our personal as well as our professional time (Chapter 41). You should therefore be sure to include your personal activities and projects in your budget and, later, your schedule and tracking.

- A general rule of thumb is that **college professors assign two hours of homework for every hour of classroom time.** But be flexible: some of your classes will probably require more or less time. (If you don't know how much time you should be putting into your homework, ask your professor.)

- Since school is currently your professional priority, any "optional" study sessions and test prep sessions should also be priorities. Schedule them in.

- Be sure to budget at least some time for all the Investment Categories listed in Chapter 43.

- Be sure to include travel and prep time for each activity. For example, when budgeting for your workout, include the time it takes to travel to and from the gym, change into your workout clothes before your workout, and shower and dress after it.

- For biweekly, monthly, and other non-weekly commitments, just budget the average weekly time. (A four-hour monthly appointment would be budgeted for an hour a week.) Your schedule won't work out exactly, but doing this works well enough—especially if you underschedule, see below—and is *much* easier than trying to work out a "perfect" budget that accounts for every minute.

When you're done, add up the hours per week. If you're like most people, your ideal time budget will come in at 150 to 200 hours per week. Time to cut back...

(3) Eliminate as many of your time expenses from your budget as you can. I offered some suggestions for this—like quitting unwanted activities and relationships, doubling up with roommates or friends for chores, cutting back on escapism, and getting frugal—back in Chapter 44. But maybe you can come up with some other ideas. Be ruthless! The goal—

which no one actually ever achieves but is still worth aiming for—is zero time expenses, with all your time going to investments.

If you can't eliminate an expense entirely, "trim" it. (Recalling that Good Time Managers value small increments of their precious time.) If you can cut 15 minutes from an expense, you absolutely should do that.

When you're done eliminating and trimming expenses, add up all your commitments again. Hopefully, you're now much closer to 119 hours.

(4) Sort your investments into three groups: high-, medium-, and low-priority. High-priority investments are those you must do and those you really want to do. Low-priority ones are the ones you could live without. The medium-priority ones will be somewhere in the middle. And within each of those groups...

(5) Rank your investments from most to least important.
Yes, your rankings will probably be somewhat arbitrary and imprecise, but in the process of doing this, you'll give serious thought to, and make tough decisions about, what's truly important to you. **A major purpose of time management is to encourage yourself to make these kinds of difficult, yet vital, decisions consciously and deliberately in advance, instead of impulsively during a scheduling conflict, the way Poor Time Managers do.** I think you know what's coming next...

(6) Eliminate as many of the low-priority investments from your time budget as you can. And any that you can't eliminate, trim as much as you can. Be careful not to eliminate any of the investment *categories* from your budget, however. It's important to do at least some self-care, planning and management, etc. every week.

When you're done eliminating and trimming your low-value investments, add up all your commitments again. Probably, you're now even closer to 119 hours, but still not there. So now it's time to...

(7) Eliminate, or trim, your medium-priority investments. This is the point at which budgeting can get really tricky, because now you're cutting back on stuff you really want to be doing. You could be asking yourself to give up an exciting extracurricular project, or a couple of fun workouts a week, or an extra night or two of socializing. But (you remind yourself) productivity work and time management are all about getting real. Pretending you have time to do something when you really don't is *not* an option.

Postponing is sometimes an option. I once knew someone who was trying to write her thesis at the same time she was working full-time *and* training for a marathon. Needless to say, she wasn't making much progress. "Thesis now, marathon later," I suggested. Presto! Progress on thesis!

251

You're probably even closer to your 119 hours now. But you're probably not quite there (because there are so many investments that need to be squeezed into the week). So now it's time to...

(8) Trim your high-priority investments. Now, budgeting becomes an almost Buddhist discipline, forcing you to acknowledge and accept what may be life's most painful reality, our tragically limited amount of time. It will probably help if you take some time to mourn your losses, as discussed in Chapter 23; also, if you remember that you're making these sacrifices for the best possible reason: your personal liberation. **Please remember, too, that, when all is said and done, you probably will have enough time to get done everything you *need* to get done, and even much of what you *want* to get done, if you use your time well.** GTMs derive some solace and motivation from that truth, but it's often lost on the poor PTMs, who remain in stubborn denial about both their time constraints and the potential of time management to mitigate their losses. So, they struggle on under the delusion that if they could only somehow, magically, "get their act together," they'd be able to "do it all."

GTMs also know that the goal isn't to squeeze every possible activity into our time budget but, rather, to eliminate as many of the inessential and less-essential activities as possible, so that we have abundant time for the essentials. Or, to put it another way: **an important time management strategy is to not have too many activities to manage in the first place**. Sure, you can reclaim little bits of your time here and there: by walking to class, for instance (thus getting in some exercise), or doing some schoolwork while you eat lunch. These kinds of habits are absolutely worth cultivating, so long as you don't go overboard. (Remember: if it feels stressful or deprivational, you've crossed the line into perfectionism.) You also want to specialize, decline, delegate, and use Operating Principles as much as possible. While helpful, however, these are not definitive solutions, the way frugality (Chapter 44) and radically emptying out your schedule are.

(9) When you arrive at your goal (e.g., 119 hours), **take a moment to stop and appreciate the achievement.** It's a meaningful one.

But you're not quite done yet...

The Genius of Underscheduling

Remember how, in Chapter 41, Sophie was careful not to schedule a social lunch on the same day she had a test? She obviously understands the importance of **underscheduling**, which you accomplish by: (a) allocating generous time for your day's important activities, and (b) leaving a few unscheduled hours in your weekly schedule. Underscheduling helps you to accommodate both the unexpected tasks, like when you need to help a friend or stranger, and the irregular (biweekly, monthly, etc.) ones.

PTMs, sadly, resist doing it. Chronically behind in their work and other obligations, perfectionistically attached to suffering and pressure, and grandiosely refusing to accept their time limitations—not to mention, the laws of physics (you can't be in two places at once)—they have a strong compulsion to schedule every single moment of their lives.

With all that in mind, let's return to our budgeting process:

(10) Cut and trim some more. In particular, see if you've eliminated as many time expenses and low-value investments as possible. A good goal to aim for would be anywhere from three to five unscheduled hours per week.

Finally, we have a vitally important step that many people forget...

(11) Show your time budget to your mentor(s). (In this case, perhaps, your advisor.) And ask the all-important question, "Am I using my time in the right way to achieve my goals?" This will not only get you some incredibly valuable feedback, it will show your mentor that you're really on the ball.

Sample Time Budget

Table V, below, shows a sample time budget for a very busy undergraduate who not only goes to school full-time but has a job (or serious athletic or arts commitment) and also wants to maintain a good social life. It's also realistic in terms of the human need for daily down time and escapism.

Table V: Sample Time Budget for a Full-Time Student

Activity	Hrs/Week*	Notes
Classes	18	16 hours in class, plus 2 hours of travel time.
Homework	32	Rule of thumb: 2 hours of homework for every hour of class time.
Extracurricular	12	E.g., a job, athletic team, arts group, activist group, etc.
Self-Care	14.5	An hour per day for personal grooming and other personal care, plus 7.5 hours a week for exercise (e.g., three gym sessions or yoga classes).
Meals	14	A half-hour for all breakfasts and lunches, and a full hour for all dinners (includes cooking and cleanup time).

Activity	Hrs/Week*	Notes
Socializing/ Recreation	7	Two or three recreational events per week (in addition to any recreation you're doing during other activities, such as meals or extracurricular activities).
Escapism	10.5	1.5 hours per day for social media, gaming, television, etc. (See Chapter 44.)
Errands	4	Laundry, shopping, cleaning, etc. and Chores
Activism/ Community Work	2	Whichever cause you care most about. (Could be a three-hour meeting or event every two weeks, plus some emails. If you're already doing serious activism under the "Extracurricular Activity" category above, then you can allocate this time elsewhere.)
Planning/ Management	2	Includes research and meetings with career advisors, etc. Also reviewing the week's time use—see next chapter.
Total	116	(Out of 119 hours total = underscheduling!)

*All time estimates include commuting and preparation time.

This student obviously has a full schedule, which includes not just a full course load but a significant job or other extracurricular commitment. Their schedule also includes a decent amount of time for recreation and socializing (seven hours each week for dinners and another seven for recreational events), and doesn't neglect activism or planning. It also allows 1.5 hours each day for social media, gaming, television, and other escapism, and a decent 14.5 hours each week for self-care. Still, it's a bit too jammed in my view. Many students with jobs must work more than 12 hours a week to pay the bills, and some athletes, performers, and others with a serious extracurricular commitment would also have to budget more than 12 hours a week for that. Also, many students have a weekly counseling or medical appointment that could easily take up two hours a week, including commute. Budgeting for only one hour of escapism a day—thereby freeing up a valuable 3.5 hours per week for these kinds of priorities—might be one solution, and you might also be able to trim the Errands category to gain an additional hour per week.

Please let this sample time budget serve as a guide for you as you create your own in Exercise 29.

Exercise 29

Go ahead and create your own Time Budget using the process outlined in this chapter. Take your time and pay attention to your feelings, especially while cutting and trimming activities. If you feel sad or conflicted about not being able to do everything you'd like, that probably means you're doing your budgeting right! Please use the solutions discussed above and in Chapter 23 to process those feelings.

50. Scheduling and Tracking Your Time

After finishing your Time Budget, your next step is to create a weekly **schedule**. Download a form for this from www.hillaryrettig.com, or photocopy a page from a daily planner. Then use this process:

1. First, fill in your **obligatory/fixed commitments**: classes, job, medical/counseling appointments, etc.
2. Figure out when, during the day, you're at your **highest energy,** and schedule your study time then. Also, if you have any time left over, schedule your exercise and any other priorities you find challenging or might be tempted to skip. Keep this time "sacred" for those activities, doing your best to never, ever schedule anything else during it.
3. As much as possible, schedule your homework and other important tasks in **chunks** of an hour or more. You need these chunks because: (a) interruptions are "expensive" time-wise (as discussed in Chapter 5), (b) it can take a while to immerse ourselves in a task—although nonperfectionism can help to reduce that immersion time a lot, and (c) because tough creative and intellectual challenges usually require sustained focus and concentration.
4. Set up **routines**—meaning that, whenever possible, try to do the same thing at the same time and in the same place each day. This sounds boring, but (as discussed in Chapter 45) it simplifies your life and helps you conserve your precious time, energy, and cognitive capacity.

5. Bonus points, as always, if you **show your schedule to your advisor or another mentor** and ask for feedback.

Tracking

Once you've developed your schedule, you should start using it. And for a while, at least, you should also track your time use. Tracking trains you to be mindful of your time use, thus making it easier for you to stick to your schedule. Here's how to do it:

1. **Download the tracking form** from www.hillaryrettig.com. Or create your own from a spreadsheet. It should be a grid, with columns for Monday through Sunday, and a row for each of your activities, including your personal ones. Also, a row to record the amount of procrastination you do each day—Stay cool! No judgments or punishments here!—and other rows to record the time you wake up and go to bed each day. Finally, there should be a Total box at the end of every column and row, and a box for recording Notes at the end of each row, after the Total.

2. **Keep the sheet with you**, in either electronic or printed form, as you go through your day.

3. *Every 15 minutes*, **put a check mark on the activity you just worked on.** So, if you do two hours of math homework on Monday, you'll have entered eight check marks in the "Monday/Math" box. You track every 15 minutes for two important reasons: (a) it's easy to forget what you've done, even an hour later, and (b) frequent check-ins keep you alert and mindful of your time use, thus helping you to stay on schedule.

4. **Record any time you spend procrastinating.** Record what kind of procrastination you did, and why you did it, in the Notes box.

5. Also **record your daily wake-up and go-to-bed times.** It's best, from the standpoint of productivity, to wake up and go to bed at the same time most days, so this is how you track that. Also, you can use this data to see how sleep deprivation affects your productivity.

6. On Day 5 of your week, **check for rows with few or no checkmarks**—meaning, tasks you've skimped on, or maybe skipped entirely. Be sure to devote some time to those.

7. At the end of the week, **add up all the horizontal and vertical totals** and record those in the appropriate boxes.

8. **Analyze the results and, if needed, make a plan to do better next week.** First, take a moment to appreciate the times you did

stick to your schedule, and the work you did get done. Then *nonper-fectionistically* (without judgments or punishments) look at the times you didn't stick to your schedule and see if you can figure out how to resolve the obstacles that caused you to derail. (Do that systematically using Chapter 9's Obstacle Identification and Resolution technique.) Also, if needed, tweak your budget and schedule so that they better fit the realities of your time use. (They're "living" documents that you should feel free to change at any time as your needs, situation, and priorities change.)

9. **Repeat** the entire process the following week.

10. Some people track for just a couple of weeks after starting with a new schedule, just to get used to it. Others track for their whole career—or beyond, if they're also tracking their personal time. And some track just in a few areas. (I continue to track my writing and exercise times, just to make sure that, no matter what else is happening in my life, those crucial tasks get done.) Do whatever works for you.

So that's Values-Based Time Management! Like all the work in this book, you want to take it "to the max." The harder you rock it, the more benefit you'll receive from it.

Don't settle for being a Good Time Manager, in other words, when you can be a *Great* Time Manager!

Exercise 30

Create a weekly schedule from Exercise 29's Time Budget, then track your time for at least a couple of weeks. Pay particular attention to your stress level and emotions during that time. Hopefully, as you improve at using your time, you'll also get happier and less stressed. Paying attention to those kinds of positive changes can help you to stay motivated to continue the practice.

CONCLUSION

Liberating Yourself and the World

A funny thing happens to a lot of people after they graduate from college: they start to settle.

They settle for jobs they don't want, but that provide a paycheck.

For relationships that bore or stress them, but that they can't bring themselves to end.

For towns they don't like, because moving's a hassle.

And for governments and other systems that neglect and exploit them because, "It's always been that way" or, "What can one person do?"

You can watch it happen and, unfortunately, probably will. Decade after decade, you'll see more and more of your classmates "settle down" and, in some cases, get stuck.

Please don't let that happen to you.

Now, don't get me wrong: there's no such thing as a perfect situation, and so everyone does eventually have to settle, sooner or later. Difficult times tend to require even more settling than usual, moreover—and, as noted in the Introduction, you are graduating at an *exceptionally* difficult time. (In the midst of an historically terrible economy and job market, not to mention multiple serious political, ecological, and other crises.) So don't feel bad about any decisions you need to make, even if they're not the ones you'd make if, say, jobs were more abundant and secure, or the political situation less concerning.

At the same time, however, don't settle preemptively, or more than you have to. Out there, somewhere, are a career, place, lifestyle, and relationships that will make you happy—or, at least, happier than the alternatives. These are definitely worth working toward and, if necessary, fighting for. (And as my own story in the Introduction illustrates, even if you happen to be reading this in your late 20s or 30s, or even in your 40s or beyond, it's not too late to start!)

Your life has value and meaning—and not just to you, but the rest of us. You may be just one small thread in the vast tapestry that we call life, but you matter. If most of the threads in our tapestry shine, then it will be a vibrant work of beauty. If most don't, then the tapestry—and life itself—will be dull. Best of all, you already have most of what you need to shine. Nonperfectionism, the Joyful Dance, Values-Based Time Management, and the other techniques in this book will take you far, especially if you use them not just for your work but your play, relationships, and other important areas of your life. And let's add **authenticity** to your list of foundational values. By that I mean that the trajectory of your life, and of your individual days, should align as much as possible with your true goals, values, needs, and desires. Put another way: **you should mostly be doing the things you want to be doing, in the company of those with whom you'd mostly like to be doing them.** (As discussed in Chapter 46, if you focus on the things you love, the community often naturally follows.)

Authenticity isn't a goal so much as a path. You walk it by listening to, and then acting on, that quiet inner voice that tells you what's working and not working for you. Also, you want to cherish and nurture your vision of the "ideal" career and life you'd like to have. Sure—you don't want to perfectionistically cling to that vision too tightly, or get upset when you fall short of achieving aspects of it. But it should always be there in the background of your thoughts, informing, guiding, and inspiring you. Writer Neil Gaiman offered a terrific example of this in a commencement speech he gave at the University of the Arts:

> Something that worked for me was imagining that where I wanted to be—an author, primarily of fiction, making good books, making good comics and supporting myself through my words—was a mountain. A distant mountain. My goal.
>
> And I knew that as long as I kept walking towards the mountain I would be all right. And when I truly was not sure what to do, I could stop, and think about whether it was taking me towards or away from the mountain. I said no to editorial jobs on magazines, proper jobs that would have paid proper money, because I knew that, attractive though they were, for me they would have been walking away from the mountain.[79]

---

[79] https://www.uarts.edu/neil-gaiman-keynote-address-2012

Do your best to stay on the path, even during—especially during—difficult times. Take bold steps toward your destination when you can, and small steps when you can't. Enjoy the successes, and persevere through the setbacks. And remember that it's your community, more than any other single factor, that will determine your success. Surround yourself with supporters, mentors, and encouragers, and they'll likely accelerate your progress. But surround yourself with naysayers, cynics, and *dis*couragers, and you'll likely stall.

Similarly, always strive to surround yourself with empowered and effective people, including Good Time Managers, since that will tend to maximize your own empowerment and effectiveness. The goal, really, is to **"live among the wise,"** as the Buddha put it—and it's even more important to do that online than off, so that you can avoid, as much as possible, social media's rampant perfectionism and other toxicities.

Likewise, be selective in the media you consume. We all have our need for escapism, but, as much as possible, your "inputs" should delight and inspire you, not bore you or drag you down.

Speaking of community, empowered and authentic people seek happiness, health and success not just for themselves but others. That's partly because they want to "pay it forward" for help they themselves received and/or privilege they benefited from, and partly because they know that you can't be truly happy or successful while those around you are suffering. And it's also because, on a deeper level, having your authentic needs met gives you the intellectual and emotional capacity to respond to others' needs with kindness, generosity, and care. Empowered and authentic people, in other words, do their best to see others not merely as competitors, or exploitable resources, or obstacles to their own (or society's) "progress," but as the unique and valuable individuals they are—and, yes, that absolutely does include the precious nonhumans with whom we share the planet.

All of which brings us to my final piece of advice: *trust*.

Trust yourself: your skills, resources, capacities, and commitment. Trust that you *are* enough and *have* enough to succeed, especially if you use the techniques in this book to minimize your perfectionism, unmanaged time, and other barriers. (As I've noted earlier, you may not actually have enough if you are being seriously disempowered by poverty, bigotry, violence, and/or other conditions, but it's even more important, in such situations, to use the techniques I've discussed to reclaim whatever power you can.)

Trust that you can have a satisfying, fulfilling, and, at least sometimes, joyful life and career. They may not be exactly the life and career you are currently envisioning—possibly not even close. But any path built on empowerment and authenticity will have its substantial rewards. Trust the path.

Trust, also, your community. You are surrounded by visionary and powerful teachers, healers, creators, communicators, and seekers after equality and justice in all their forms. Find them, and live and work as much as possible among them.

Trust that, whenever you find yourself needing help, it will be there. (Help is, in fact, abundant.)

Most of all, trust in the possibility of positive growth and change, both for individuals and societies, because—despite the easy, and often loud, pessimism of the doom-mongers—the evidence for that is all around us.

In fact, you're holding a bit of that evidence in your hands right now.

My own journey brought me to writing this book, and your own journey brought you to reading it. I am grateful for both of our journeys and wish you well, with all my heart, as you continue on yours.

Hillary Rettig
Kalamazoo, MI
September 2021

APPENDICES

CAREER AND LIFE STRATEGIES

Appendix 1: Creating the Career You Really Want

Note: As I mentioned way back in the Introduction, the job market for college graduates is currently (Summer 2021) historically weak. Moreover, some graduates, as always, will face additional barriers due to poverty, discrimination, or other factors. The techniques outlined in this Appendix obviously can't entirely neutralize, or compensate for, these kinds of structural barriers. But they should make it easier for you, despite whatever barriers you're facing, to look for work.

And they should also boost your odds of success.

Many people will tell you to be realistic when planning your career, but I think you should aim sky high. That's because some people actually do manage to achieve their dream career—and even if you're not one of the lucky ones, you'll probably get a better outcome aiming high than if you settle right out of the gate.

Obviously, it's not enough to simply want a career: you have to plan and prepare for it. "In dreams begin responsibilities," as the Irish poet William Butler Yeats said. The chief requirement for any stellar career is probably connections, and you may feel like you don't have any. But your professors can be your first, and you can use the techniques in this chapter and the rest of this Appendix to find others.

Stellar careers also often require money for things like specialized training or to start a small business. While this absolutely can be an impediment, I wouldn't assume that it's a terminal one. Many jobs offer a tuition-reimbursement benefit that you can use to get your training, for instance, and there are also nonprofit business development organizations that can either provide you with a microloan or help you approach banks, investors, and other funding sources. The important things are that you plan (see below) and consult lots of mentors.

So go for your dream job! Here's a six-step process that will help you get started:

(1) Research. Read at least two years of back issues of your field's main trade magazine—meaning, the magazine most people in your field go to for news, articles, updates, trends, personnel announcements, etc. A professor or librarian can tell you what it is, and your school library should have a subscription. Read the new issues as they come out, and also follow two or three of your field's leading blogs or other social media accounts. (They'll be mentioned in the magazine.) The goal is to learn your field's history and trends, and also the major problems that everyone is trying to solve: information that can help you to figure out your entry point and strategy. (If your field is globalizing, for instance, your bilingual/bicultural skills might be an asset.) This research can also help you to figure out how best to present your professional specialty (Chapter 46) to potential employers.

Don't forget to work with your college's career center during this and every phase of your career hunt. Along with helping you with research and planning, they can also help you to improve your resume-writing and interviewing skills. They might even be able to connect you with alumni in your field who can provide you with advice and referrals. (If they don't, then you should research those alumni yourself and reach out to them: see Appendix 3, below.)

(2) Plan. A few pages ought to do it. (Yeah, you should Joyfully Dance through this project, too. The Joyful Dance isn't just for schoolwork.) Start with where you'd like to be in 20 years and then work backward in five-year intervals (20, 15, 10, and five years). For each of those milestones, list your career goals, the major steps it will take to achieve them, and the major investments (e.g., of time and money) you'll need to make.

When you reach the five-year mark, switch to annual planning (years one through five), still covering the same information.

As part of this process, you should also start to problem-solve around your anticipated obstacles—lack of contacts, money, etc.—while, at the same time, figuring out just how much you're willing to work and sacrifice to achieve your goal. Generally speaking, the higher you aim, the more sacrifices you'll need to make. People seeking to be at the top of many fields, for instance, often must move to an area that's a hub for that field. And would-be entrepreneurs often have to commit to living on a low income for many years while they're building their business. It's a great sign if you don't actually see the needed sacrifices as being too big—or as sacrifices at all, compared with the joy of following your dream. Conversely, if the sacrifices seem huge, that might be a sign that you should choose a different path.

Because of the sacrifice, or for other reasons entirely, you may decide, in the process of doing all this research and planning, that you don't actually want to pursue this particular career. That's fine—and an excellent result, really. (Far better to discover this "on paper" than in real life.) Start researching and planning for a career you're more interested in. Or, if you're having trouble choosing, try some of Chapter 24's solutions to ambivalence, and also ask your college's career center for help.

(3) Show your plan to your mentors. Ask for their feedback. This should gain you not just useful information and perspective, but your mentors' respect, because mentors know that a willingness to plan—and, especially, to have one's plan critiqued—is a hallmark of a serious person. When speaking to mentors, don't forget to ask these two important network-building questions: (1) "Do you know anyone who can help me with task X?," and (2) "Is there anyone else you know who could give me some good feedback on my plan?"

More on mentors in Appendix 3.

(4) Develop some social media chops. Employers in all fields crave employees with social media expertise, and often hire young people specifically to help with this. So familiarize yourself with the main social media platforms *as they are used by successful companies and professionals in your field.* Be prepared to discuss your knowledge of this during interviews (with specific examples, especially about how social media helped create a success or was used to solve a problem). Also, systematically (meaning, in an organized or structured way) study at least one platform, so that you know how to do things on it that most users can't. Play to your strengths: if you like writing, choose a text-based platform, and if you're more visual, choose an image-based one.

(5) Participate. Join your field's main trade association. The trade magazine will tell you what that is, or you can ask a professor. Avoid organizations whose primary focus is lobbying or providing insurance: your goals are professional development and networking, so look for one that offers lots of meetings, classes, networking opportunities, etc. Memberships can be expensive, so ask about a student rate or discount.

Once you've joined, diligently read the organization's newsletter. Attend whatever local meetings you can plus, if possible, the annual national or international meeting. (Ask both the organization and your school for a scholarship or travel stipend.) If the organization has a student subgroup, join it and be active in it.

After you graduate, join the main (non-student) group and volunteer in a *visible* position, like on the association's blog or an event-planning committee.

(6) When you're ready, **start applying for work.** If you've followed the above steps, you should be a much stronger candidate, and already possibly on potential employers' radar. Check out my free ebook *It's Not You, It's Your Strategy* for a good job-search strategy. (Download English and Spanish versions at www.hillaryrettig.com.)

(7) Especially early in your career, **look for jobs that will allow you to grow your skills, get great mentoring, and make great connections.** (Title and salary are less important, in other words.) And throughout your career, seek out empowering workplaces that are run on principles of equality, transparency, kindness, compassion, and justice.

(8) Stay focused. There will almost certainly be times, during your career, when you feel confused, stalled, or even hopeless. Or, when you're tempted to take another, possibly easier-seeming or better-paying, path "just for a while." Try not to let these kinds of transient feelings, events, and opportunities derail you. Keep "walking towards the mountain," as Gaiman put it—and please remember that living frugally, as discussed in Chapter 44, is one of the best insurances against having to take a higher-paying job just to get by.

Yes, you can change your mind and your plan. Try not to do so impulsively, however, or out of fear or confusion. If you are still committed to your Plan A, but can't figure out how to make it work, talk to your mentors.

Appendix 2: More Career Advice

Below are short answers to common career-related questions. Remember that, no matter which path you take, Career Task #1 is *always* nonperfectionism, Career Task #2 is *always* research and planning, and Career Task #3 is *always* to find, and work with, great mentors.

"How can I find work when I'm a liberal arts major?" Great question! People are always blathering on about how liberal arts majors can't get jobs, but the truth is that many employers actually favor them.[80] These employers are looking for candidates with *demonstrated* communications, teamwork, and leadership skills, so don't just join projects or clubs, lead them.

For an extra advantage, do a bankable minor like marketing or statistics. Fluency in a second language also helps. Also, buff up your social media skills as described in the previous chapter.

"I want to be a professional artist, craftsperson, or performer." That's great! The world needs more visions and voices. These can be tough fields to succeed in, and yet some people do succeed. I've taught entrepreneurship to hundreds of creative people of all types, and here is my advice for anyone on that path:

1. *Take an entrepreneurship class taught by someone* **with actual small business experience**. It doesn't have to be geared toward artists: in fact, there are advantages to being in a room full of caterers, locksmiths, hair stylists, and others, and seeing what your business has in common with theirs. If your school happens to offer an excellent

---

[80] See, for example: www.cnbc.com/id/100642178, www.theladders.com/career-advice/liberal-arts-major-hire, and www.historians.org/publications-and-directories/perspectives-on-history/april-2017/history-is-not-a-useless-major-fighting-myths-with-data.

entrepreneurship class taught by someone with first-hand knowledge, I'd take it. If not, don't worry: many nonprofits, community colleges, and other venues offer such classes, and you can take one after you graduate.

2. *Do an apprenticeship*, i.e., work with a successful artist in a position that allows you to observe how they run their business. (By "successful," I mean someone whose business is stable and provides at least a part-time income.) You do this to gain a real-world understanding of what the business entails, versus the stereotypes and hype the media often present, and also to gain some contacts and learn who the good suppliers, galleries, agents, banks, and other business partners are. Try to get a paid gig, but I wouldn't rule out an initial unpaid internship with the right person, so long as they are committed to doing a lot of mentoring.

3. *Make a business plan.* A few pages detailing what you will sell, to whom, and for how much will be fine. Include at least three years of "income statements" (a.k.a., "profit-and-loss statements") showing how the money will flow in and out of your business. (Your entrepreneurship class should teach you how to do all this, and you can also download a Marketing Exercise from www.hillaryrettig.com.) When you're done, show your plan to your teacher and other mentors and ask for feedback.

In my experience, would-be entrepreneurs who skip the above steps almost always fail. By the way, you'll also need exceptional time management skills (Part V) to succeed, because entrepreneurship is a busy, busy gig.

"I want to do a non-arts business." Great! Entrepreneurship of any kind is a really satisfying path. The above advice also applies.

"I want a community organizing or activism job." Excellent! I am always thrilled to hear when someone wants to pursue this path, both because we need as many community organizers as possible, and because social justice work can be incredibly personally rewarding. Paid jobs with top organizations tend to be competitive but you can boost your odds of being hired by: (1) networking (often via volunteering and attending conferences, as discussed in Appendix 3); and (2) being a terrific applicant. (Again, see my ebook, *It's Not You, It's Your Strategy.*)

A lot of activist learning is experiential, but you should read up on the basics. Some good books for that are Becky Bond and Zack Exley's *Rules for Revolutionaries*, adrienne maree brown's *Emergent Strategy*, Nick Montgomery and carla bergman's *Joyful Militancy* (a book that's really about nonperfectionist activism, although they don't use that phrase), Alexandra Bradbury,

Mark Brenner, and Jane Slaughter's *Secrets of a Successful Organizer*, Jane F. McAlevey's *No Shortcuts*, and my own *The Lifelong Activist*. Also, please read a few sales and marketing books—including Dale Carnegie's classic *How to Win Friends & Influence People*—because the techniques are very relevant and powerful, and absolutely can be used nonexploitatively to promote social good.

Keep in mind, too, that many other types of careers—including in politics, government, medicine, education, and certain businesses such as vegan foods or renewable energy—will also allow you to make a great social justice contribution.

"I can't decide what I want to do!" There may be many reasons for your ambivalence—because that's what we're talking about—including fear of failure and fear of success. Or, you might be self-censoring because you think that your desired career is somehow unacceptable or unattainable. "What makes you think *you* can be a [insert career type]?" someone might have said to you once. Or, "You'll never make a living doing that!"

I say...nuts to all the naysayers! The ability to do what you love as your primary career is a tremendous gift that you give yourself over the years and decades of your life, and absolutely worth striving for. The first step would be to deal decisively with any ambivalence using journaling, nonperfectionism, and the other solutions discussed in Chapter 24. Doing so will hopefully strengthen your clarity and commitment, so that you can then proceed wholeheartedly with your research, planning, and consultations with mentors.

What if it turns out that you don't actually have a strong career preference? It's okay to try a few different careers after graduation. (The career equivalent of trial and error.) As mentioned in Chapter 24, another common reason for ambivalence is that we don't have enough information to make a decision. Working for a while in a field you are considering is a good way to get that information.

Appendix 3: Working with Mentors

The more ambitious you are, the more mentors you need.

Generally speaking, there are two types: (1) those who are further along a professional or personal path than you and can advise you on how to proceed, and (2) those who can teach you a useful skill, such as how to ace a job interview, purchase a home, or cook a nutritious meal. You want to have at least one mentor for every important professional and personal endeavor, and it's okay if some of your mentors—like your mental-health counselor, personal trainer, and/or personal finance consultant—are paid.

Obviously, all of the faculty and educational staff you've worked with are potential mentors, and you shouldn't hesitate to ask them for advice or support both before and after graduation. (If you're hesitant, please review Chapter 10's discussion on the importance of asking for help.) You probably also already know a few other people who can mentor you in crucial areas. Sooner or later, however, you'll probably need to reach out to a stranger for mentorship. Perhaps you'll need to follow up on a referral from a professor, or contact a potential mentor you've heard about through a professional or other organization. Don't be shy about approaching such potential mentors: most people do want to help. At the same time, however, successful people tend to get asked for help a lot, including by people who aren't serious. When approaching a potential mentor, therefore, make sure they know you're one of the serious ones by making a knowledgeable, focused, personalized, and well-prepared request for assistance:

- "Knowledgeable" means it's clear that you understand your field, including how to behave professionally within it.

- "Focused" means your request is clear and concise, and the favor you're asking for is obvious and doable. (If the recipient has to puzzle over what, exactly, you're asking for, that's not good.)
- "Personalized" means it should be obvious why you're asking that person, in particular, for help.

Below is a sample email from a student to a potential mentor who works at a company they'd like to work for:

Subject: Referred by Dr. Carol Referrer

Dear Dr. Alcantara:

I'm a senior at XYZ College majoring in materials engineering, and my career goal is to work in the field of renewable energy. After graduation, I will be seeking an entry-level scientific position at a leading company in the field, with ABC Company being my top choice. My energy engineering professor, Dr. Carol Referrer, therefore suggested I contact you. Would you be available to talk for a few minutes about opportunities at ABC Company? I am available either by telephone or teleconference at your convenience.

I am attaching my resume and would like to highlight my sophomore and junior summer internships working at LMN Utilities, where I assisted with solar cell efficiency studies. This research has led to a research paper, currently in submission at *Prestigious Solar Publication*, and I am listed as a coauthor.

Thank you for your time and consideration. I look forward to your reply.

Sincerely,

Trina Salas

We use the referrer's name in the subject line to maximize the chances that the email will stand out via a personal connection. (Compared with a more generic subject line, such as "Seeking Advice" or "Hoping to Work at ABC Company.") Also, please note the email's "professional" letter format and tone. Better, in such cases, to be "too professional" than "not professional enough."[81]

---

[81] It's true that some so-called "professional" behaviors reflect historical bias and exclusion, however, it's easy enough, these days, for nearly anyone to write a professional email, especially if they make use of resources on the Internet or at their university career center. Even in situations where it takes more time and money to be "professional"—for instance, your interview appearance—there is lots of help available. For example, you can use thrifting (see Chapter 44) to get an interview suit, or consult one of the nonprofits listed here: https://jailstojobs.org/need-a-suit-these-organizations-will-give-you-one-and-

Finally, note that Trina does *not* ask Dr. Alcantara to "be my mentor." What you're asking for is a favor, not a relationship: if the relationship is destined to develop, it will. (In fact, you may never actually need to use the word "mentor" when interacting with your mentors.)

A note similar to the above should yield a good response from many potential mentors. If you don't get such a response, or any response at all, don't sweat it. This happens to everyone, and there could be many reasons for it, including some that have nothing to do with you or your request. (The person you wrote to could be busy, or dealing with some professional or personal problems.) Take another look at your note to see if you can improve it, then reach out to others.

Some final suggestions:

Ace the meetings. If a mentor agrees to talk with you, that's fantastic. Be prompt, prepared, and professional, and don't go past the agreed-upon time. (Although if the mentor is enjoying the conversation, they might, which is fine.)

Focus on problem-solving. As opposed to how frustrated or miserable the situation is making you feel. (Save that for your friends or a counselor.)

Follow through. Meaning, do what your mentor tells you to do. This would seem to be a no-brainer, but plenty of people trouble others for advice which they then fail to follow. When you do that, you not only waste your mentor's time, but send a message that, as a sports coach I know once put it, you're "uncoachable." Most mentors are quick to shift their time and energy away from the uncoachable ones, and toward other, more productive relationships.

It's not that mentors are infallible, or that you have to follow their advice every single time: it's that you should follow it most of the time, and only not follow it when you have a good reason.

Build your network. Always ask questions like, "Do you know anyone else whom I should be talking to about this?"

Stay in touch even when everything's okay. If you just contact your mentors when you need help, they'll feel used. So contact them once or twice a year just to let them know (briefly) how things are going. Mentors especially like hearing your good news, which should, of course, include a "thank you" for their ongoing contribution to your success.

Reciprocate. While it can be hard to figure out what you can offer a mentor with more skills, experience, and contacts than you have, most mentors do appreciate receiving articles on topics of mutual interest, and also having their work shared on social media and elsewhere.

more/.

Learn to recognize mentor relationships that aren't working. This could be because the person isn't a competent mentor, or because the two of you aren't a good fit. You can also "outgrow" a mentor, in which case, hopefully, you'll graduate to "colleague" status.

Be a Mentor. Yes, YOU should be a mentor! It's a great way to do good while also growing your skills and your network. You can mentor people in any professional or personal specialty (Chapter 46), as well as in nonperfectionism, the Joyful Dance, Values-Based Time Management, and the other techniques in this book. Sharing your hard-won skills, techniques, and insights with others will not only put wings on your own career and life, it will help those with whom you're sharing to also soar.

Acknowledgments

I gratefully acknowledge the assistance and support of:

James Wilkinson, whose influence in the field of undergraduate education has been immense. I am honored to be among the many people whose work he has supported and encouraged, and even more honored by his friendship.

Lee Busch, who provided yet another fantastic book cover, as well as valuable strategic advice.

Martin Rowe, a brilliant editor whose assistance greatly improved this book.

Christopher Sturr and Eli Massey, for fantastic copy editing.

Joan Frantschuk for a fantastic book and page design.

My diligent manuscript readers: Paul Busch, John Falcone, Julia Falcone, Cristina Florea, Julia Ftacek, Kerry Langdon-Fisher, and Arvind Thomas.

For valuable advice and assistance: Liz Alton, Erin Boydston, Alexis Diller, Cory Doctorow, Lisa Falcone, Elizabeth McCullough, Michael A. McDonald, Sanjoy Mahajan, Daniel M. Pink, Lauren Rosenthal, Zick Rubin, Karen E. Sprole, and the late Ralph Deal.

My family, and especially my sisters, for walking the path with me, even when it wasn't easy.

Jan Tobochnik for his unending support and generosity, as well as ongoing terrific advice.

My workshop students and coaching clients. You have been a constant source of learning, insight, and inspiration.

If This Book Has Helped You...

If this book has helped you, please support my work by:

- Leaving a review on your favorite online bookseller. (Even a one- or two-line review is great!)
- Emailing any comments or suggestions for the next edition to me at hillaryrettig@gmail.com.
- Signing up for my mailing list at www.hillaryrettig.com. (You'll find many free articles there, and also information about my workshops.)
- Inviting me to lead a workshop at your school, arts, community, parenting, or other group. (Email me at hillaryrettig@gmail.com with information about your group, and some possible dates.)

Thank you!

Hillary

About the Authors

Hillary Rettig

Along with the book you're holding, Hillary Rettig is also author of *The 7 Secrets of the Prolific: The Definitive Guide to Overcoming Procrastination, Perfectionism, and Writer's Block* (Infinite Art, 2011) and *The Lifelong Activist: How to Change the World Without Losing Your Way* (Lantern Books, 2006). She has taught productivity and time management classes at top educational, community, arts, and business organizations throughout the United States. Her articles have appeared in dozens of online and offline publications including *Wired*, *Working Woman*, *Psychology Today*, *Fortune*, *Future Buzz*, *Time Management Ninja*, *Tomorrow's Professor*, *Authors Helping Authors*, and *The Thesis Whisperer*.

From 2001 – 2012, she worked as a business coach and microlender at two nonprofit agencies in Boston, roles in which she helped hundreds of people from all backgrounds start and grow businesses in fields including art, technology, personal services, professional services, manufacturing, distribution, and retail.

Hillary is also a vegan, a free software/free culture advocate, and a lover of life, dogs, and social justice in all its forms. She is also a living kidney donor, and a former foster mother to four teenage Sudanese refugees (a.k.a., "Lost Boys"), now all adults living independently.

Hillary was born in the Bronx, spent time in Ithaca, New York, and Boston, Massachusetts, and now lives in Kalamazoo, Michigan, with her partner Jan Tobochnik, a physics professor at Kalamazoo College.

Learn more about Hillary and her work at www.hillaryrettig.com.

James Wilkinson (Foreword)

Harvard University professor emeritus James Wilkinson is a global leader in the field of undergraduate pedagogy. After receiving his doctorate in history from Harvard in 1974, he taught European history at Boston University and from 1985 – 1988 was founding director of BU's Teaching Center. In 1988 he joined the Harvard faculty, and from then through his retirement in 2007, served as director of Harvard's Derek Bok Center for Teaching and Learning. (He remains affiliated with the Center as a senior associate.)

In 2009, Dr. Wilkinson became the organizer of The International Conference on Improving University Teaching (IUT), the premier international meeting on university teaching. The IUT Conference examines topics relevant to students, faculty, and staff in higher education as well as to representatives of business and organizations concerned with higher education.

Dr. Wilkinson has received fellowships from the Guggenheim Foundation and National Endowment for the Humanities, as well as numerous other honors and awards.

Other Books by Hillary Rettig

The 7 Secrets of the Prolific

The Lifelong Activist

The Journey is the Reward

Index

Page numbers in **bold** indicate tables.